Student Resource Manual

for use with

Personal Finance

Eighth Edition

Jack R. Kapoor
College of DuPage

Les R. Dlabay
Lake Forest College

Robert J. Hughes
Dallas County Community College

Boston   Burr Ridge, IL   Dubuque, IA   Madison, WI   New York   San Francisco   St. Louis
Bangkok   Bogotá   Caracas   Kuala Lumpur   Lisbon   London   Madrid   Mexico City
Milan   Montreal   New Delhi   Santiago   Seoul   Singapore   Sydney   Taipei   Toronto

Student Resource Manual for use with
PERSONAL FINANCE
Jack R. Kapoor, Les R. Dlabay, Robert J. Hughes

Published by McGraw-Hill/Irwin, an imprint of The McGraw-Hill Companies, Inc., 1221 Avenue of the Americas, New York, NY 10020. Copyright © 2007 by The McGraw-Hill Companies, Inc. All rights reserved.

No part of this publication may be reproduced or distributed in any form or by any means, or stored in a database or retrieval system, without the prior written consent of The McGraw-Hill Companies, Inc., including, but not limited to, in any network or other electronic storage or transmission, or broadcast for distance learning.

1 2 3 4 5 6 7 8 9 0 CUS/CUS 0 9 8 7 6 5

ISBN-13: 978-0-07-319949-8
ISBN-10: 0-07-319949-4

www.mhhe.com

The McGraw-Hill Companies

STUDENT RESOURCE MANUAL

This publication is designed to help you learn and apply personal financial planning concepts. This *Student Resource Manual* supplements *Personal Finance* (Kapoor, Dlabay and Hughes Eighth Edition; McGraw-Hill, 2007) and will guide you through the content of the book. You will be given opportunities to learn, test, and apply personal financial topics.

Each chapter of the *Student Resource Manual and Casebook* has the following features:

Chapter Overview	This introductory paragraph provides an overview of the main topics and concepts developed in the chapter.
Objectives	These instructional goals from the introductory page of each chapter in the textbook offer a framework for desired behaviors related to chapter content.
Key Terms	This feature lists the vital words related to chapter content. The definitions of these terms are in the margins within each chapter for your review.
Pretest	This section allows you to assess your initial knowledge of the chapter material with a ten-item true-false quiz.
Self-Guided Study Questions	These open-ended questions are keyed to textbook headings and provide you with an opportunity to develop a knowledge of the content and concepts of a chapter.
Post Test	After reading and studying the material of a chapter, ten completion and ten multiple choice questions help you measure your mastery level.
Problems, Applications, and Cases	Several activities are provided to allow you to use personal financial planning concepts. These include computational exercises, financial planning activities, and situations requiring examples or further research.
Supplementary Cases	Real-world situations are presented for you to use your research and analytical skills related to personal financial decision making.
Supplementary Reading	To expand the content of *Personal Finance*, recent articles from *Business Week* are included in the Resource Manual. Each article is accompanied by study questions.

The answers to the pretests, post tests, problems, applications, and cases are presented at the end of this publication. These are provided so you can assess your knowledge based on the various tests and exercises in this Resource Manual.

CONTENTS

Chapter

1	Personal Financial Basics and the Time Value of Money	1
2	Financial Aspects of Career Planning	17
3	Money Management Strategy: Financial Statements and Budgeting	33
4	Planning Your Tax Strategy	48
5	The Banking Services of Financial Institutions	60
6	Introduction to Consumer Credit	73
7	Choosing A Source of Credit: The Costs of Credit Alternatives	99
8	Consumer Purchasing Strategies and Legal Protection	117
9	The Finances of Housing	132
10	Home and Automobile Insurance	146
11	Health and Disability Insurance	161
12	Life Insurance	189
13	Investing Fundamentals	211
14	Investing in Stocks	232
15	Investing in Bonds	253
16	Investing in Mutual Funds	270
17	Real Estate and Other Investment Alternatives	292
18	Retirement Planning	312
19	Estate Planning	334
	Answers to Pretests, Post Tests, and Problems, Applications, and Cases	357

1 PERSONAL FINANCE BASICS AND THE TIME VALUE OF MONEY

Chapter Overview

This chapter provides the foundation for *Personal Finance* and the study of financial planning. The chapter starts with a discussion of decision making, including consequences of choices and the evaluation of associated risks. Next, the opportunity costs, or trade-offs, of decisions are considered in relation to personal and financial resources. This is followed by coverage of the personal, social, and economic factors that make up the financial planning environment. Next, the steps of the financial planning process are discussed, along with the main components of financial planning (obtaining, planning, saving, borrowing, spending, managing risk, investing, and retirement and estate planning). Finally, strategies for creating and using a financial plan are introduced.

Learning Objectives

After studying this chapter, you will be able to:

Obj. 1 Analyze the process of making personal financial decisions.

Obj. 2 Develop personal financial goals.

Obj. 3 Assess the personal and economic factors that influence personal financial planning.

Obj. 4 Determine the personal and financial opportunity costs associated with personal financial decisions.

Obj. 5 Identify strategies for achieving personal financial goals for different life situations.

Key Terms

adult life cycle	future value	personal financial planning
bankruptcy	inflation	present value
economics	liquidity	time value of money
financial plan	opportunity cost	values

Pretest

True-False

_____ 1. (Obj. 1) Every person uses decision-making techniques every day.

_____ 2. (Obj. 2) The risks associated with financial decisions are easy to measure.

_____ 3. (Obj. 3) Ideas and principles that are considered correct, desirable or important are examples of opportunity costs.

_____ 4. (Obj. 4) Financial opportunity costs can be measured using time value of money calculations.

_____ 5. (Obj. 3) A career change can influence a person's financial decisions.

_____ 6. (Obj. 3) Inflation results in increased buying power for consumers.

_____ 7. (Obj. 1) Financial planning starts with setting personal economic goals.

_____ 8. (Obj. 1) Financial planning requires an ongoing reevaluation and revision of financial goals.

_____ 9. (Obj. 5) Liquidity is the ability to convert financial resources into useable cash without a loss of value.

_____ 10. (Obj. 5) The primary purpose of a financial plan is to report a person's or household's current financial situation.

Self-Guided Study Questions

Obj. 1

The Financial Planning Process (p. 4)

1. What is personal financial planning?

2. What are some advantages of personal financial planning?

3. What are the steps of the financial planning process?

4. How do opportunity costs influence decision making?

5. What types of risks affect personal financial decisions? How can these risks be considered when making financial choices?

6. Why is information important for successful financial decisions? What are the main sources of financial planning information?

Obj. 2

Developing Personal Financial Goals (p. 9)

7. How does timing affect goals?

8. What are four qualities of effective financial goals?

Obj. 3

Influences on Personal Financial Planning (p. 13)

Life Situation and Personal Values (p. 13)

9. What factors affect a person's life situation?

10. How do values affect financial planning?

Economic Factors (p. 13)

11. What does the study of economics involve?

12. What function does supply and demand serve?

13. What are the main financial institutions that operate in our society?

14. How do global business activities affect individuals in our society?

15. How are people on fixed incomes, lenders of money, and borrowers of money affected by inflation?

16. What does the consumer price index (CPI) measure?

17. How do changing interest rates influence personal financial decisions?

Obj. 4

Opportunity Costs and the Time Value of Money (p. 16)

Personal Opportunity Costs (p. 17)

18. What are some examples of opportunity costs that cannot be measured in terms of money?

Financial Opportunity Costs (p. 17)

19. What are some examples of the time value of money affecting personal financial decisions?

20. How is interest computed?

21. How are future value calculations used in financial planning?

22. What information is provided by present value calculations?

Obj. 5

Achieving Financial Goals (p. 20)

Components of Personal Financial Planning (p. 20)

23. What are the eight areas of financial planning that require decisions by all people at some time in their lives?

24. Why is a savings and investment program a necessity for future financial security?

25. What problems can the overuse of credit cause?

26. What are some common types of investments?

Developing a Flexible Financial Plan (p. 24)

27. What is a financial plan?

Implementing Your Financial Plan (p. 24)

28. What are some examples of short-term and long-term financial strategies that can help a person achieve his or her financial goals?

Post Test

Completion

1. (Obj. 1) _____ _____ _____ is the process of managing your money to achieve personal economic satisfaction.

2. (Obj. 3) The stages in the family situation and financial needs of an adult are referred to as the _____ _____ _____.

3. (Obj. 1) The second stage of the financial planning process is to develop financial _____.

4. (Obj. 1) If you decide to use your savings to pay for school instead of going on vacation, this is an example of _____ _____.

5. (Obj. 3) _____ is the study of how wealth is created and distributed.

6. (Obj. 4) The _____ _____ _____ _____ refers to increases in the amount of money as a result of interest earned.

7. (Obj. 3) A rise in the general level of prices is referred to as _____.

8. (Obj. 5) _____ is the ability to readily convert financial resources into usable cash without loss in value.

9. (Obj. 3) _____ are ideas and principles that a person considers correct, desirable and important.

10. (Obj. 5) A financial _____ is a formalized report that summarizes your current financial situation, analyzes your financial needs, and recommends a direction for your financial activities.

Multiple Choice

_____ 1. (Obj. 1) The main purpose of personal financial planning is to
   A. plan for retirement.
   B. control your spending habits.
   C. reach personal economic goals.
   D. increase the amount in your savings.

_____ 2. (Obj. 1) The first step in financial planning is to
   A. create a financial plan of action.
   B. analyze your current situation.
   C. develop financial goals.
   D. implement your financial plan.

_____ 3. (Obj. 4) Which of the following time value of money computations would be used to determine the value of $100 three years from now?
   A. Future value of a single amount
   B. Future value of a series of deposits
   C. Present value of a single amount
   D. Present value of a series of deposits

_____ 4. (Obj. 3) An example of a personal factor that would affect financial planning is
   A. inflation.
   B. household size.
   C. interest rates.
   D. tax laws.

_____ 5. (Obj. 3) Prices in the American economy are most influenced by
   A. government.
   B. supply and demand.
   C. taxes.
   D. interest rates.

_____ 6. (Obj. 3) Increased consumer borrowing is likely to cause
   A. an increase in interest rates.
   B. a decrease in interest rates.
   C. lower taxes.
   D. reduced consumer prices.

_____ 7. (Obj. 1) The final step of the financial planning process is to
   A. implement the financial plan.
   B. create a financial plan of action.
   C. develop financial goals.
   D. re-evaluate your actions.

_____ 8. (Obj. 5) _____ is necessary to have funds available for long-term financial security.
   A. Borrowing
   B. Spending
   C. Saving
   D. Liquidity

_____ 9. (Obj. 5) Making a will is involved in the _____ component of financial planning.
   A. spending
   B. obtaining
   C. managing risk
   D. estate planning

_____ 10. (Obj. 5) The main purpose of a financial plan is to
   A. budget for current spending.
   B. determine your insurance needs.
   C. recommend financial activities.
   D. plan risk management activities.

Problems, Applications, and Cases

1. Compute the future or present value for the following:

    a. What is the future value of $430 earning 8 percent for two years?

    b. What is the future value of $200 deposited each year for six years earning 6 percent?

    c. What is the present value of $700 earning 7 percent for 12 years?

    d. What is the present value of a withdrawal of $300 at the end of each year for 8 years with an interest rate of 8 percent?

2. For each of the following life situations, (a) suggest some short-term and long-term goals that would be unique to this group; and (b) recommend specific financial activities that could help these individuals achieve these goals.

Life situation	Short-term goals	Long-term goals	Financial activities
Single person, age 43, no dependents			
Married couple, both working, children ages 3 and 7			
Married couple, ages 56 and 51, no dependent children			
Divorced woman with a 10-year-old daughter			
Married couple, one income, child age 14 and dependent parent, age 73			

3. Using the Internet, *The Wall Street Journal*, the business section from the newspaper, or business periodicals such as *Business Week*, *Forbes*, and *Fortune*, obtain current information on various economic conditions. Indicate how this information might affect a person's financial decisions.

Economic indicator	Current trend	Source of information	Possible impact on financial planning
Inflation; Consumer prices			
Interest rates			
Employment			
Consumer spending; Retail sales			

4. Listed here are the main components of financial planning. For each situation below, indicate which area is being neglected. More than one may apply to a situation.

- obtaining
- planning
- saving
- borrowing
- spending
- managing risk
- investing
- retirement and estate planning

   a. Alice Kendall does not have a will to make sure that her children will receive her financial resources should she die. _____

   b. Janet and Brad Collins spend money as they need or want without a budget. _____

   c. Ken and Barb Kolar rent an apartment but don't believe they need insurance for their furniture or other personal belongings. _____

   d. John Brubeck charges frequent restaurant visits and clothing purchases to his credit cards and other charge accounts.

e. Mona Collins can't get a promotion at her place of employment because she lacks adequate education. _____

f. Joyce and Tom Hallar are not able to save more than a few dollars each month. _____

g. Bill Cartwright had to borrow money to pay taxes he owes for last year. _____

h. Jeanne Holland has $14,000 in a savings account that pays five and one-half percent interest. _____

5. With the use of a telephone directory, advertisements in local newspapers, the Internet, information from friends, and by contacting one or more financial advisors, develop a list of people available in your community who provide financial planning assistance. Obtain the following information:

   a. Name, address, telephone number, and e-mail
   b. Area of expertise, training, and background
   c. Type of fee charged
   d. Comments from previous customers

   (Note: Refer to Appendix A for additional questions to ask when selecting a financial planner.)

6. Based on the format in Exhibit 1-10, outline a financial plan for you or your household.

Supplementary Case 1-1: Winners Can Still Be Losers*

Topic: Financial Planning and Budgeting

Text Reference: pp. 4-25

Poor personal financial management is the most important cause of bankruptcy and the greatest cause of anxiety in American households. Consider the case of Erika Earnhart of Lexington Park, Maryland, who won $1 million in the Maryland lottery. Erika says she is in debt, lives in a trailer park, and is unable to work because of a knee injury.

"I thought I'd be on easy street the rest of my life," said Erika. "Now I live from April to April. I admit I've had some fun, but it's not everything it's cracked up to be."

Each April, Erika receives her annual $50,000 check, a prize guaranteed for 20 years. Erika spent the first $50,000 on a four-bedroom house, gifts of money to her parents and sister, a Volkswagen, and some travel. She did not pay taxes on this money, so when her second check came, she had to pay $18,000 in taxes on the first year's winnings plus advance taxes for the second year. Consequently, the second annual windfall immediately plunged from $50,000 to about $20,000.

Now—after two divorces, a still unresolved child custody case, two knee operations without any health insurance to defray the costs, and moves to Michigan, Colorado, California, and back to Maryland—Erika is broke. She sold her house and lives in a nearly new, extra-wide trailer. She visits her bank frequently. The bank vice president does not even ask Erika the purpose of her visit. He knows that Erika is borrowing against her next lottery check, and he just needs to know what amount she wants to withdraw. "When I got this year's check, I already owed the bank $10,000," she said.

There are still several checks to come, but Erika said that if she had known what would happen after she won the million dollars, "I'd have torn up the ticket or put it in someone else's name." Still she continues to play the Maryland lottery periodically in the hope of winning again, "to pay off my debts."

Erika's financial woes demonstrate that using money effectively is one of the biggest problems in the lifetime of any individual or family. But personal financial planning and money management are skills that can be learned, developed and enjoyed.

---

*Adapted from "'I'm Broke,' Says Winners of Lottery," *Chicago Tribune*, October 11, 1984, sec. 1A, p. 32.

The job of managing your money is lifelong. Some people do it well and live smoothly and pleasantly, free from monetary cares and worries. They enjoy the pleasures and satisfactions of a full life. Others ineptly stumble from one financial mess to the next. They never seem to solve their personal financial problems. Some families can live comfortably and save money on an annual income of $30,000. Others, with annual incomes of more than $100,000 can't make ends meet. Most of us work hard for our money. We should make an additional effort to see that it is managed and used wisely.

Case Questions

1. What financial planning mistakes did Erika Earnhart make?
2. How did the misuse of credit contribute to Erika's problems?
3. Did Erika's changing household situation affect her financial planning difficulties? Explain.
4. If you were in a situation similar to Erika's, how would your actions differ from her actions?

Supplementary Case 1-2: Emily's Personal Financial Plan

Topic: Developing a Financial Plan

Text Reference: pp. 4-25

Emily Burton, 23, completed college two years ago with a degree in physical therapy. The major cost of her education was covered by a scholarship. Through wise planning by her parents, Emily has $32,000 which they set aside for her education. This fund consists of savings certificates and stocks that increased in value over the years.

Emily works for a hospital in Lincoln, Nebraska, and earns $32,000 a year. In about three years, she would like to go to graduate school to get a master's degree. Then she would like to buy a house. Emily wants to live on her salary and invest the $32,000 for her education and future needs.

Case Questions

1. How did Emily benefit from her parents' financial planning?
2. What decisions does Emily need to make regarding her future?
3. How could various personal and economic factors influence Emily's financial planning?
4. What would be the value of Emily's $32,000 in three years if it earned an annual interest rate of 7 percent?

Supplementary Case 1-3: Maternity Leave for Margo

Topic: Financial Planning

Text Reference: pp. 9-25

Having children has always been important to Margo Sanchez; however, so has her career. Within the next few years, she would like to take a leave of absence from her employment to start a family. To obtain the necessary financial resources for this goal, Margo estimates that she will need to accumulate $16,000 over the next four years.

Currently Margo and her husband, Alex, rent an apartment and have a combined household income of $53,000. While they have very few debts, their savings consist of less than $2,000.

Case Questions

1. How does Margo's personal goal affect her financial planning activities?
2. What information sources might be helpful to Margo when making decisions related to her goal?
3. What amount would Margo need to deposit today for that amount to grow to $16,000 in four years at a 6 percent annual interest rate?
4. What actions would you suggest for Margo and Alex?

Supplementary Reading 1

Anne Tergesen, "Three Generations, One Roof", October 31, 2005.

Three Generations, One Roof

More and more households are doubling up. Here's how to make it work

Stacey Egan was nine months pregnant with her third child when she called off her family's search for a home in Rye, N.Y., a New York City suburb where the median-priced home now sells for over $1.3 million. The Egans had outgrown the two-bedroom condo they had purchased in Rye in 2000. But they were tired of watching $850,000 fixer-uppers get snapped up before they even had a chance to bid. "Anytime an affordable house would come on the market, it would sell in a day," she says.

So about a year ago, Egan and her husband, Michael, a compliance officer for a Wall Street firm, did what a growing number of families are doing: They moved back in with (her) mom and dad, whose five-bedroom empty nest in Rye has plenty of room for a growing family.

Yes, the extended family is making a comeback. In many cases, generations are squeezing under one roof, sometimes by refurbishing basements or building extensions for the in-laws or grandkids. They're also living in family compounds that feature garage apartments or guest cottages. In response to surveys of homebuyers, builders are offering second master bedrooms and "accessory" units, such as so-called granny flats, and guest homes in a growing number of mainly upscale housing developments. And Dallas-based CTX Mortgage () offers a mortgage for multifamily households in Florida that considers the senior generation's income when qualifying -- without requiring them to be listed on the loan.

According to the latest U.S. Census data, the number of households with three or more generations living under one roof grew 38% from 1990 to 2000, vs. 8% for those with just two generations. Doubling up is most common in states where home values have soared as well as in places with large populations of immigrants from countries accustomed to multigenerational living. Extended households now account for 5.6% of California's total, vs. almost 4% nationally. And 8.2% of Hawaii's households are multigenerational. With the affordability of starter homes at a 15-year low, the pressure to double up is likely to remain.

BETTER LIFE
Those living in three-generation households say the arrangement can solve a host of financial and practical problems. Most obviously, money saved on rent can fund a downpayment on a separate home later. It can also allow breadwinners to stay home with kids or start businesses. Some say they enjoy a better quality of life, with shorter commutes and access to better schools. One extended clan discovered that for the price of two three-bedroom homes on quarter-acre lots in Atherton, Calif., they could jointly finance something far more grand -- a five-bedroom place on an acre with a pool and a 1,200-square-foot guest house for the grandparents. "In our case, one plus one equaled three," says Peter Clark, chief financial officer at a Silicon Valley technology firm whose family lives with his in-laws, Richard and Ann Dorst.

Families also say that by living together, they're better able to meet evolving needs, from child care to eldercare. Clark says his in-laws at times have been "like second parents" to his three daughters. But "when they get older, we'll be there if they need anything."

Such arrangements have lots of challenges, however. As with marriage, the division of household bills and chores can be sources of conflict. There are privacy issues. Families who live together permanently may also need to work out an estate plan -- without stepping on other heirs' toes. When children are involved, parents and grandparents may have to resolve differences over child rearing.

Moving back to the nest can be hard on the ego, too. "The stereotype is that adults who live with their parents are losers," says Jeffrey Mordan, a private-school art teacher whose family moved into his wife's childhood home in Hill Town, Pa., two years ago, in part to finance the master's degree in teaching he'll earn in 2007. Sometimes, too, it's easy to lapse into past patterns, with parents dictating rules and adult children reverting to childlike roles.

If you're thinking about giving mom and dad the guest room or suspect you may soon be sharing close quarters with a boomerang child, here are tips from families living in extended households.

Make a Plan
Long before purchasing a family compound or calling a moving van, hash out a written plan for dividing the finances, chores, and space, advises John Graham, professor of international business at the University of California at Irvine's Paul Merage School of Business, who is writing a book with his sister, Sharon Niederhaus, about extended family living. Other topics might include house guests and parties.

If you'd prefer a temporary arrangement, agree on a timetable. Grandparents should be clear about how much child care they're willing to do. Parents should ask the household's other adults to respect their approach to child rearing.

Privacy
Families say an extended arrangement works best when each branch can retreat to its own space. Separate units are ideal. But in many locales, zoning laws or deed restrictions prohibit guest homes and granny flats, says Andy Gianino, president of The Home Store, a Whately (Mass.) builder of custom modular units. Additions may also trigger an increase in property taxes or insurance premiums.

Families who share single-family residences can enhance privacy by occupying bedrooms on separate floors or opposite ends of the house. Mordan's in-laws, Fran and Terry Gery, converted a ground-floor multipurpose room into a master bedroom suite -- a project that's been on their "to do" list for years. The Mordans and their two young children have the three bedrooms upstairs.

For families who live close by, knock before popping in. You can even reserve specific times for the immediate family to be alone. "Because of our busy schedules, dinner was the only time my husband and I could be with my daughter as a family. Fortunately, my mom did not feel she had to be part of our dinner," says Jill Ridky-Blackburn, whose mother, Lillian Ridky, now 90, moved into attached living quarters on the family's Chapel Hill (N.C.) property about 11 years ago.

Finances
There are many approaches to dividing the bills. The Clarks and Dorsts evenly split fixed costs, such as property taxes and insurance. Why? Each owns about 50% of the property. But they allocate utility, phone, and cable bills on a per capita basis. In some cases, the generation with greater resources writes the checks. Parents might waive rent to help a child maximize savings and move out sooner. The key, according to Niederhaus, is for everyone to contribute, be it rent or yardwork.

Of course, even the closest families have arguments. To minimize conflict, veterans suggest various strategies. But there are great rewards, too. "We've gotten to know one another as families rarely do," says Fran Gery. "It's going to be hard to break apart."

Anne Tergesen

Study Questions

1. What factors could create the type of life situation discussed in this article?

2. What special financial planning actions need to be addressed in this situation?

2 FINANCIAL ASPECTS OF CAREER PLANNING

Chapter Overview

A person's career and work situation is frequently overlooked in financial planning. Your career will influence the financial resources you have available for spending, savings, and investing. In addition, a career interacts with a person's lifestyle, interests, and values, all of which influence financial decisions. This chapter provides a basic understanding of career planning, job selection, and obtaining an employment position. Included is practical information regarding career information sources, creating a resume and cover letter, and interviewing. Finally, material on evaluating a job offer and considering a career change is presented.

Learning Objectives

After studying this chapter, you will be able to:

Obj. 1 Describe the activities associated with career planning and advancement.

Obj. 2 Evaluate the factors that influence employment opportunities.

Obj. 3 Implement employment search strategies.

Obj. 4 Assess the financial and legal concerns related to obtaining employment.

Obj. 5 Analyze the techniques available for career growth and advancement.

Key Terms

cafeteria-style employee benefits
career
cover letter
informational interview
job
job creation
mentor
networking
résumé

Pretest

True-False

_____ 1. (Obj. 1) Increased education increases a person's potential earning power.

_____ 2. (Obj. 1) A person's career selection influences many aspects of his or her lifestyle.

_____ 3. (Obj. 1) Aptitude tests are designed to measure a person's interests.

_____ 4. (Obj. 2) Foreign competition has resulted in fewer manufacturing jobs in the United States.

_____ 5. (Obj. 3) An informational interview is designed to gather information about a career or an organization.

_____ 6. (Append) References are not usually included on a résumé.

_____ 7. (Append) A functional résumé is suggested for individuals with diverse skills who may be seeking employment in a new career area.

_____ 8. (Append) A screening interview is designed for in-depth discussion with the finalists for a job.

_____ 9. (Obj. 4) Salary is only one of the financial factors that should be considered when accepting an employment position.

_____ 10. (Obj. 5) Continuing career education can involve both formal and informal methods of training.

Self-Guided Study Questions

Obj. 1

Career Choice Factors (p. 44)

1. Describe the differences between a job and a career.

Trade-Offs of Career Decisions (p. 44)
2. What are some trade-offs a person may face when making a career decision?

Career Training and Skill Development (p. 44)
3. What is the common relationship between education and income?

4. What traits are commonly associated with successful individuals?

Personal Factors (p. 45)
5. How can aptitude tests and interest inventories assist a person with career planning?

6. How does a person's personality affect career decisions?

Career Decision Making (p. 46)
7. How would the career activities of a person seeking an entry-level position differ from a person planning to change careers?

Obj. 2
Career Opportunities: Now and in the Future (p. 47)
Social Influences (p. 47)
8. How can demographic and geographic trends affect job opportunities?

Economic Conditions (p. 49)

9. What types of employment opportunities would be most affected by higher interest rates?

Trends in Industry and Technology (p. 49)

10. How have foreign businesses affected career opportunities?

11. What career areas are likely to have the most demand in the next few years?

Obj. 3
Employment Search Strategies (p. 50)

Obtaining Employment Experience (p. 51)

12. How can a person obtain work-related experience without having a job?

Using Career Information Sources (p. 51)

13. What are the main sources of career planning information and assistance?

14. In what ways could the *Occupational Outlook Handbook* and the Internet assist a person with career planning decisions?

15. What is the value of personal and business contacts in the career planning process?

Identifying Job Opportunities (p. 54)

16. What are some methods for finding available employment positions?

Applying for Employment (p. 55)

17. How does a résumé differ from a cover letter?

Obj. 4

Financial and Legal Aspects of Employment (p. 55)

Accepting an Employment Position (p. 55)

18. What factors of the working environment of an organization should be considered when evaluating a job offer?

19. What factors affect a person's salary?

Evaluating Employee Benefits (p. 56)

20. What is the advantage of a cafeteria-style employee benefits program?

21. What analytical techniques could be used to assess the financial value of employee benefits?

22. How do tax-deferred employee benefits differ from tax-exempt benefits?

Your Employment Rights (p. 58)

23. What are some rights employees have that are protected by law?

Obj. 5
Long-Term Career Development (p. 59)
24. What daily work activities can contribute to long-term career success?

Training Opportunities (p. 59)
25. What are some common sources of continuing education experiences?

Career Paths and Advancement (p. 60)
26. How can a mentor contribute to your career development?

Changing Careers (p. 60)
27. What factors might a person consider when deciding whether or not to change employment situations?

Appendix: Résumés, Cover Letters, and Interviews (p. 67)

Developing a Résumé (p. 67)
28. What are the main components of information on a résumé?

29. Should a career objective be presented on a résumé?

30. What types of school and community experiences are relevant work experiences?

Types of Résumés (p. 68)

31. How does a chronological résumé differ from a functional résumé?

32. When should a targeted résumé be used?

Creating a Cover Letter (p. 71)

33. What is the purpose of a cover letter?

34. What are the main sections of a cover letter?

The Job Interview (p. 72)

35. What actions are suggested before going to an interview?

36. How does a screening interview differ from a selection interview?

37. What actions could be taken after an interview to add to a person's chances of successful job hunting in the future?

Post Test

Completion

1. (Append.) A(n) _____ interview is an initial meeting, usually brief, that reduces the pool of job candidates to a workable number.

2. (Append.) A(n) _____ résumé is used to apply for a specific job.

3. (Obj. 1) An employment position that is obtained mainly to earn money is commonly referred to as a(n) _____.

4. (Obj. 5) A(n) _____ is an experienced employee who serves as a teacher and counselor for a less experienced person in a career field.

5. (Obj. 3) A(n) _____ _____ is designed to express your interest in a job and obtain an interview.

6. (Append) The _____ résumé presents your education, work experience, and other information in a reverse time sequence.

7. (Append) The purpose of a(n) _____ interview is to gather information about a career or an organization.

8. (Obj. 1) A commitment to a profession that requires continued training and offers a clear path for occupational growth is a(n) _____.

9. (Append.) A(n) _____ interview is limited to the finalists in a job search.

10. (Append.) The _____ résumé emphasizes a person's abilities and skills in categories such as communication, supervision, and training experiences.

Multiple Choice

_____ 1. (Obj. 1) Aptitudes refer to
   A. Areas of interest.
   B. natural abilities.
   C. skills requiring technical training.
   D. supervisory skills possessed by managers.

_____ 2. (Obj. 3) The purpose of an informational interview is to
   A. obtain career information.
   B. select a job for which to interview.
   C. make a final selection of an employee.
   D. select the best candidates for a position.

_____ 3. (Append.) The item least likely to be included on a résumé is
   A. volunteer work.
   B. school club activities.
   C. employment experience.
   D. references.

_____ 4. (Append.) A _____ résumé would be best for a person with many skills who is applying for employment in a new career area.
   A. targeted
   B. functional
   C. chronological
   D. placement

5. (Obj. 3) The purpose of a cover letter is to
   A. obtain career planning information.
   B. determine the jobs available in an organization.
   C. apply for a specific position.
   D. inquire about employee benefits with a prospective employer.

6. (Append) The final section of a cover letter should
   A. express your interest in the job.
   B. request the opportunity for an interview.
   C. highlight portions of your background.
   D. communicate your career goals.

7. (Append.) The purpose of a screening interview is to
   A. obtain information on a career area.
   B. select the best candidate for an available position.
   C. make an initial contact with an employer.
   D. discuss the working environment with current employees.

8. (Append.) The final step in the interview process involves a(n) _____ interview.
   A. selection
   B. transition
   C. screening
   D. informational

9. (Obj. 4) Which of the following is considered a long-term employee benefit?
   A. Salary
   B. Overtime pay
   C. Profit sharing
   D. Paid vacations

10. (Obj. 4) A cafeteria-style employee benefits program is designed to
    A. minimize taxes for workers.
    B. reduce benefit costs for the company.
    C. meet the needs of individual employees.
    D. provide food service for workers while on the job.

Problems, Applications, and Cases

1. With the use of the Web, *Business Week*, other business periodicals, and the daily newspaper, obtain information about increased or decreased career opportunities based on the following factors that influence the job market. (Refer to text pages 47-49 for additional information.)

Factor	Influence on the job market
Economic trends	
Industry trends	
Technology	
Social factors	
Geographic trends	

2. Investigate one or more careers in which you are interested. Be sure to use information from the library, mass media sources, the Internet, your campus placement office, community organizations, professional associations, and personal and business contacts.

3. Conduct a personal inventory of your background, and prepare a chronological résumé (refer to text pages 68-69). Your data should include information in the following areas:

   a. personal data

   b. career objective

   c. education

   d. experience

   e. related information

   f. references

   If a functional or targeted résumé (see text pages 70-71) is more appropriate for your personal situation, create one of these personal information sheets.

4. Select a specific job opportunity and develop a cover letter (see text page 72) that would be appropriate. This correspondence should have the three main sections:

   (1) the introductory paragraph

   (2) the development section (one or two paragraphs)

   (3) the concluding paragraph

5. Talk to several people who have recently interviewed for a job and obtain information on the questions they were commonly asked. (Or refer to Exhibit 2-E, text page 74, for sample questions.) Make notes as to how you would respond to these questions.

Interview question	Possible response

6. Contact one or more companies to obtain information about the types of employee benefits they offer, or talk to friends who work to gather this data (see text pages 56-58).

Company		
Paid holidays		
Vacation time		
Sick days		
Health insurance		
Life, other insurance		
Retirement program		
Profit sharing		
Other benefits:		

Supplementary Case 2-1: Wise Career Choices

Topic: Job Search Strategies

Text Reference: pp. 51-55; 59-61

Barb Collins was recently promoted from regional sales manager to vice president of marketing for a telecommunications company. Many people would say they could never achieve that kind of success. However, Barb also had that attitude when she graduated from college eight years ago. What changed her attitude and put her on a successful career path? She didn't always take the right actions, but after awhile Barb started to learn from every experience.

During college, Barb majored in history and also took several English, psychology, math, computer, and business classes. When she graduated, she wasn't sure how to get a job. Barb obtained help with her résumé from the career placement office on campus. Not sure about the type of work she wanted to do, Barb sent out letters and résumés to nearly 200 companies that advertised positions open. She received very few responses and was invited to interview for only three jobs. None of the three interviews went well.

To pay her living expenses, Barb took a job as a sales clerk. One day, Barb was talking to her supervisor, Joan Sanders, about the trouble she was having getting a job that used more of her skills. Joan suggested that Barb visit some companies for which she would like to work.

Joan also advised Barb to strengthen her career planning portfolio before the visits. First, she told Barb to make sure her résumé communicated the skills and experiences the company wanted. Barb had completed several class projects involving field research, human relations, and communication skills. Her campus activities demonstrated leadership and organizational planning. These qualifications were not clearly presented on her current résumé. Joan also stressed the importance of emphasizing in an interview how Barb's past accomplishments would benefit the employer in the *future*.

Next, Joan suggested that Barb prepare questions about the jobs available, the skills required, and the working environment of the company. These questions would show her personal initiative and desire to work for that company.

Finally, Joan encouraged Barb to talk to as many people as possible at different companies, both on and off the job, and to ask questions about everything related to their companies and their duties. This information would prepare Barb to better target her job search.

Things started to go a little better with Barb's career planning activities. She started to get more interviews, but still no job. Then, one day, while talking to someone while waiting for an interview, she heard about a company that was opening a new sales office in the neighboring city. It was at this company that Barb Collins became vice president of marketing.

Case Questions

1. How could Barb Collins have improved her chances of getting the job she wanted before meeting Joan Sanders?

2. What types of school and work experiences helped Barb obtain the job she wanted?

3. Which of Joan's suggestions do you believe will be most helpful to you when planning a career or changing jobs?

Supplementary Case 2-2: A Dead-End Career Path

Topic: Career Planning Activities

Text Reference: pp. 50-55

Joanne Nash has tried to get a sales job for three months. She has applied for a position with companies that sell everything from automobiles and electronic products to medical supplies and restaurant equipment. Joanne has always worked in an office. She completed two years of college and took several business courses. She sees sales as a chance to meet interesting people and earn a higher salary.

During interviews, Joanne displays a very pleasant and outgoing personality. The company representatives like talking with her, but they have not offered her a job due to her limited knowledge and her limited sales experience.

Case Questions

1. As a career counselor, what suggestions would you offer Joanne?

2. What experience might Joanne have that could be adapted to a sales career?

3. How could a specific career objective be valuable to Joanne?

4. What types of career information materials could Joanne use to improve her chances of obtaining a sales job?

Supplementary Case 2-3: A Midlife Career Search

Topic: *Changing Careers*

Text Reference: pp. 50-55

Bob Thomas faces a difficult situation—two children in college, a dependent parent, and a job eliminated in a corporate merger. After 20 years with the company, Bob, age 47, must seek employment elsewhere. Bob's wife still has her job. Her income, however, will not support all of the family's financial obligations. Bob has the options of taking out his pension funds, leaving them in the same pension plan, or transferring them to a different retirement account.

During the two decades Bob was with the company, he was promoted several times. He started as an accounting clerk, then became credit manager, and most recently served as manager of the company's southeastern regional office.

Bob's former employer will allow him to continue his health insurance coverage. Bob, of course, will be required to pay monthly premiums. The company is also providing a career consultant to assist former employees with their job search.

Case Questions

1. How can the family's spending be revised to cope with financial difficulties while Bob is between jobs? What sources of funds are available to Bob and his family?
2. What actions should Bob consider regarding his pension funds?
3. What employment skills is Bob likely to have that will make him an attractive prospect to other organizations?
4. What career planning advice would you recommend to someone in Bob's situation?

Supplementary Reading 2

Michelle Dammon Loyalka, "Tips for Going Palm on Palm", June 28, 2005.

Tips for Going Palm on Palm

National Handshake Day provides a chance to examine one of the most overlooked aspects of business. Here's how to improve your move

Forget about putting your best foot forward. In the professional world, it's all about the handshake. While it may seem like nothing more than a fleeting formality, locking palms is serious business.

Studies show that the mere act of shaking hands makes people twice as likely to remember you, and with just a few quick pumps, you can say a lot about yourself: Too much oomph, and you appear domineering. Come on too soft, and exude incompetence. Fret too much, and you're headed for a clammy clasp that'll send your fellow shaker into instant recoil.

But the right shake, on the other hand, can convey openness, respect, confidence, and vitality. "It says 'I'm a person of substance, I'm to be taken seriously,'" says Marjorie Brody, author of several books on business etiquette and professionalism, including the recently released *Help! Was That a Career Limiting Move?*

PREPARE YOUR PAW. In her 25 years as an executive coach, speaker, and author, Brody has learned to appreciate the gesture's importance. "The handshake is the official business greeting," says the founder and CEO of Philadelphia-based Brody Communications. "It's absolutely your chance to make a first impression, and most of us just don't think about it."

That's why Brody Communications recently applied with *Chase's Calendar of Events* -- a directory of more than 12,000 special days, weeks, and months, established in 1957 and published by McGraw-Hill (MHP) -- to get some recognition for a good grip. So mark your calendars and prepare your paw, because from now on, June 28 is officially National Handshake Day.

To ring in this new, unlikeliest of special days, BusinessWeek Online asked some top experts for their take on one of the most overlooked aspects of business.

Technique
Like anything, proper technique will take you a long way. To launch a metacarpal encounter, Brody advises that you wait until you're about three feet away from the target before you extend your right arm -- at a slight angle across your chest and with your thumb up. Once you've made contact, lock hands, thumb joint to thumb joint, and commence pumping. But don't get carried away. You've got time for two, maybe three well-executed pumps before you should disengage.

Peter Post, great-grandson of the legendary matron of manners, Emily Post, and director of the Emily Post Institute, says the most important thing is to carefully moderate your squeeze. "A bone-crusher is not good, and a limp, dead fish is just awful," he says. "But a firm handshake is great."

Women
In modern U.S. culture, be it in a business or social situation, Post says everyone needs to be shaking -- men and men, women and men, and women and women. "This idea that somehow women don't have to shake hands or shouldn't shake hands is for the birds," says Post, who writes a syndicated weekly newspaper column, *Etiquette at Work*.

But, even in the 21st century, getting palmy with a member of the opposite sex gives some men the shakes. That's because, once upon a time, a gentleman wouldn't make a move for a woman's hand unless she offered it first. Though that's not proper protocol anymore, many men mistakenly stick to this bygone tradition, which can make for an awkward first encounter, Brody says.

Her advice: "Women, automatically get your hand out there because so many men will wait for you."

Confusion also still lingers regarding the appropriate cross-gender grip. Brody says under no circumstances should a man "tone down" his shake, and, for that matter, neither should a woman: "It's not the bent wrist, it's not 'grab me at the fingers,' it's not 'kiss my ring,'" Brody says. Instead, she advises, both men and women can avoid appearing condescending, domineering, wimpy, or whiny by cultivating a single, solid, universal clasp.

Frills

Of course, the secret to a satisfying shake isn't all in the hands. Post says the whole purpose of this culturally-condoned extremity embrace is to set people at ease and help establish a relationship. "A good handshake is a handshake that makes a person feel welcome and appreciated," he says.

If, like the Donald, you're a bit squeamish about going palm on palm with a room of strangers (Trump is notorious uncomfortable with the germs involved in handshaking), Post says get over it. Refusing someone's outstretched hand -- or even showing a hint of reluctance to partake in a shake -- can really put a damper on an otherwise promising encounter.

For Marilyn Holt, whose work at Seattle-based Holt Capital frequently involves connecting business owners with venture capitalists, making a solid connection is particularly important. "If people think you're a worm when they shake your hand, they're not going to invest in your company," she says.

That's why she suggests getting the whole body involved. "Shaking hands does make a difference, but you need to follow through with other behaviors," she says. "Looking people in the eye, smiling, and saying hello are equally important."

You may also want to consider spicing things up with a few frills. Frank Maguire, a corporate speaker who was one of Federal Express' (FDX) founding executives, says he warms up his handshakes by adding an extra hand. While additions like that may seem small, or even over the top, they can go a long way. "Those are little gestures that make all the difference," he says.

Preparation

To Maguire, the main concern isn't so much about style or skill as it is about awareness. "People just don't make an effort to put forth an impression," he says. "They're just not conscious of it."

So, since you never know when you'll be called to proffer up your palm, it's best to be prepared. Always dry your hands thoroughly after washing, and keep food and drinks in your left hand so you won't be caught off guard. And if your hands are sweat-prone, keep a handkerchief handy, for everyone's sake.

But in the end, good old-fashioned practice is the best preparation. "Most people are totally unaware of how their handshake comes across," Brody says. "Let's face it, we've never been trained." She suggests finding a friend, sharing a few shakes, and then getting some feedback.

Despite Brody's championing of the age-old ritual, the National Handshake Day pioneer won't have a chance to celebrate herself: She's scheduled for a solid day of teleconferencing. Anyone for a cybershake?

Michelle Dammon Loyalka

Study Questions

1. What guidelines should be considered when shaking hands?

2. How might a handshake affect a person's success in a job interview?

3 MONEY MANAGEMENT STRATEGY: FINANCIAL STATEMENTS AND BUDGETING

Chapter Overview

Successful money management is based on organized financial records, accurate personal financial statements, and effective budgeting. This chapter offers a discussion of the importance and type of financial documents. This is followed by an explanation of the components and procedures for preparing personal financial statements—the balance sheet and the cash flow statement. Next, the chapter covers the basics of developing, implementing, and evaluating a budget. Finally, savings techniques for achieving financial goals are discussed.

Learning Objectives

After studying the chapter, you will be able to:

Obj. 1 Recognize the relationships among financial documents and money management activities.

Obj. 2 Design a system for maintaining personal financial documents.

Obj. 3 Develop a personal balance sheet and cash flow statement.

Obj. 4 Create and implement a budget.

Obj. 5 Relate money management and savings activities to achieving financial goals.

Key Terms

assets	deficit	net worth
balance sheet	discretionary income	safe-deposit box
budget	income	surplus
budget variance	insolvency	take-home pay
cash flow	liabilities	
cash flow statement	liquid assets	
current liabilities	long-term liabilities	
	money management	

Pretest

True-False

_____ 1. (Obj. 2) Most financial records and documents should be stored in a safe-deposit box.

_____ 2. (Obj. 3) A balance sheet reports the current financial position of an individual or family.

_____ 3. (Obj. 3) An individual retirement account (IRA) is an example of a liquid asset.

_____ 4. (Obj. 3) Your net worth is computed by adding total assets to total liabilities.

_____ 5. (Obj. 3) If your assets exceed your liabilities, this is referred to as insolvency.

_____ 6. (Obj. 3) Wages, salaries, and commissions are cash inflows.

_____ 7. (Obj. 3) If a person's payments are greater than income for a month, this will decrease net worth.

_____ 8. (Obj. 4) Food, clothing, and transportation expenses are commonly referred to as fixed expenses.

_____ 9. (Obj. 5) A budget deficit occurs when actual spending exceeds planned spending.

_____ 10. (Obj. 5) Future value computations are used to determine the amount in savings at some later date.

Self-Guided Study Questions

Obj. 1

Planning for Successful Money Management (p. 78)

Opportunity Cost and Money Management (p. 78)

1. What are examples of trade-offs associated with money management decisions?

Components of Money Management (p. 78)

2. What are the major money management activities encountered by most people?

Obj. 2

A System for Personal Financial Records (p. 79)

3. Why is an organized financial records file important?

4. What is the purpose of a safe-deposit box?

5. What suggestions could be offered to a person designing a system for organizing and storing financial records and documents?

Obj. 3

Personal Financial Statements for Measure Financial Progress (p. 81)

6. What are the main purposes of personal financial statements?

The Personal Balance Sheet: Where Are You Now? (p. 81)

7. What is the purpose of a balance sheet?

8. What are the three categories of assets?

9. How do current liabilities differ from long-term liabilities?

10. How is a person's or household's net worth computed? What does this number represent?

11. What is insolvency?

Evaluating Your Financial Position (p. 84)

12. What information does a debt ratio, a current ratio, and other ratios provide?

The Cash Flow Statement: Where Did Your Money Go? (p. 84)

13. What purpose does a cash flow statement serve?

14. What are common sources of income?

15. What are commonly used categories for cash outflows?

16. What is the effect of a negative cash flow on a person's financial position?

Obj. 4

Budgeting for Skilled Money Management (p. 88)

17. What purposes does a budget serve?

Starting the Budgeting Process (p. 88)

18. What factors affect your daily financial choices?

19. What are some common financial goals?

20. What information sources are available to assist a person in developing a budget?

21. What is the difference between fixed and variable expenses?

22. What is a budget variance?

23. What factors should be considered when reviewing a budget for possible changes?

Characteristics of Successful Budgeting (p. 93)

24. What are the qualities of a successful budget?

25. What types of financial recordkeeping systems are available for maintaining budget information?

Obj. 5

Money Management and Achieving Financial Goals (p. 95)

26. What relationship exists among the balance sheet, cash flow statement, and a budget?

Identifying Savings Goals (p. 96)

27. What are common reasons for saving?

Selecting a Savings Technique (p. 97)

28. What are methods that can be used to increase a person's savings?

Calculating Savings Amounts (p. 97)

29. How can the time value of money be used to reach savings goals?

Post Test

Completion

1. (Obj. 3) _____ assets are cash and items of value that can easily be converted to cash.

2. (Obj. 4) A budget _____ is the difference between the amount budgeted and the actual amount received or spent.

3. (Obj. 3) A(n) _____ _____ reports the assets, liabilities, and net worth of a family or individual.

4. (Obj. 3) A person's earnings after deductions is referred to as _____ _____.

5. (Obj. 3) Amounts owed to others are called _____.

6. (Obj. 3) A summary of cash receipts and payments for a period of time is reported on a(n) _____ _____ _____.

7. (Obj. 3) _____ is the financial position in which your total liabilites are greater than the value of your assets.

8. (Obj. 4) Budget _____ are amounts allocated for various spending categories.

9. (Obj. 3) The difference between total assets and total liabilities is referred to as _____ _____.

10. (Obj. 2) A(n) _____ _____ is a private storage area at a financial institution that offers maximum security for valuables.

Multiple Choice

_____ 1. (Obj. 2) Which of the following items is most likely to be stored in a safe-deposit box?
   A. Paycheck stubs
   B. Savings' certificates
   C. Income tax returns
   D. Bank statements

_____ 2. (Obj. 3) The purpose of a balance sheet is to
   A. report a person's or family's financial position.
   B. serve as a plan for spending.
   C. report current income and expenses.
   D. project a person's or a family's future financial position.

_____ 3. (Obj. 3) Which of the following would be an example of a liquid asset?
   A. A savings account
   B. Furniture
   C. Stocks and bonds
   D. An individual retirement account

_____ 4. (Obj. 3) The net worth of an individual or family is determined by
   A. subtracting expenses from income.
   B. adding income and expenses.
   C. adding assets and liabilities.
   D. subtracting liabilities from assets.

_____ 5. (Obj. 3) Which of the following would result in an increase in net worth?
   A. Reduced income
   B. Reduced spending
   C. Increased amounts owed to others
   D. Decreased value of personal belongings

_____ 6. (Obj. 3) A common example of a fixed expense is
   A. food.
   B. telephone.
   C. rent.
   D. clothing purchases.

_____ 7. (Obj. 3) The purpose of a cash flow statement is to
   A. budget for future spending.
   B. report current income and payments.
   C. summarize assets and liabilities of an individual or family.
   D. project the future value of investments.

_____ 8. (Obj. 4) The main purpose of a budget is to
   A. determine the future value of investments.
   B. plan spending.
   C. determine a person's current financial situation.
   D. report assets and liabilities.

_____ 9. (Obj. 4) A budget _____ occurs when actual spending exceeds budgeted spending.
   A. surplus
   B. deficit
   C. restriction
   D. reduction

_____ 10. (Obj. 5) Which of the following time value of money computations would be used to determine the value of $100 three years from now?
   A. Future value of a single amount
   B. Future value of a series of deposits
   C. Present value of a single amount
   D. Present value of a series of deposits

Problems, Applications, and Cases

1. Develop a financial document and records filing system based on the categories and information presented on pages 79-80 of the text.

2. Create a balance sheet and income statement based on the following information for Gail Johnson; date the balance sheet September 30 of the current year and the income statement for the month ended September 30 of the current year.

Balance sheet data
Cash in checking account $460
Retirement account $7,690
Value of furniture $2,560
Credit card balances $563
Value of automobile $5,600
Jewelry $340
Auto loan balance $1,239
Savings certificate $3,000
Cash value of life insurance $2,298
Cameras $980
Savings accounts $1,256
Value of clothing $1,800
Credit union loan $315
Value of stereo $1,150
Amount owed to dentist $76
Antiques $2,100

Cash flow statement data
Food (home and away) $467
Gifts $45
Electricity $67
Rent $810
Clothing $108
Take-home pay $2,078
Auto loan payment $211
Water $22
Auto insurance $38
Telephone $43
Interest earned on savings $34
Heat $47
Cable television $26
Personal care/reading materials $63
Medical expenses $65

3. Through library research, the Internet, and discussion with others, determine the common budget category percentages for such expenses as food, housing, transportation, clothing, personal care, entertainment/recreation, and savings.

4. Conduct a survey of common financial goals of families and individuals. Categorize these goals using the following headlines:

Short-term goals (less than two years)	Intermediate goals (2-5 years)	Long-term goals (over 5 years)

5. Create a budget for a month similar to Exhibit 3-7 (page 90 in text).

6. For each of the following living expenses, decide if the item is generally fixed or variable:

	Fixed or variable expense?
a. Personal care	
b. Transportation	
c. Mortgage payments	
d. Telephone	
e. Gifts	
f. Loan payments	
g. Food	
h. Savings	

Supplementary Case 3-1: A Money Management Mess

Topic: Financial Records and Savings Goals

Text Reference: pp. 79-80; 95-98

Jeff Conrad completed high school two years ago. Afterward, he continued to live with his parents while attending college across town. He had a part-time job as a sales and inventory clerk at a department store. With his income, he was able to pay his school expenses and save $1,000. Since his parents paid for housing and food, he was able to make car payments, buy clothes, and spend money on entertainment activities.

During the past two years, Jeff never kept track of his spending habits. His financial record-keeping consisted of depositing half of his income in a checking account and half in a savings account. Whenever he needed to pay a bill or make a purchase, he would write a check. If he didn't have enough money in checking, he would transfer funds from savings to checking. When he decided to get his own apartment, he didn't have a realistic picture of his finances and living expenses.

During the first few months in his apartment, Jeff was able to work full-time and could pay his bills on time. When school started in September, however, his income decreased since he worked fewer hours. Also, he had to use most of his savings to pay for tuition and books. These school costs were higher than those he had paid the previous year.

As time passed, Jeff had other expenses, such as automobile repairs, insurance for his car and other property, and medical bills. The cost of food, electricity, and telephone was higher than he had anticipated. Jeff's financial independence was not as pleasant as he had hoped it would be.

Budgeting and an understanding of living expenses are skills that many people learn only after difficult experiences. An ability to plan and document spending is the starting point of successful money management and effective financial planning.

Case Questions

1. What actions could Jeff Conrad have taken to prepare for his financial independence from his parents?

2. What common problems did Jeff encounter because he did not have an organized system of financial records and documents?

3. How effective would Jeff's financial record-keeping system be for developing personal financial statements and a budget? Explain.

4. What are common savings goals for persons in Jeff's situation? What money management activities would be most effective in achieving these goals?

Supplementary Case 3-2: Beth's Unbalanced Books

Topic: Personal Financial Statements

Text Reference: pp. 81-87

Beth Lyons is employed as a word processing supervisor for an investment company. She lives in a small house about 20 minutes from work, and she drives a two-year-old car. She is making payments on both the house and the car. Beth has a steady income and can afford to buy many other items. She recently redecorated several rooms in her house, and during each of the past five years she has taken a vacation.

Even though Beth handles business records and documents at work, she is frequently late in making payments to her creditors. Also, the insurance coverage for her home and car is not adequate to cover their value.

Beth has the following assets and liabilities:

Savings/investment account, $800
Market value of automobile, $11,000
Mortgage balance, $66,000
Household possessions, $18,500
Credit card balances, $8,600
Market value of home, $83,000
Checking account balance, $340
Personal loans, $1,700

Case Questions

1. Which financial documents does Beth need?
2. How could Beth become better organized in handling her personal finances?
3. Compute Beth's net worth based on the data provided.
4. How would a personal balance sheet and a personal cash flow statement assist Beth in her financial planning?

Supplementary Case 3-3: Mismanaged Money

Topic: Personal Financial Statement and Budgeting

Text Reference: pp. 81-96

Julie and Ralph Palmer have been married six years. They have a combined income of $50,000. With total assets of $110,000, they have only $500 in savings. Their liabilities total $80,600.

Each time the Palmers have a substantial amount of savings, they spend it for such things as vacations, furniture, or home entertainment equipment. Currently, their annual expenses include $11,325 listed as "unaccounted for." This amount is in addition to the amounts they spend for food, housing, utilities, transportation, loan payments, insurance, donations, gifts, and taxes. The Palmers live in a town house, but they would like to buy a detached house.

Case Questions

1. What is the net worth of the Palmers? What is your opinion of their current financial position?
2. How could the Palmers improve their financial position?
3. What changes would you suggest in the Palmers' budgeting techniques?
4. How could the Palmers be more effective in their financial planning?

Supplementary Reading 3

Lindsey Gerdes, "Online Extra: Personal Finance for Freshmen," *Special Report*, November 14, 2005

Online Extra: Personal Finance for Freshmen

College students need money smarts if they want to succeed after graduation. Increasingly, schools are offering assistance

Undergrads who believe GPAs and test scores determine whether they can go to graduate school should consider another number: their credit score. Some law and medical schools encourage -- and a few actually require -- admitted students to submit their credit score to help the school decide if applicants have the means and commitment to complete the degree. Georgetown Law School urges students with severe credit issues to defer for a year while getting their finances in order. "The decisions they make today have a cumulative impact on practicing law," says Ruth Lammert-Reeves, Georgetown's assistant dean for financial aid. According to Reeves, bar examiners in states such as California and New York take an applicant's observance of fiduciary responsibility into consideration. The Medical College of Wisconsin even reserves the right to deny admittance if a student doesn't provide a clean credit report. SURPRISE DISCOVERY. Such actions may seem harsh, but institutions say they want to ensure that financial ignorance doesn't jeopardize a student's graduate education or career aspirations. "I believe we're moving into more of an advocacy role to teach them to be wise and cautious about money issues and spending habits," says Anthony Sozzo, associate dean for student affairs at New York Medical College. Sozzo, who also teaches a two-hour financial-planning seminar to students each year, says the school "strongly encourages" students to submit a credit check upon acceptance, and 100% comply with the request. A bonus: Some students have discovered credit-report errors or identity-theft issues that they were then able to correct. Undergraduate institutions are also getting in on the act, helping newly independent 17- and 18-year-old students just beginning to understand this responsibility. "I tell my students, you have to leave Ohio State with two products," says Tally Hart, director of financial aid at Ohio State University. "One is an excellent academic record reflecting the great course work. The second is a great financial record." "IN MY CORNER." After research showed that students were much more likely to drop out of school because of "outside pressures" -- such as finances and a part-time job -- than poor grades, Hart developed a seven-week "Success Series." Every freshman is required to complete several sessions on such issues as debt management, academic engagement, and leadership, in order to receive credit for a mandatory Survey 100 class. Sessions on savings and investing, credit-card abuse, and identity theft are particularly popular. Freshmen retention has improved each year since the program was founded in 2001, according to Hart. Students aren't necessarily the only ones that benefit when their financial knowledge is boosted. Chapman University, in Orange County, Calif., hired financial coaching company InsideTrack in 2003 and continues to recoup the program's cost, thanks to higher retention rates. Founded in 1999, InsideTrack provides coaches who schedule weekly one-on-one meetings with students to discuss progress in areas like personal finance and academics, recommend useful on-campus resources, and help them cut through administrative red tape. In most cases, the university itself foots the bill. "I just thought it was exceptional to have somebody in my corner," says 26-year-old Nicole Marai, an undergraduate student at Chapman. An InsideTrack coach helped her clear up an important financial-aid issue. Marai, who juggles going to school with working and raising a 4-year-old son, found it too time-consuming to handle alone. BEYOND FREE LUNCH. Students who don't face such immediate financial concerns often think financial-literacy courses are unnecessary, but their parents may beg to differ -- even those footing the bill for college. "They really want to know that students learn how to handle life after college as well," says Mahnaz Mahdavi, professor of economics at Smith College. Parents who have made a substantial investment in their children's future realize that a well-educated and financially savvy young person is more likely to thrive in post-graduate life -- and is less likely to require further financial support. Mahdavi is also director of the Women's Financial Education Program that Smith has offered to its all-female student body since 2001. The impetus for the program was research suggesting that women generally have far less basic financial knowledge than their male counterparts have. She says she made the quartet of voluntary eight-week courses -- which cover entrepreneurship, personal finance, interpreting financial news, and investing -- appealing by offering them on a weekly basis for an hour at lunchtime. Free lunch is even provided. After taking their final exams, seniors also are encouraged to attend "From Backpack to Briefcase," a three-hour course that covers subjects ranging from types of insurance to retirement plans. Roughly 25% of Smith students choose to participate in these noncredit courses -- a respectable but hardly spectacular turnout. PEER PERSUASION. Some colleges have found that offering for-credit financial-literacy courses within their curriculums provides students with additional incentives to attend. "Students can fulfill a requirement and get information they can use for the rest of their lives," says Melinda Burke, director of the University of Arizona's Terry J. Lundgren Center for Education and Research, of the school's "Money, Consumers, and the Family" course. Arizona also offers peer-to-peer financial counseling, an increasingly popular method of reaching out to students, through a student group called Credit-Wise Cats. The Cats are affiliated with Students in Free Enterprise (SIFE), a global nonprofit organization that encourages student-led community outreach on four topics, including personal financial-success skills. Morgan Clevenger, SIFE's financial-literacy program director, feels students may be more comfortable discussing financial issues with SIFE members than with adults. "They're at the same level," says Clevenger of the peer counselors from 96 universities who participate in the program. While financial-literacy initiatives are becoming increasingly common at U.S. colleges and universities, many schools still simply incorporate financial tips into freshman orientation and leave it at that. Such an approach isn't adequate, believes research consultant Lana Low, who interviewed 125 institutions for a 2004 financial-literacy study done for educational-consulting firm USA Funds. "I think financial literacy should become part of the fabric of an institution," Low says. She points out that financial pressures continue to build throughout students' time at college, as they often accrue more and more debt. Despite the various approaches schools are taking, the reality is that plenty of undergrads must learn the hard way: Their financial education begins only after having been denied a loan or forced to delay graduate studies.

Lindsey Gerdes, New York

Study Questions

1. What are some of the common personal financial planning mistakes of beginning college students?

2. What actions might be taken to avoid these errors?

4 PLANNING YOUR TAX STRATEGY

Chapter Overview

The basics of taxes and their relationship to financial planning are presented in this chapter. The material starts with a brief discussion of types of taxes. Next, the fundamental aspects of federal income taxes are presented, including taxable income, deductions, exemptions, tax rates, and tax credits. The information on filing your federal income tax return covers filing status, types of tax forms, basic steps for completing Form 1040, tax assistance sources, and audit procedures. Finally, the chapter concludes with a discussion of tax planning strategies related to purchasing decisions, investment alternatives, and retirement plans.

Learning Objectives

After studying the chapter, you will be able to:

Obj. 1 Describe the importance of taxes for personal financial planning.

Obj. 2 Calculate taxable income and the amount owed for federal income tax.

Obj. 3 Prepare a federal income tax return.

Obj. 4 Identify tax assistance sources.

Obj. 5 Select appropriate tax strategies for different financial and personal situations.

Key Terms

adjusted gross income (AGI)	inheritance tax	tax avoidance
average tax rate	investment income	tax credit
capital gains	itemized deductions	tax deduction
earned income	marginal tax rate	tax-deferred income
estate tax	passive income	tax evasion
excise tax	standard deduction	tax-exempt income
exclusion	taxable income	tax shelter
exemption	tax audit	

Pretest

True-False

_____ 1. (Obj. 1) Federal income tax is based on a person's earnings.

_____ 2. (Obj. 1) Inheritance taxes are also referred to as gift taxes.

_____ 3. (Obj. 1) An excise tax is a sales tax on specific goods and services.

_____ 4. (Obj. 2) Earned income refers to money received in the form of dividends or interest

_____ 5. (Obj. 2) Medical expenses, real estate property taxes, and home mortgage interest may qualify as itemized deductions for federal income tax purposes.

_____ 6. (Obj. 2) A tax credit is a deduction that reduces the amount of taxable income.

_____ 7. (Obj. 2) Most employees are required to make quarterly payments for estimated taxes owed.

_____ 8. (Obj. 3) The Form 1040A is used by a taxpayer who plans to itemize deductions.

_____ 9. (Obj. 4) A correspondence tax audit requires a person to report to a local IRS office.

_____ 10. (Obj. 5) An IRA is an example of a tax-exempt investment.

Self-Guided Study Questions

Obj. 1

Taxes and Financial Planning (p. 106)

1. What are common goals for tax planning efforts?

2. What is the main purpose of taxes?

3. What are the main types of taxes paid by individuals and households?

4. How does an excise tax differ from a general sales tax?

Obj. 2

Income Tax Fundamentals (p. 107)

Step 1: Determining Adjusted Gross Income (p. 107)

5. What is taxable income?

6. How does earned income differ from investment income?

7. What is the difference between tax-exempt income and tax-deferred income?

Step 2: Computing Taxable Income (p. 109)

8. How do deductions and exemptions affect taxes?

Step 3: Calculating Taxes Owed (p. 112)

9. What procedure is used to determine the amount of taxes due?

10. What is the difference between the marginal tax rate and the average tax rate?

11. What is a tax credit?

Making Tax Payments (p. 113)
12. What is the purpose of the tax withholding system?

13. Who must make estimated quarterly payments?

Deadlines and Penalties (p. 115)
14. What is the purpose of Form 4868?

Obj. 3

Filing Your Federal Income Tax Return (p. 115)

Who Must File? (p. 115)
15. Who is required to file a federal income tax return?

16. What are the main filing status categories?

Which Tax Form Should You Use? (p. 116)
17. What factors affect a person's decision to file the Form 1040EZ, Form 1040A, or Form 1040?

Completing the Federal Income Tax Return (p. 116)

18. What determines if a person receives a refund or owes an amount for taxes due?

Obj. 4

Tax Assistance and the Audit Process (p. 120)

Tax Information Sources (p. 120)

19. What services does the IRS provide to assist taxpayers in preparing their tax returns?

Tax Preparation Software (p. 123)

20. What are the main benefits of using tax preparation software?

Electronic Filing (p. 123)

21. What procedures are involved with online filing of taxes?

Tax Preparation Services (p. 124)

22. What individuals and organizations are available to help people with their tax returns?

What if Your Return is Audited? (p. 125)

23. What is a tax audit?

24. What are the main types of IRS audits?

25. What is the appeal process for an IRS audit?

Obj. 5

Tax Planning Strategies (p. 126)

26. What is the difference between tax avoidance and tax evasion?

Consumer Purchasing (p. 127)

27. What types of interest payments are tax deductible?

28. What are some job-related tax deductions?

Investment Decisions (p. 128)

29. What are the benefits of tax-deferred investments?

Retirement Plans (p. 129)

30. How do individual retirement accounts, Keogh plans, and 401(k) plans provide tax benefits for workers?

Post Test

Completion

1. (Obj. 2) A tax _____ is an amount subtracted directly from the amount of taxes owed.
2. (Obj. 1) A tax imposed on specific goods and services is a(n) _____ tax.
3. (Obj. 5) A(n) _____ _____ is a profit realized from the sale of a capital asset such as stocks, bonds, or real estate.
4. (Obj. 4) A detailed examination of your tax return by the IRS is called a(n) _____ _____.
5. (Obj. 2) _____ income is money received by an individual for personal effort.
6. (Obj. 1) A(n) _____ tax is levied on the value of property bequeathed by a deceased person.
7. (Obj. 2) _____ _____ are expenses that a taxpayer is allowed to deduct from adjusted gross income, such as real estate property tax and home mortgage interest.
8. (Obj. 2) A deduction from adjusted gross income for yourself, your spouse, or qualified dependents is a(n) _____.
9. (Obj. 5) Tax _____ income includes interest from municipal bonds.
10. (Obj. 2) An amount not included in gross income is a(n) _____.

Multiple Choice

1. (Obj. 1) An estate tax is based on
   A. income.
   B. property value.
   C. earnings.
   D. retirement benefits.

2. (Obj. 1) A tax on specific goods and services is a(n)
   A. social security tax.
   B. general sales tax.
   C. corporate income tax.
   D. excise tax.

3. (Obj. 2) Money received in the form of dividends or interest is commonly referred to as _____ income.
   A. investment
   B. earned
   C. passive
   D. excluded

4. (Obj. 2) Which of the following is an example of an itemized deduction?
   A. Child care expenses
   B. Expenses to travel to work
   C. Real estate property taxes
   D. Life insurance premiums

5. (Obj. 2) An exemption is a deduction from adjusted gross income for
   A. yourself and your dependents.
   B. money earned while living in a foreign country.
   C. money donated to charity.
   D. earnings from stocks and bonds.

6. (Obj. 2) Which of the following people is most likely to be required to make quarterly estimated tax payments?
   A. A person who is employed by a non-profit organization
   B. A person with excessive federal income tax withheld from his or her pay
   C. An employee of a government agency
   D. A person who earned large amounts of dividends and interest

7. (Obj. 3) Which of the following filing status categories would most likely be used by a person who is married with a dependent child, and is living apart from the spouse?
   A. Single
   B. Head of household
   C. Married filing separate return
   D. Married filing joint return

8. (Obj. 4) Government-approved tax experts who prepare tax returns are
   A. enrolled agents.
   B. IRS agents.
   C. auditors.
   D. accountants.

9. (Obj. 4) Which type of IRS audit requires a visit to your home or office?
   A. Research
   B. Office
   C. Correspondence
   D. Field

_____ 10. (Obj. 5) Interest paid on a(n) _____ is fully deductible as an itemized deduction.
   A. credit card
   B. auto loan of less than $20,000
   C. home equity loan
   D. personal cash loan from a credit union

Problems, Applications, and Cases

1. Based on the following information, determine the amount of taxable income for Joanna Thompson. (Refer to text pages 107-113 to review this material.)

    gross income $37,000

    exclusions $3,400

    exemption value $2,050

    standard deduction $3,000

    taxable income $ _____.

2. Obtain current income tax forms and instructions. Use this material to prepare your own taxes. IRS Web site: www.irs.gov

3. Conduct a survey of people who prepare their own taxes and people who have someone else prepare their taxes. What are the main reasons given for the method of tax preparation selected by various individuals?

Supplementary Case 4-1: Taxes and Financial Planning

Topic: Tax Planning Activities

Text Reference: pp. 107-115; 126-131

Bob and Connie Martin have always considered themselves careful in their budgeting and savings activities. They never use credit cards; they pay all bills, including their monthly rent, on time; and they have several thousand dollars in savings certificates. However, tax planning is an area of weakness in what the Martins believe to be good financial planning and money management habits. Each year, they pay much more in taxes than they need to; quite often, they have had to take money out of savings to make their tax payment.

Case Questions

1. How might the Martins' housing situation be changed for better tax planning?
2. What savings and investment alternatives might reduce the Martins' tax liability?
3. What could the Martins do to prevent having to pay the government tax owed?
4. What additional suggestions with regard to effective tax planning could be offered to the Martins?

Supplementary Case 4-2: Taxes for a Home-Based Business

Topic: Tax Planning

Text Reference: pp. 107-120

In an effort to spend more time with their family and to have more flexible careers, Doris and Bob Hannon have decided to leave their current jobs and start a home-based business. They have years of experience in the areas of graphic arts, sales, marketing, and computers. As a result, the Hannons are operating a combination promotion and design company. Their main clients include local businesses and others who need brochures, newsletters, and promotional materials.

To get things started, the Hannons set up a portion of their home as an office and design studio. They purchased appropriate office equipment, computers, and software. The Hannons also had to purchase a variety of supplies and encountered more start-up costs than they estimated.

Next, they had to promote their business. They distributed fliers, put ads in local newspapers, and visited many businesses. One weekend, Doris and Bob attended a trade show of companies from around the state. This gave them names of potential clients for their services.

To keep up with personal living expenses, the Hannons received monthly interest payments from federal government securities and municipal bonds. In addition, Bob maintains a part-time job at a local retail store.

During their first year of business, the Hannons were able to generate $43,000 in revenue for the company. The expenses for the business were either $28,500 or $47,800 depending on what they included!

Doris asked, "Well Bob, did we make money or did we lose money?" "I'm not sure," Bob responded. "I'm not sure."

Case Questions

1. What are the main tax benefits of owning your own business?
2. What types of taxable income must the Hannons report for federal income tax purposes?
3. What factors could have accounted for the differences in total expenses for the Hannon's business?

Supplementary Reading 4

Lewis Braham, "Time for a Yearend Checkup", Personal Business, October 31, 2005.

Time For A Yearend Checkup

If you want to fund a new wing at your alma mater or start a foundation to benefit hurricane victims, now's the time to do it. According to the Katrina Emergency Tax Relief Act of 2005, donors to any charity in 2005 are allowed to deduct the entire contribution come tax time instead of the usual maximum of 50% of adjusted gross income. What's more, contributions exceeding your income can be carried forward for five years.

This is but one new feature of the tax code worth taking advantage of before 2005 ends. Other perks are extensions or hikes of existing benefits and deductions. For instance, like last year, taxpayers may opt to deduct their state sales tax instead of their income tax, a perk for residents of the nine states without income taxes and for shoppers in general. "This is the last year sales taxes will be deductible," says Bob Scharin, editor of the journal *Practical Tax Strategies*. "If you're planning on making a substantial purchase -- a car, jewelry, appliances -- do it before the year ends."

If you have a large amount of appreciated stock, it might be good to start "gifting" it to your children or grandchildren, says tax analyst Mark Luscombe of CCH Tax & Accounting. Long-term capital-gains tax rates are currently only 5% for people with incomes lower than $29,700 this year -- most children fall into this category -- compared with 15% for those with higher incomes. You can give up to $11,000 a year to a recipient without having to pay the gift tax. And you can exceed that limit as long as you don't give more than $1 million in your lifetime. But children under age 14 cannot receive more than $14,000 a year without being subject to the "kiddie tax" -- they're taxed at the donor's rate after that level.

Of course, not everything in the tax code this year is a gift. Millions of Americans will suffer again from the alternative minimum tax (AMT), which disallows deductions for people in high income brackets -- and sometimes for those in the middle, too. In fact, an AMT exemption, created in 2001, expires at the end of this year. Unless Congress votes to extend it, the ranks of AMT sufferers will explode. "About 3 million people will be subject this year," says tax expert Martin Nissenbaum of Ernst & Young. "Next year there'll be 12 million to 13 million unless something is done." Because of that risk, Nissenbaum recommends that taxpayers not subject to the AMT this year accelerate their deductions, such as paying January real estate taxes in December, to avoid taking a hit next year.

When doing your tax checkup, also consider the following:

-- Higher-education deduction: Individuals may take a $4,000 deduction to pay for college expenses if their income does not exceed $65,000 ($130,000 for married couples). Those with incomes lower than $80,000 ($160,000 for married couples) may take a $2,000 deduction.

-- IRA contributions: You have until Apr. 15, 2006, to contribute up to $4,000 ($4,500 if you're 50 or older) for 2005.

-- Medical expenses: These must exceed 7.5% of your adjusted gross income to be deductible. If you're near that threshold, you may want to have elective surgery or dental work done now and pay for it before yearend.

Lewis Braham

Study Questions

1. What types of tax changes occur on a regular basis?

2. How can taxpayers stay informed on various tax law changes?

5 THE BANKING SERVICES OF FINANCIAL INSTITUTIONS

Chapter Overview

Using savings plans, checking accounts, and other financial services is a primary personal financial planning activity. This chapter starts with an overview of these services followed by a discussion of the changing environment of financial services caused by technology and economic conditions. Next, discussion of the different types of financial institutions is offered along with the factors to consider when selecting one. Coverage of choosing and using savings plans includes material on the types of accounts that are available. Finally, selection and use of checking and other payment accounts is presented.

Learning Objectives

After studying this chapter, you will be able to:

Obj. 1 Identify factors that affect selection and use of financial services.

Obj. 2 Compare the different types of financial institutions.

Obj. 3 Compare the costs and benefits of various savings plans.

Obj. 4 Identify the factors used to evaluate different savings plans.

Obj. 5 Compare the costs and benefits of different types of payment accounts.

Key Terms

annual percentage yield
asset management account
automatic teller machine
certificate of deposit
commercial bank
compounding
credit union

debit card
demand deposit
money market account
money market fund
mutual savings bank
NOW account
overdraft protection

rate of return
savings and loan association
share account
share draft account
time deposits
trust

Pretest

True-False

_____ 1. (Obj. 1) Increased borrowing is a quick source of cash, however your net worth is reduced.

_____ 2. (Obj. 1) Savings accounts are also referred to as *time deposits*.

_____ 3. (Obj. 1) A debit card allows a financial institution customer to charge purchases that can be paid for later.

_____ 4. (Obj. 1) *Demand deposits* refer to money in checking accounts.

_____ 5. (Obj. 2) A mutual savings bank is the financial institution that offers the widest range of services.

_____ 6. (Obj. 4) The more frequent the compounding on savings, the lower the rate of return that is earned.

_____ 7. (Obj. 3) Savings certificates usually have a higher liquidity than a regular savings account.

_____ 8. (Obj. 5) A Smart card is a type of checking account.

_____ 9. (Obj. 5) An activity checking account is designed for people who write many checks each month.

_____ 10. (Append.) A blank endorsement requires the words "for deposit only."

Self-Guided Study Questions

Obj. 1

A Cash Management Strategy (p. 138)

Meeting Daily Money Needs (p. 138)

1. What are common sources of quick cash?

Types of Financial Services (p. 139)

2. What are the main financial services used by most consumers?

3. How do demand deposits differ from time deposits?

4. What are the benefits of an asset management account?

Electronic Banking Services (p. 140)

5. How does a debit card differ from a credit card?

6. What services are available with an electronic banking system?

7. What are "web-only" banks?

Opportunity Costs of Financial Services (p. 141)

8. What common trade-offs are present when selecting financial services?

Financial Services and Economic Conditions (p. 141)

9. How can changing interest rates affect use of financial services?

Obj. 2

Financial Institutions (p. 142)

10. What types of organizations are considered to be "financial supermarkets"?

Deposit Institutions (p. 142)

11. How are commercial banks organized and chartered?

12. What are the main services of a savings and loan association?

13. How does a mutual savings bank differ from other financial institutions?

14. What are the main advantages of using a credit union?

Other Financial Institutions (p. 144)

15. How does a money market fund operate?

16. What costs are associated with using a pawnshop or check-cashing outlet?

Comparing Financial Institutions (p. 145)

17. What factors are commonly considered by consumers when selecting a financial institution?

Obj. 3

Savings Plans (p. 147)

18. What are the main types of savings instruments available to consumers?

19. What are the main types of certificates of deposit?

20. How does a money market account differ from a money market fund?

21. What are the benefits of U.S. savings bonds?

Obj. 4

Evaluating Savings Plans (p. 150)

22. How does frequency of compounding affect the yield in a savings plan?

23. What is the purpose of the Truth-in-Savings law?

24. What is liquidity?

25. What is the purpose of the Federal Deposit Insurance Corporation?

26. What restrictions and fees may be associated with a savings account?

Obj. 5

Payment Methods (p. 154)

27. What are the common types of electronic payments and checking accounts available to consumers?

Evaluating Checking Accounts (p. 156)
28. What factors should be considered when comparing different types of checking accounts?

Managing Your Checking Account (p. 158)
29. What are the benefits of a joint checking account?

30. What are the different types of endorsement? When is each appropriate?

31. What is the purpose of a bank reconciliation? What steps are involved in the process?

Other Payment Methods (p. 159)
32. What types of payment forms are available other than personal checks?

Post Test

Completion
1. (Obj. 2) A(n) _____ _____ _____ _____ specializes in savings accounts and loans for mortgages.
2. (Obj. 4) The percentage of increase in the value of savings due to earned interest is referred to as the _____ _____ _____.
3. (Obj. 1) _____ deposits are money held in checking accounts.
4. (Obj. 5) A(n) _____ _____ _____ is an interest-bearing checking account at a credit union.

5. (Obj. 1) A(n) _____ _____ _____ is a computer terminal for banking transactions.

6. (Obj. 3) A savings plan that requires you to leave a certain amount on deposit for a set time period in order to receive a certain interest rate is a(n) _____ _____ _____.

7. (Obj. 1) A complete financial services program for a single fee is referred to as a(n) _____ _____ _____.

8. (Obj. 2) A(n) _____ _____ is a non-profit financial institution.

9. (Obj. 4) Interest that is earned on previously earned interest is called _____.

10. (Obj. 1) Savings accounts and savings certificates are referred to as _____ deposits.

Multiple Choice

_____ 1. (Obj. 2) Financial services would usually be most expensive at a
   A. credit union.
   B. check cashing outlet.
   C. commercial bank.
   D. financial supermarket.

_____ 2. (Obj. 1) Which of the following would be an example of a demand deposit?
   A. A savings account
   B. A savings certificate
   C. A checking account
   D. A money market account

_____ 3. (Obj. 2) Traditionally, the widest range of financial services has been offered by
   A. credit unions.
   B. investment companies.
   C. mutual savings banks.
   D. commercial banks.

_____ 4. (Obj. 1) The purpose of a trust is to
   A. combine all financial services into one account.
   B. earn high rates of return on savings.
   C. manage funds for another person.
   D. obtain highly liquid investments.

_____ 5. (Obj. 4) _____ refers to the earnings received on savings.
   A. Yield
   B. Compounding
   C. Liquidity
   D. Insolvency

6. (Obj. 4) Which of the following savings plans has the highest liquidity?
   A. An interest-earning checking
   B. A savings certificate
   C. A U.S. savings bond
   D. An individual retirement account

7. (Obj. 4) A return of 6 percent on a savings account for a person with a 30 percent tax rate would mean an after-tax rate of return of _____ percent.
   A. 30
   B. 6
   C. 1.8
   D. 4.2

8. (Obj. 5) Which of the following is an interest-bearing checking account?
   A. EFT account
   B. Share-draft account
   C. Activity account
   D. Share account

9. (Append.) A _____ endorsement includes the words "for deposit only."
   A. blank
   B. complete
   C. restrictive
   D. special

10. (Append.) Which of the following items would be subtracted from your checkbook balance when preparing a bank reconciliation?
    A. Interest earned
    B. Outstanding checks
    C. Deposits in transit
    D. Service charges

Problems, Applications, and Cases

1. For each of the following influences on financial institutions and services, list an observed change that has occurred in recent years in your community.

Factor affecting financial services	Recent changes in financial institutions or services in your community
Legislative actions	
Economic conditions	
Technology	

2. Survey people in your community to determine which financial institution is strongest with regard to each of the following factors

    a. variety of services offered

    b. personal service

    c. convenience (location, hours, electronic banking services)

    d. return on savings

    e. low-cost checking

3. Survey several local financial institutions to compare the features of their savings plans (refer to text pages 147-154).

4. What would be the ending balance of the following savings accounts?

    a. $560 earning 7% (compounded annually) after one year

    b. $700 earning 8% (compounded quarterly) after three years

    c. $235 earning 5% (compounded annually) after two years

    d. $1,290 earning 12% (compounded monthly) after one year

5. With the use of the Internet (www.federalreserve.gov), *The Wall Street Journal, Business Week*, and other sources of current business news, update the interest rates presented on page 143.

6. Conduct a survey of checking services at financial institutions in your community. Also refer to text pages 155-158 for information on evaluating various types of checking accounts.

7. Prepare a bank reconciliation based on the information given below; also refer to text pages 159-160.

   Bank statement balance $436

   Unadjusted checkbook balance $234

   Total of outstanding checks $293

   Monthly service charge $4

   Deposit in transit $87

   Corrected (adjusted) checkbook balance $ _____

Supplementary Case 5-1: Evaluating Financial Institutions

Topic: Comparing Financial Institutions

Text Reference: pp. 142-146

Barb Kenton is a member of the credit union at her place of work. This financial institution offers regular savings accounts, share draft checking, and a variety of loans. It does not offer electronic banking, mortgages, or investment advice.

Barb's husband, Lance, is a manager at a department store in a local shopping center. Recently, an investment company opened a store in the mall. It offers free checking, low-cost loans, investment assistance, insurance, and real estate service. Lance believes that Barb and he should do business with this nationally known company.

Case Questions

1. What are the benefits of doing business with the credit union instead of the investment company?
2. What factors should Barb and Lance consider when they compare financial institutions?
3. What recommendations would you make to Barb and Lance about their use of financial services?

Supplementary Case 5-2: Selecting Financial Services

Topic: Comparing Financial Services

Text Reference: pp. 142-146; 155-158

Fran Hubbard lives with her two children and her father, Jerry. Although Jerry is retired, he is still very active in part-time consulting work and with various community volunteer programs. While Fran pays most of the household bills through her checking account, her father also wants to maintain his own checking account. Currently, Jerry's account requires a minimum balance of $1,500, pays a low interest rate, and has a $12 monthly charge if the balance falls below the minimum.

In recent weeks, unexpected expenses have resulted in Jerry's checking account balance dropping below the minimum balance. Jerry's pension checks are automatically deposited to his account, and he really likes the convenience of that service. In addition, Jerry is able to access various cash machines with the debit card from his bank.

Case Questions

1. What stated and implied factors probably encouraged Jerry to select his current checking account?
2. What alternatives may be available to Jerry for his checking services?
3. How might Fran and her father coordinate their financial services to minimize costs and maximize the services they receive?

Supplementary Case 5-3: Rate of Return versus Liquidity

Topic: Comparing Savings Plans

Text Reference: pp. 147-154

Martin Hoy recently obtained a bonus for a special project at work. His friends think that he should take a trip or buy a new car. However, Martin has decided to save these funds for the future.

Martin might like to buy a house in the next couple of years. Or he might want to go back to college for an advanced degree. In addition, his mother may need some financial assistance in her later years.

In viewing his alternatives, Martin has narrowed his choices to the following:

- Deposit the funds in a money-market account that earns 5.78 percent.
- Buy U.S. savings bonds, currently paying 5.67 percent.
- Purchase two-year certificates of deposit earning 6.83 percent.

Case Questions

1. What factors should Martin consider when deciding among the various savings plans?
2. Which of Martin's options has the greatest liquidity? When might liquidity be preferred over higher rate of return?
3. What action would you recommend for Martin?

Supplementary Reading 5

Justin Hibbard, "Banks Go Beyond Toasters", Personal Business, December 20, 2004.

Banks Go Beyond Toasters
Signing up for a package of services can give you convenience and discounts

Zach Maxfield spends a lot of time talking to bank salespeople. As an associate at Second Curve Capital, a New York hedge fund that specializes in bank stocks, he regularly phones branches to gauge their sales acumen. But nothing prepared him for the woman who answered his call at a Bank of America (BAC) branch in October. "I knew that banks were going crazy for cross-selling lately, but I didn't realize just how crazy," he says. All Maxfield wanted was the current money-market rate. But the woman pitched him a package that included two checking accounts, two savings accounts, a credit card, a debit card, and online banking.

Would you like fries with that? If you've heard that line, you're familiar with cross-selling. By offering discounted products to complement the one you're already buying, companies look to get more business. Banks have gone gaga for this approach, and to many people that's welcome news. According to research firm TowerGroup, 70% of U.S. consumers would like to have all of their accounts at one financial institution -- as opposed to the average of four they now have them spread across.

If you have at least three accounts and a combined balance of $10,000 or more, you're likely to benefit from a bank package. By aggregating accounts, you could save hundreds of dollars a year in fees and qualify for higher rates on savings and lower rates on loans. But if you don't maintain the minimum balance, watch out -- you'll get soaked on fees. Don't sign up for a package before shopping around and calculating the potential savings.

WAIVING FEES
Start by figuring out which packages you qualify for. Most let you combine balances from several accounts to meet a minimum and avoid fees. For example, if you keep the total deposits in your checking, savings, certificates of deposit, and individual retirement accounts above $10,000, you qualify for Bank of America's Prima package and a waiver of $20 a month in service charges. Other packages have age requirements. For customers who are 50 or older, Wachovia (WB) offers Crown Classic Banking, which provides benefits such as no fees on early CD withdrawals for health-related emergencies.

You may be able to sign up for a package at your current bank without changing your accounts. That's what happened when Cheryl Hansen visited the Wells Fargo (WFC) branch in Wallingford, Wash., earlier this year. "It was a no-brainer," she says. She and her husband already had about 10 accounts at the branch, including payroll for their lamp shop. By rearranging them into a personal package and a small-business package, the branch manager reduced the Hansens' monthly service charges without changing any account numbers or transferring balances.

If your accounts are spread across several banks, do some research before uprooting your finances. Calculate the total savings you stand to gain and compare the price of each service in a package to its stand-alone price. For example, the 10 free online stock trades that go with the Wells Fargo Portfolio Management Account are worth nearly $250 when you compare them to what they would cost with an individual WellsTrade account. Make sure to check prices at other companies, too. Online brokerages such as Scottrade offer unlimited trades for $7 a piece, which may be better for heavy traders. (Wells charges $24.95 a trade after the 10 freebies run out.)

Take a similar approach when considering bonus interest rates. If one bank charges a much higher rate on car loans than another, it doesn't matter if you can knock off a quarter point because you sign up for a package. The same goes for interest on deposits. Bank of America's Prima package pays 2% annual yield on a $10,000 nine-month CD, which is better than the 1.73% on the bank's comparable stand-alone CD. But if you deposit the same amount for a full year with no withdrawals, ING Direct pays 2.75%.

Of course, that only matters if you care about getting the best CD rate. The value of a package doesn't come from any one product but from the total savings. Wells Fargo, for example, claims its Portfolio Management Account can save customers up to $871 a year, vs. the cost of setting up all the accounts separately. That would be hard to beat by assembling your own package of products from multiple institutions.

Finally, it's worth asking: Do you need all of the products in a package? Maybe not, but as long as you maintain a minimum balance, most banks won't charge for products you don't use. Moreover, you may not need all of the products today, but you might want them later. Think of them as the extras you get with your value meal.

Justin Hibbard

Study Questions

1. What benefits are associated with packages of financial services?

2. What actions should eb taken when evaluating financial services?

6 INTRODUCTION TO CONSUMER CREDIT

Chapter Overview

This chapter defines consumer credit and analyzes its advantages and disadvantages. The importance of consumer credit in our economy is explained and uses and misuses of credit are discussed. Financial and personal opportunity costs of using credit are emphasized. Next, two types of consumer credit—closed-end and open-end credit—are differentiated. Then, general rules of measuring credit capacity such as debt payments-to-income ratio and debt-to-equity are explained. This is followed by coverage of building and maintaining credit rating. Next, the information that creditors look for in granting or refusing credit is identified, and the Equal Credit Opportunity Act is explained. Then, the steps in avoiding and correcting credit mistakes are outlined, and the provisions of the Fair Credit Billing Act are described. Finally, strategies for complaining about consumer credit are introduced, and the major consumer credit laws are summarized.

Learning Objectives

After studying this chapter, you will be able to:

Obj. 1 Define consumer credit and analyze its advantages and disadvantages.

Obj. 2 Differentiate among various types of credit.

Obj. 3 Assess your credit capacity and build your credit rating.

Obj. 4 Describe the information creditors look for when you apply for credit.

Obj. 5 Identify the steps you can take to avoid and correct credit mistakes.

Obj. 6 Describe the laws that protect you if you complain about consumer credit.

Key Terms

capacity
capital
character
closed-end credit
collateral
conditions
consumer credit

Consumer Credit Reporting Reform Act
credit
credit bureau
debit card
Equal Credit Opportunity Act (ECOA)
Fair Credit Billing Act (FCBA)

Fair Credit Reporting Act (FCRA)
home equity loan
interest
line of credit
open-end credit
revolving check credit

Pretest

True-False

_____ 1. (Obj. 1) Credit is an arrangement to receive cash, goods, or services now and pay for them in the future.

_____ 2. (Obj. 1) There are not many valid reasons for using credit.

_____ 3. (Obj. 2) With open-end credit, you pay back one-time loans in a specified period of time and payments are of equal amount.

_____ 4. (Obj. 2) Incidental credit is a credit arrangement that has no extra costs and no specific payment plan.

_____ 5. (Obj. 3) The debt payments-to-income ratio is calculated by dividing monthly debt payments (not including house payments) by net monthly income.

_____ 6. (Obj. 3) The debt-to-equity ratio is calculated by dividing total liabilities by net worth.

_____ 7. (Obj. 4) The Equal Credit Opportunity Act is not very specific about how a person's age may be used in credit decisions.

_____ 8. (Obj. 5) In case of a billing error, notify the creditor within 60 days after the bill was mailed.

_____ 9. (Obj. 5) If you think that your credit bill is wrong, you must notify the creditor in writing within 10 days after the bill was mailed.

_____ 10. (Obj. 6) The Fair Credit Reporting Act gives you the right to know what your credit file contains.

Self-Guided Study Questions

Obj. 1

What Is Consumer Credit? (p. 168)

1. What is the meaning of consumer credit?

The Importance of Consumer Credit in Our Economy (p. 168)

2. Why is consumer credit a major force in our economy?

Uses and Misuses of Credit (p. 169)

3. What are the uses and misuses of credit?

Advantages of Credit (p. 170)

4. How can credit be used to your advantage?

Disadvantages of Credit (p. 170)

5. What are the disadvantages of using credit?

Obj. 2

Types of Credit (p. 172)

6. What are the two types of consumer credit?

Closed-End Credit (p. 172)

7. Give examples of closed-end credit

8. What are the most common types of closed-end credit?

Open-End Credit (p. 173)

9. How does open-end credit differ from closed-end credit?

10. Give examples of open-end credit.

11. What is incidental credit?

12. What is a line of credit?

13. What is revolving check credit?

14. What is cobranding?

15. How do debit cards differ from credit cards?

16. What is a smart card?

17. How do you protect yourself against debit/credit card fraud?

18. What are travel and entertainment cards?

19. What is a home equity loan?

20. How much can you borrow with a home equity loan?

Obj. 3

Measuring Your Credit Capacity (p. 180)

21. What is the importance of a family budget in measuring your credit capacity?

Can You Afford a Loan? (p. 180)

22. How can you determine whether you can afford a loan?

General Rules of Credit Capacity (p. 180)

23. What are the general rules of measuring credit capacity?

24. How can debt payments-to-income ratio and debt-to-equity ratio be used to measure credit capacity?

Cosigning a Loan (p. 181)

25. What would you do if a friend or relative asked you to cosign a loan?

26. Why are cosigners asked to wholly or partially repay the loan?

27. What are a few caveats to consider if you do cosign a loan?

Building and Maintaining Your Credit Rating (p. 182)

28. What steps would you take in building and maintaining your credit rating?

Credit Bureaus (p. 182)

29. What is a credit bureau?

Who Provides Data to Credit Bureaus? (p. 182)

30. Who provides data to credit bureaus?

What's in Your Credit Files? (p. 183)

31. What information is contained in your credit files?

Fair Credit Reporting (p. 183)

32. What is the purpose of the Fair Credit Reporting Act?

Who May Obtain a Credit Report? (p. 183)

33. Can anyone obtain your credit report?

Time Limits on Adverse Data (p. 184)

34. How long can a credit bureau keep adverse information in your credit file?

Incorrect Information in Your Credit File (p. 184)

35. What can you do if there is incorrect information in your credit file?

What Are the Legal Remedies? (p. 185)

36. Do you have any legal rights and remedies if a credit bureau refuses to correct mistakes in your credit file? Explain your answer.

Obj. 4

Applying for Credit (p. 186)

A Scenario From the Past (p. 186)

37. Which federal consumer credit law starts all credit applicants off on the same footing?

38. What does the Equal Credit Opportunity Act (ECOA) state?

What Creditors Look For: The Five Cs of Credit Management (p. 186)

39. What do creditors look for when they extend credit to their customers?

40. Describe the five Cs of credit.

41. Does public assistance affect your creditworthiness? Explain.

42. Does the ECOA cover your application for a mortgage or a home improvement loan?

What if Your Application Is Denied? (p. 189)

43. What steps can you take if your application for credit is denied?

Obj. 5

Avoiding and Correcting Credit Mistakes (p. 189)

44. What are the major provisions of the Fair Credit Billing Act?

45. How does the Fair Credit Billing Act (FCBA) define a billing error?

In Case of Billing Error (p. 191)

46. What steps can you take if you think your bill is wrong or you want more information about it?

Your Credit Rating During the Dispute (p. 191)

47. What happens to your credit rating during the dispute?

Defective Goods or Services (p. 191)

48. Can you withhold payment on damaged or shoddy goods or poor services that you have purchased with a credit card?

Identity Crisis: What To Do If Your Identity Is Stolen

49. What can you do if your identity is stolen?

Obj. 6

Complaining About Consumer Credit (p. 194)

50. What should be your first step if you have a problem with your creditor?

Complaints About Banks (p. 195)

51. What can you do if you have complaints about banks?

Protection Under Consumer Credit Laws (p. 195)

52. What protections are available to you under consumer credit laws?

53. What are the Truth in Lending and Consumer Leasing Acts?

54. What is the Equal Credit Opportunity Act?

55. What is the Fair Credit Billing Act?

56. What is the Fair Credit Reporting Act?

57. What are the provisions of the Consumer Credit Reporting Reform Act?

Your Rights Under Consumer Credit Laws (p. 196)

58. What are your rights under consumer credit laws?

Post Test

Completion

1. (Obj. 1) _____ is an arrangement to receive cash, goods or services now and pay for them in the future.

2. (Obj. 2) With _____ _____ _____, you pay back a one-time loan in a specified period of time and the payments are of equal amounts.

3. (Obj. 2) With _____ _____ _____, loans are made on a continuous basis and you are billed periodically to make at least a partial payment.

4. (Obj. 2) _____ _____ _____ is the maximum amount of credit you can use.

5. (Obj. 4) By _____, we mean the borrower's attitude toward his or her credit obligations.

6. (Obj. 4) By _____, we mean the borrower's financial ability to meet credit obligations.

7. (Obj. 4) _____ is a valuable asset pledged to assure loan payments and is subject to seizure upon default.

8. (Obj. 3) Experts suggest that you spend no more than _____ _____ of your net income on credit purchases.

9. (Obj. 3) Most of the information in your credit file may be reported for only _____ _____.

10. (Obj. 5) _____ _____ _____ _____ sets the procedure for promptly correcting billing mistakes, for refusing to make credit card payments on defective goods, and for promptly crediting your payments.

Multiple Choice

1. (Obj. 1) In which period did the use of installment credit explode on the American scene?
   A. During the colonial times
   B. Before WWI
   C. In the early 1900s
   D. In the 1980s

2. (Obj. 1) Perhaps the greatest disadvantage of using credit is
   A. the temptation to overspend.
   B. to use it as leverage.
   C. that you fail to carry cash.
   D. that it results in bankruptcies.

3. (Obj. 2) Which is a good example of an open-end credit?
   A. A mortgage loan
   B. An automobile loan
   C. An installment loan
   D. A VISA and MasterCard loan

4. (Obj. 2) A credit arrangement in which loans are made on a continuous basis and you are billed periodically is called a(n)
   A. closed-end credit.
   B. installment sales credit.
   C. single lump-sum credit.
   D. open-end credit.

5. (Obj. 4) The borrower's attitude toward his or her credit obligation is known as
   A. capacity.
   B. character.
   C. capital.
   D. collateral.

6. (Obj. 4) The borrower's financial ability to meet credit obligations is called
   A. conditions.
   B. character.
   C. collateral.
   D. capacity.

7. (Obj. 3) Spend no more than __ percent of your net income on credit payments.
   A. 5
   B. 10
   C. 20
   D. 35

_____ 8. (Obj. 3) Which law regulates the use of credit reports, requires the deletion of obsolete information, and gives you access to your credit file?
   A. The Fair Credit Reporting Act
   B. The Fair Credit Billing Act
   C. The Truth in Lending Act
   D. The Equal Credit Opportunity Act

_____ 9. (Obj. 5) Which law sets the procedure for promptly correcting billing mistakes and for promptly crediting your payments?
   A. The Fair Credit Reporting Act
   B. The Fair Credit Billing Act
   C. The Truth in Lending Act
   D. The Equal Credit Opportunity Act

_____ 10. (Obj. 6) If you have a complaint against a bank regarding the violation of federal credit laws, the best place to complain is the
   A. U.S. Department of Commerce.
   B. U.S. Department of Labor.
   C. Consumer Protection Agency.
   D. Federal Reserve System.

Problems, Applications, and Cases

1. Do you wish to learn what is in your credit file? Check the Yellow Pages under Credit Bureaus or Credit Reporting Agencies. If several are listed, call to find the one that keeps your file.

2. Directions: Identify the type of credit described in each of the following examples and circle your answer.

   a. A consumer makes purchases at All Goods Department Store using an All Goods credit card.

       incidental   closed-end   open-end

   b. A consumer pays a bill for long-distance telephone calls made last month.

       incidental   closed-end   open-end

   c. A doctor's office allows patients to pay their bills in installments, but does not charge interest on the unpaid balance.

       incidental   closed-end   open-end

   d. A loan from a credit union is paid back in 24 bimonthly payments.

       incidental   closed-end   open-end

   e. A contract is signed that states the terms and conditions of paying an orthodontist's fee.

       incidental   closed-end   open-end

   f. A local hospital sends a patient a bill for $50 for emergency room treatment.

       incidental   closed-end   open-end

   g. A consumer pays for dinner using a credit card issued by the restaurant.

       incidental   closed-end   open-end

   h. A bank credit card is used to make purchases at several retail stores.

       incidental   closed-end   open-end

   i. Furniture, Inc., requires customers to sign a contract each time they purchase a new item.

       incidental   closed-end   open-end

   j. An "overdraft protection" agreement allows a consumer to write a $150 check when his account balance is only $100.

       incidental   closed-end   open-end

   (Reprinted courtesy of Office of Public Information, Federal Reserve Bank of Minneapolis.)

Credit Use Surveys

3. **Would You Use Credit?**

   Directions: Decide if you would use credit to make the following purchases. In the appropriate box, give the reasons for your decisions.

	Yes	No	Maybe
a. Would you use credit to buy a home or pay for a college education?			
b. Would you use credit to purchase appliances, furniture, etc. for a home?			
c. Would you use credit to pay for overdue bills?			
d. Would you use credit to purchase gasoline or food?			
e. Would you use credit instead of cash or checks to make several purchases in one store?			
f. Would you use credit to purchase an item that costs $8.50?			
g. Would you use credit to purchase an item on sale?			
h. Would you use credit to pay for a vacation?			
i. Would you use credit if you couldn't save enough money to buy something you wanted?			
j. Would you use credit to make a purchase even if you would pay cash?			

4. Directions: List examples of the four types of credit you or your family use (Column I). Under Columns II, III, and IV (optional), describe how you use and repay credit.

I Credit Sources	II How often is credit used?	III How is credit repaid?	IV How much is spent on monthly credit payments?
Public utility Ex: city water 1.	Every day	Paid quarterly	Approx. $30
2.			
Incidental 1.			
2.			
Open-end 1.			
2.			
Closed-end 1.			
2.			

(Reprinted courtesy of Office of Public Information, Federal Reserve Bank of Minneapolis.)

5. Alyssa purchased a dress from Amy's Boutique, a store in her home town, for $85 with her Discover Card. Before she paid her bill, she noticed that a seam was ripped and tried unsuccessfully to return the dress. Can Alyssa withhold payment?

6. Mark gets his television repaired by a local Ace TV Repair Shoppe. He uses a bank credit card to pay the $150 repair charge. A week later the TV breaks down again. Mark is fed up with Ace TV, so he calls a different repair shop. Can he withhold the payment of $150?

7. Amy purchases a $55 pair of shoes at DeKalb Shoemart, about 25 miles away from her home. She charged the shoes with her MasterCard. The heel falls off the shoe the next week. Can Amy withhold payment?

Supplementary Case 6-1

Topic: Applying for Credit and Getting It

Text Reference: pp. 186-189

Allison Allmart, a recent divorcee, applied for credit at Friendly Finance Company. She was denied credit and received a form letter stating that information had been obtained from a consumer reporting agency. The letter included the name, address, and phone number of Anytown Credit Bureau.

Allison called Anytown Credit Bureau to find out what information it had given the finance company. She was told that it generally did not give out such information on the phone but that she could come to the office to learn the contents of her credit file. Allison said that she would be able to come at 1 p.m. on Monday.

When Allison arrived at the credit bureau, she was asked to show her driver's license and one other piece of identification. A trained interviewer talked with her and revealed that the inquiry from Friendly Finance Company was the only inquiry about her that the credit bureau had received during the past six months. The only other information in her file was that an account held five years earlier with AAA Department store had been paid. Allison was surprised at the lack of credit information in her file, but she explained that until recently she had lived in a different state. The interviewer asked whether she could provide the names of her creditors there. The credit bureau would then check with those firms and add any new credit information. Allison did so and then applied for credit again at Friendly Finance Company. This time, she was granted credit.

Case Questions

1. Why did you think Ms. Allmart was denied credit?

2. Was it legal for the Friendly Finance Company to deny her credit request?

3. How could Ms. Allmart have avoided being denied credit the first time?

Supplementary Case 6-2

Topic: Measuring Credit Capacity

Text Reference: pp. 180-181

Hank Hansen, a recent college graduate, is 24 years old, single, and employed as a computer operator at a local manufacturing company. He recently purchased a two-bedroom condominium, and he plans to marry his high school sweetheart when she graduates from college in two years.

Hank's net monthly income is $2,000. He spends the following amounts each month for essential items:

Mortgage loan	$600
Utilities	130
Food	260
Transportation	130
Clothing	40
Medical expenses	40
Total	$1,200

Hank wants to buy a $10,000 car, and he has a down payment of $2,000. He figures that automobile insurance will be about $900 a year but that if he buys this new, fuel-efficient car, he will save about $30 a month on transportation.

Case Questions

1. How much can Hank spend on credit payments each month?
2. What percentage of his net monthly income can Hank spend safely on credit (not including housing) payments?
3. Will Hank get a loan from a bank if he applies for it?

Supplementary Case 6-3

Topic: *Credit Cards*

Text Reference: *pp. 174-175*

A Hard Lesson on Credit Cards

Parents of college students, beware: The empty-nest syndrome you're experiencing may end up as empty-wallet syndrome. The moment your kids step on campus, they become highly-sought-after credit card customers. To establish relationships, they hope will extend well beyond the college years, card marketers are offering students everything from free T-shirts to chances to win airline tickets as enticements to sign up. As a result, college students now have heavy card debts. Some 14 percent have balances of $3,000 to $7,000, and 10 percent owe amounts exceeding $7,000, according to Nellie Mae, a nonprofit student loan provider in Braintree, Massachusetts.

"Students who have no history with credit are being handed it on a silver platter," say Gerri Detweiler, education adviser for Debt Counselors of America, a consumer advocacy group in Rockville, Maryland. As long as they are over 18, students can get a card without asking mom or dad to cosign. But when they get into trouble, they often go running to their folks for help. Jason Britton did—and then some. Now 21 and a senior at Georgetown University in Washington, Britton racked up $21,000 in debt on 16 cards over four years. "When I first started, my attitude was: 'I'll get a job after college to pay off all my debt,'" he says. He realized he dug himself into a hole when he couldn't meet the minimum monthly payments. Now he works three part-time jobs, and his parents are helping him pay his tuition and loans.

Case Questions

1. Why should parents of college students beware?
2. How do credit card marketers entice college students?
3. Where do students turn for help when they get into debt trouble?

Supplementary Reading 6-1

Mara Der Hovanesian, "The Deeper The Hole, The Better For Business", *Business Week*, Jan. 10, 2005, p. 126.

The Deeper The Hole, The Better For Business

When is bad debt good business? A small cadre of public collection agencies that specialize in the purchase of unpaid credit-card obligations and other bills is expected to get a lift next year as the so-far resilient consumer starts to show some signs of overload.

Consumers have borrowed a bundle in recent years—to the tune of over $2 trillion in credit card and auto debt, according to the Federal Reserve. Add mortgages and the figure jumps to nearly $10 trillion. All in all, the average U.S. household is deeper in the hole than it was four years ago, carrying debt of about $9,200, up from $7,200.

Since household income isn't keeping pace with debt growth, more consumers are getting close to the edge. Credit card charge-offs, or the bad debt that banks and others write off the books, were expected to hit a record $65 billion in 2004, up from $57.3 billion in 2003, according to the Nilson Report, a consumer credit newsletter. Nilson forecasts the market for such debts will increase to $2.8 trillion by 2010.

Who makes money on these bad debts? If they aren't trying to collect on the loans internally or through a third-party collection agency, lenders—banks, credit unions, auto finance companies, and retailers—sell these bad loans in bundles to specialty companies, such as Englewood Cliffs (N.J.)-based Asta Funding Inc., NCO Group in Horsham, Pa., Portfolio Recovery Associates of Norfolk, Va., and San Diego's Encore Capital Group. The loans are typically sold at 3 cents to 5 cents on the dollar.

The more bad debt on the market, the less expensive the portfolios are. "Right now the banks are doing well, and delinquencies are low, so the market, and pricing, are a little tight," explains Andrew Zaro, CEO of Cavalry Investments LLC. It bought $1.7 billion worth of receivables through Sept. 30, a 55% increase from the third quarter of 2003, and a boost of its total portfolio to $13 billion. But with interest rates on the rise, the dollar sliding, and inflation looming, execs such as Zaro are betting the tides will soon turn. "Eventually...some of the debtors will have trouble meeting their obligations," he says.

Even so, consumers need not be in dire straits for these businesses to boom. Portfolio Recovery Associates went public last fall at $13, for instance, and hit $35 by yearend. Asta Funding had a record $22 million profit for the year ended Sept. 30, a 92% jump. Gary Stern, Asta's CEO, expects to exceed the $2.8 billion in purchases it made last year. "We're looking for more to buy," he says.

Ultimately, collection companies make their money from bad-debt portfolios by working out reasonable solutions with borrowers. The old days of terrorizing customers with threats is self-defeating, says Cavalry's Zaro: "If you don't help them, you don't help yourself."

Mara Der Hovanesian

Study Questions

1. Who makes money on consumers' bad debts?

2. Why will some debtors have trouble meeting their debt obligations?

Supplementary Reading 6-2

"Managing Debt and Credit", *Standard & Poor's Special Report Library.*

Managing Debt and Credit

Credit is defined by Dun & Bradstreet's moto as "Man's Confidence in Man." However, the definition of credit today is more like "Man's Confidence in Himself." Using credit today means you have confidence in your future ability to pay that debt. Forty years ago, your grandparents may have paid cash for their homes and their cars, a largely unheard-of (and most likely impossible) event today. If they borrowed money at all, chances are it was from a relative or friend, and not a financial institution.

Today debt and instant credit are part of our everyday lives. The convenience of instant credit, however, has taken its toll. Many individuals use credit cards to spend more than they earn, and a few of these people actually build themselves a debt prison from which some never emerge. On the other hand, those who never use credit can be denied a loan or credit when they have a justifiable need or use for it. Using credit establishes a history of financial responsibility; until you establish a credit history, your chances of qualifying for an important loan such as a mortgage are greatly reduced.

Installment debt and **revolving credit** are two ways of borrowing. Installment debt allows you to purchase items at a competitive interest rate: for example, 6 to 7 percent for a 30-year home mortgage and about 9 percent for a car loan. The loan is paid back on an amortizing schedule: monthly payments of a fixed amount that remain constant over the life of the loan. At first, most of the monthly payment consists of interest. In later years, principal begins to be paid down. Installment debt is easily budgeted and the debt is eliminated on a pre-determined date.

A revolving line of credit, also called "open-ended credit," is made available to you for use at any time. Credit cards—such as Visa, MasterCard, and department store cards—are examples of revolving credit. When you apply for one of these cards, you receive a credit limit based on your credit payment history and income. When you use the credit line, you must make monthly minimum payments based on the total balance outstanding that month. Some lines of credit will also have an annual account fee.

While revolving credit is a convenient way to borrow, it can also become an endless pit of minimum payments that barely cover the interest due. As you pay off your debt, the minimum payment is also reduced, thus extending your payoff period and consequently the interest you pay. Paying just the minimum due on a $2,000 credit card loan could mean making monthly interest payments for 10 or more years! Many cards charge rates of interest as high as 18 percent annually. If you have a good **credit history**, you may qualify for a lower rate, however, a few late payments will push your interest rate higher. Also, carrying a balance on a credit card can make it harder for you to obtain less expensive types of financing.

Revolving credit, in addition to being convenient, eliminates the need to carry a lot of cash, and helps bridge small timing differences between income and expenses. The itemized monthly statements also can help you track your expenses. Some people can easily yield to the temptation that the convenience of credit cards offers. Impulse buying, failing to compare costs, and purchasing large items you can't afford are all downfalls brought on by always-available purchasing power.

Installment Debt vs. Revolving Debt

Beginning Balance	$2,500	$2,500
Interest Rate	10%	18.5%
Years to Repay	4	30*
Interest Cost	$544	$6,500

*Paying 2 percent minimum monthly payment.

Excerpted with permission from Standard & Poor's *Special Report Library*

Study Questions

1. Why are debt and instant credit part of our everyday lives?

2. What are the two types of credit? Give examples of each.

Supplementary Reading 6-3

Brian Grow, "New Sharks in the Web Surf", *Business Week*, March 28, 2005, p. 14.

New Sharks in the Web Surf

THE PERILS OF a high-tech world keep getting worse. Spam is growing more sophisticated. Viruses plague PCs. And cell phones, PDAs, and voice-over-Internet protocol (VoIP) networks, used to make inexpensive calls over the Web, are being targeted by hackers. Now even more insidious threats may be on their way.

•**Pharming** It's a new twist on "phishing," where e-mails from fake banks and credit-card companies try to entice Web surfers to give up their passwords. Pharming plants malicious code on users' computers by e-mail. So when they visit a trusted Web site and are least likely to expect a scam, the malcode goes to work logging keystrokes—or delivering fake pop-up windows that appear as if they're from that Web site—to pilfer personal data.

In the past month, says security firm **Proofpoint,** pharms known as "Banker" and "Goldun" have surfaced. Last year, "Korgo" hit 4,000 U.S. Web surfers, says the **SANS Internet Storm Center.**

•**Bluesnarfing & Bluebugging** Exploiting Bluetooth, the wireless standard that links cell phones and headsets, is the new craze. A fairly benign version called "bluejacking" involves sending text messages to unwitting owners of cell phones and PDAs.

The latest variant: sending viruses, or bluebugging. Users in the U.S. and Europe have been hit. The problem could get worse. On Mar. 10, Finnish security firm **F-Secure** identified "Commwarrior" as the first virus that can spread through Bluetooth and cell-phone networks. What's next? Bluesnarfing: hijacking the cell phone and PDA data.

Halting this new onslaught of hackers may be tough. Says Gary Steele, head of Proofpoint: "Whether it's e-mail, VoIP, or the Web, they'll come after you." In a digital world, there's no place to hide.

Brian Grow

Study Questions

1. What are the perils of a high-tech world?

2. What is "pharming"? How does it work?

Supplementary Reading 6-4

Source: www.fdic.gov/consumers, "New Studies Highlight Different ID Thefts", July 20, 2005.

New Studies Highlight Different ID Thefts

Here's a look at some new studies that can help you better understand the common causes of identity theft—situations in which a crook uses someone else's personal information to commit fraud—and how the crime is committed.

The Federal Trade Commission's latest annual report on consumer complaints shows that ID theft topped the list for the fifth year in a row, accounting for 39 percent of all consumer fraud complaints filed with the FTC during 2004. Credit card fraud was the most common form of reported identify theft (28 percent of the total), followed by phone or utilities fraud (19 percent) and bank fraud (18 percent). See the FTC's announcement at www.ftc.gov/opa/2005/02/top102005.htm.

A study released by the Council of Better Business Bureaus (BBB) and Javelin Strategy & Research shows that ID theft is more likely to occur as the result of a lost or stolen wallet or checkbook, not because of Internet-related fraud. The study also says that friends, family members, neighbors or in-home employees make up half of all identity thieves. To read the report and recommendations for consumers, go to www.bbb.org.

And the FDIC released a study on "account hijacking," which is the unauthorized access and misuse of existing account information, primarily through online "phishing" scams (fraudulent e-mails asking recipients to verify or provide confidential financial information).

The FDIC report offers some "best practices" that financial institutions and their regulators can consider using to help protect consumers from online fraud. Consumers also may wish to read the study to learn why phishing scams should be taken seriously. While online banking offers many benefits to consumers and there are consumer protections, people still need to be on guard against ID theft in any form.

"Most ID theft may be committed the old-fashioned way, via paper, but electronic ID theft is the fastest-growing form because of the growth in online banking," said Michael Jackson, Associate Director of the FDIC's Division of Supervision and Consumer Protection. He added that electronic ID theft "is perhaps the toughest for a consumer to detect," Why? "You're likely to know pretty quickly if you've lost your wallet," Jackson explained, "but people often go weeks or months before realizing that their personal information has been stolen online."

Source: www.fdic.gov/consumers, July 20, 2005

Study Questions

1. When is ID theft more likely to occur?

2. Who makes up half of all identity thieves?

3. What is "account hijacking"?

Supplementary Reading 6-5

Sheridan Prasso; Andrew Heller, "Painless Plastic For Shopaholics (clear cards, combined credit-debit cards)", *Business Week*, August 26, 2002, p. 14.

Painless Plastic for Shopaholics

Forget debit cards. Forget credit cards. The two are merging into a new type of card that can help people who have trouble maintaining bank balances or making minimum payments on their credit cards. Nearly a dozen companies, including Reliance Insurance and Western Union, have issued the "Clear Card" as a benefit to about 1,500 employees since January. Another dozen companies are expected to begin offering it by fall.

How does it work? Buy an $80 pair of pants, for example, and your next four paychecks will show deductions of $20. "The card is ideal for people who have had credit problems," says John Gregitis, senior vice-president of marketing at E-Duction, the company working with MasterCard to offer Clear Card. It looks like a regular MasterCard, and employees pay a $29 annual fee. Their credit limit is 2.5% of their salaries, there's no interest charge, and automatic deductions mean the card always shows a clean credit history.

Companies say offering such benefits gives them a competitive edge. Notes Wendy Carver-Herbert, a spokeswomen for Western Union, where 10% of U.S. employees use Clear Card: "We're always looking for ways to bring in talent."

Sheridan Prasso; Andrew Heller

Study Questions

1. Would you use this new type of card if your employer offered one? Why or why not?

2. How does the new card work?

3. Why are employers offering such benefits to their employees?

Supplementary Reading 6-6
A Summary of Your Rights Under the Fair Credit Reporting Act

The Federal Fair Credit Reporting Act (FCRA) promotes the accuracy, fairness, and privacy of information in the files of consumer reporting agencies. There are many types of consumer reporting agencies, including credit bureaus and specialty agencies (such as agencies that sell information about check writing histories, medical records, and rental history records). Here is a summary of your major rights under the FCRA. For more information, including information about additional rights, go to www.ftc.gov/credit or write to: Consumer Response Center, Room 130-A, Federal Trade Commission, 600 Pennsylvania Ave. N.W., Washington, D.C. 20580.

- **You must be told if information in your file has been used against you.** Anyone who uses a credit report or another type of consumer report to deny your application for credit, insurance, or employment—or to take another adverse action against you—must tell you, and must give you the name, address, and phone number of the agency that provided the information.
- **You have the right to know what is in your file.** You may request and obtain all the information about you in the files of a consumer reporting agency (your "file disclosure"). You will be required to provide proper identification, which may include your Social Security number. In many cases, the disclosure will be free. You are entitled to a free file disclosure if:
  - a person has taken adverse action against you because of information in your credit report;
  - you are the victim of identity theft and place a fraud alert in your file;
  - your file contains inaccurate information as a result of fraud;
  - you are on public assistance;
  - you are unemployed but expect to apply for employment within 60 days.

In addition, by September 2005 all consumers will be entitled to one free disclosure every 12 months upon request from each nationwide credit bureau and from nationwide specialty consumer reporting agencies. See www.ftc.gov/credit for additional information.

- **You have the right to ask for a credit score.** Credit scores are numerical summaries of your creditworthiness based on information from credit bureaus. You may request a credit score from consumer reporting agencies that create scores or distribute scores used in residential real property loans, but you will have to pay for it. In some mortgage transactions, you will receive credit score information for free from the mortgage lender.
- **You have the right to dispute incomplete or inaccurate information.** If you identify information in your file that is incomplete or inaccurate, and report it to the consumer reporting agency, the agency must investigate unless your dispute is frivolous. See www.ftc.gov/credit for an explanation of dispute procedures.
- **Consumer reporting agencies must correct or delete inaccurate, incomplete, or unverifiable information.** Inaccurate, incomplete or unverifiable information must be removed or corrected, usually within 30 days. However, a consumer reporting agency may continue to report information it has verified as accurate.
- **Consumer reporting agencies may not report outdated negative information.** In most cases, a consumer reporting agency may not report negative information that is more than seven years old, or bankruptcies that are more than 10 years old.
- **Access to your file is limited.** A consumer reporting agency may provide information about you only to people with a valid need—usually to consider an application with a creditor, insurer, employer, landlord, or other business. The FCRA specifies those with a valid need for access.
- **You must give your consent for reports to be provided to employers.** A consumer reporting agency may not give out information about you to your employer, or a potential employer, without your written consent given to the employer. Written consent generally is not required in the trucking industry. For more information, go to www.ftc.gov/credit.
- **You may limit "prescreened" offers of credit and insurance you get based on information in your credit report.** Unsolicited "prescreened" offers for credit and insurance must include a toll-free phone number you can call if you choose to remove your name and address from the lists these offers are based on. You may opt-out with the nationwide credit bureaus at 1-888-5-OPTOUT (1-888-567-8688).
- **You may seek damages from violators.** If a consumer reporting agency, or, in some cases, a user of consumer reports or a furnisher of information to a consumer reporting agency violates the FCRA, you may be able to sue in state or federal court.
- **Identity theft victims and active duty military personnel have additional rights.** For more information, visit www.ftc.gov/credit.

States may enforce the FCRA, and many states have their own consumer reporting laws. In some cases, you may have more rights under state law. For more information, contact your state or local consumer protection agency or your state Attorney General. Federal enforcers are:

TYPE OF BUSINESS	CONTACT:
Consumer reporting agencies, creditors and others not listed below	Federal Trade Commission: Consumer Response Center—FCRA, Washington, DC 20580, 1-877-382-4357
National banks, federal branches/agencies of foreign banks (word "National" or initials "N.A." appear in or after bank's name)	Office of the Comptroller of the Currency, Compliance Management, Mail Stop 6-6, Washington, DC 20219, 800-613-6743
Federal Reserve System member banks (except national banks, and federal branches/agencies of foreign banks)	Federal Reserve Board, Division of Consumer & Community Affairs, Washington, DC 20551, 202-452-3693
Savings associations and federally chartered savings banks (word "Federal" or initials "F.S.B." appear in federal institution's name)	Office of Thrift Supervision, Consumer Complaints, Washington, DC 20552, 800-842-6929
Federal credit unions (words "Federal Credit Union" appear in institution's name)	National Credit Union Administration, 1775 Duke Street, Alexandria, VA 22314, 703-519-4600
State-chartered banks that are not members of the Federal Reserve System	Federal Deposit Insurance Corporation, Consumer Response Center, 2345 Grand Avenue, Suite 100, Kansas City, Missouri 64108-2638, 1-877-275-3342
Air, surface, or rail common carriers regulated by former Civil Aeronautics Board or Interstate Commerce Commission	Department of Transportation, Office of Financial Management, Washington, DC 20590, 202-366-1306
Activities subject to the Packers and Stockyards Act, 1921	Department of Agriculture, Office of Deputy Administrator—GIPSA, Washington, DC 20250, 202-720-7051

Study Questions

1. What is the purpose of the Fair Credit Reporting Act?

2. What are your major rights under the Fair Credit Reporting Act?

3. What can you do if there is an inaccurate, incomplete, or unverifiable information in your credit file?

7 CHOOSING A SOURCE OF CREDIT: THE COSTS OF CREDIT ALTERNATIVES

Chapter Overview

All of us get into credit difficulties if we do not understand how and when to use credit. This chapter identifies major sources of consumer credit—commercial banks, savings and loan associations, credit unions, finance companies, life insurance companies, retailers, parents, and relatives. Next, in determining the cost of credit, we emphasize the finance charge and the Annual Percentage Rate (APR). Then we show how the cost of credit can be determined by calculating interest with various interest formulas. In dealing with your debts, we discuss the Fair Debt Collection Practices Act, consumer credit counseling, and the serious effects of debt. We describe various private and governmental sources that assist consumers with debt problems. Finally, we explain and distinguish between Chapter 7 and Chapter 13 bankruptcy laws to assess the choices in declaring personal bankruptcy.

Learning Objectives

After studying this chapter, you will be able to:

Obj. 1 Analyze the major sources of consumer credit.

Obj. 2 Determine the cost of credit by calculating interest with various interest formulas.

Obj. 3 Develop a plan to manage debt.

Obj. 4 Evaluate various private and governmental sources that assist consumers with debt problems.

Obj. 5 Assess the choices in declaring personal bankruptcy.

Key Terms

add-on interest method
adjusted balance method
annual percentage rate (APR)
average daily balance method
Chapter 7 bankruptcy
Chapter 13 bankruptcy
Consumer Credit Counseling Services (CCCS)
credit insurance
declining balance method
Fair Debt Collection Practices Act (FDCPA)
finance charge
previous balance method
rule of 78's
simple interest
Truth in Lending Law

Pretest

True-False

_____ 1. (Obj. 1) By evaluating your credit options, you can reduce your finance charges.

_____ 2. (Obj. 1) The least expensive loans are available from finance companies and retailers.

_____ 3. (Obj. 2) The finance charge is the total amount you pay to use credit.

_____ 4. (Obj. 2) The annual percentage rate (APR) is the percentage cost of credit.

_____ 5. (Obj. 3) If you are having trouble paying your bills, immediately turn to a debt consolidation company.

_____ 6. (Obj. 3) Paying only the minimum balance each month on credit card bills is one of the danger signals of potential debt problems.

_____ 7. (Obj. 4) A Consumer Credit Counseling Service provides debt counseling service for families and individuals with serious financial problems.

_____ 8. (Obj. 4) Most services provided by a Consumer Credit Counseling Service are not free.

_____ 9. (Obj. 5) The Bankruptcy Abuse Prevention and Consumer Protection Act of 2005 made personal bankruptcy easier.

_____ 10. (Obj. 5) A person filing for relief under the bankruptcy code is called a bankrupt.

Self-Guided Study Questions

Obj. 1

Sources of Consumer Credit (p. 206)

1. What three questions must you ask yourself before deciding whether to borrow money?

2. In what two situations should you avoid the use of credit?

3. When you need money, what kind of loan should you seek? Closed-end or open-end credit?

4. What are the sources of inexpensive loans?

5. What are the sources of medium-priced loans?

6. What are some advantages of borrowing from a credit union?

7. What are the sources of expensive loans?

8. What types of loans are made by commercial banks?

9. What types of loans are made by consumer finance companies?

10. Why do life insurance companies charge lower interest rates than some other lenders?

11. What types of loans are made by savings and loan associations?

12. What online computer services may be used to compare interest?

13. How will the smart cards facilitate banking and bill paying?

Obj. 2
Cost of Credit (p. 210)
14. What is the Truth in Lending Law of 1969?

15. What two key concepts should you consider when determining the cost of credit?

16. What is a finance charge?

17. What is the annual percentage rate (APR)?

18. How do finance charge and APR differ?

Tackling the Trade-Offs (p. 212)
19. When you choose your financing, what are the trade-offs between the features you prefer and the costs of your loan?

Calculating the Cost of Credit (p. 213)
20. How do you calculate the cost of credit?

21. What are the two most common methods of computing interest?

22. What is the simple interest formula?

23. When is the declining balance method used in calculating the cost of credit?

24. How is interest calculated with the add-on interest method?

25. What are the three methods creditors use to calculate the finance charge on open-end credit?

26. How do adjusted balance, previous balance, and average daily balance methods differ from one another?

27. How do lenders consider the effects of expected inflation in determining the cost of credit?

28. How does the new tax law affect the cost of consumer credit?

29. Why should you avoid the minimum monthly payment trap?

When the Repayment is Early: The Rule of 78's (p. 218)

30. Why do creditors use the Rule of 78's?

Credit Insurance (p. 218)

31. What is credit insurance?

32. What is the most commonly purchased type of credit insurance?

33. Distinguish among three types of credit insurance.

34. What is a better alternative to credit life insurance?

Obj. 3

Managing Your Debts (p. 221)

35. What should you do if you find it impossible to pay your bills on time?

36. What special problems are caused if you fail to pay an automobile loan?

Debt Collection Practices (p. 221)

37. What is the Fair Debt Collection Practices Act?

38. Who enforces the Fair Debt Collection Practices Act?

39. What steps should you take if a debt collector calls on you?

40. What are the major reasons for consumers not paying their debts?

Warning Signs of Debt Problems (p. 221)
41. What are the serious effects of heavy indebtedness?

Obj. 4

Consumer Credit Counseling Service (p. 225)
42. What is a Consumer Credit Counseling Service (CCCS)?

What the CCCS Does (p. 226)
43. What are the two-part activities of the CCCS?

44. Are all CCCS counseling services free for the asking?

Alternative Counseling Services (p. 226)
45. What other alternative counseling services are available to consumers?

Obj. 5

Declaring Personal Bankruptcy (p. 229)

46. What are indicators of personal bankruptcy?

47. Why has the personal bankruptcy rate increased in recent years?

The U.S. Bankruptcy Act of 1978: The Last Resort (p. 229)

48. What are the major provisions of the Chapter 7 bankruptcy?

49. What is the Chapter 13 bankruptcy?

50. What are the differences between Chapter 7 and Chapter 13 bankruptcies?

Effect of Bankruptcy on Your Job and Your Future Credit (p. 231)

51. How does a personal bankruptcy affect your job and your future credit?

52. What is the Chapter 11 bankruptcy?

Should a Lawyer Represent You in a Bankruptcy Case? (p. 231)

53. Why is an attorney needed for the Chapter 13 bankruptcy?

54. What are the monetary costs of declaring a Chapter 13 bankruptcy?

55. What are a few intangible costs to bankruptcy?

Post Test

Completion

1. (Obj. 1) Paying cash is almost always _____ than using credit.
2. (Obj. 1) The number of credit union members has been _____ steadily.
3. (Obj. 1) The _____ _____ _____ specializes in personal installment loans and second mortgages.
4. (Obj. 2) The _____ _____ is the interest computed on principal only and without compounding.
5. (Obj. 2) The _____ _____ is the total amount you pay to use credit.
6. (Obj. 2) The _____ _____ _____ is the percentage cost of credit on a yearly basis.
7. (Obj. 3) The Federal Trade Commission enforces the _____ _____ _____ _____ _____.
8. (Obj. 4) A _____ _____ _____ _____ is a local non-profit organization affiliated with the National Foundation for Consumer Credit.
9. (Obj. 5) In a _____ _____ _____, a debtor is required to draw up a petition of all assets and liabilities, and the term bankrupt is not used.
10. (Obj. 5) In a _____ _____ _____, a debtor normally keeps all or most of his or her property.

Multiple Choice

____ 1. (Obj. 1) Which of the following lenders specializes in mortgages and other housing-related loans?
   A. Commercial banks
   B. Federal savings banks (savings and loans)
   C. Credit unions
   D. Finance companies

____ 2. (Obj. 1) Which of the following lenders specializes in personal installment loans and second mortgages?
   A. Consumer finance companies
   B. Credit unions
   C. Savings and loans
   D. Commercial banks

____ 3. (Obj. 2) When creditors add finance charges after subtracting payments made during the billing period, this is called the
   A. adjusted balance method.
   B. previous balance method.
   C. average daily balance method.
   D. annual percentage rate method.

____ 4. (Obj. 2) The Truth in Lending Law
   A. sets the interest rates that creditors can charge.
   B. tells creditors how to make interest calculations.
   C. requires creditors to tell the interest calculation method to be used.
   D. was repealed by Congress in 1986.

____ 5. (Obj. 2) To determine how much interest you have paid at any point in a loan, creditors use a mathematical formula called the
   A. formula of large numbers.
   B. mathematical law of averages.
   C. Rule of 72's.
   D. Rule of 78's.

____ 6. (Obj. 3) Who enforces the Fair Debt Collection Practices Act?
   A. The Federal Trade Commission
   B. The U.S. Justice Department
   C. The U.S. Department of Labor
   D. The Better Business Bureau

_____ 7. (Obj. 3) If you cannot make your loan payments on time, first contact your
   A. friends or relatives for a quick loan from them.
   B. employers and ask for a raise in your salary.
   C. creditors at once and try to work out a modified payment plan with them.
   D. local office of a consumer finance company.

_____ 8. (Obj. 4) Which one of the following organizations is a local, non-profit organization affiliated with the National Foundation of Consumer Credit?
   A. Consumer Complaints Advisory Service
   B. Consumer Credit Counseling Service
   C. The Better Business Bureau
   D. The Federal Trade Commission

_____ 9. (Obj. 5) Usually, the largest single item of cost for a person filing a Chapter 13 bankruptcy is
   A. court cost.
   B. attorney's fee.
   C. trustee's fee.
   D. transportation cost.

_____ 10. (Obj. 5) In which type of bankruptcy are many, but not all, debts forgiven?
   A. Chapter 2
   B. Chapter 5
   C. Chapter 7
   D. Chapter 13

Problems, Applications, and Cases

1. Suppose you borrow $2,000 at 10% simple interest and repay it in one lump sum at the end of one year. How much will you owe at the end of one year?

2. Now suppose the loan is for two years and you are required to repay the loan (principal and interest) at the end of two years. What will the interest charge be?

3. What is the interest cost and the total amount due on a six-month loan of $1,500 at 13.2 percent simple annual interest?

4. Decide whether the consumer, debt collector, or creditor bears the costs described below of the Fair Debt Collection Practices Act. Circle your answers.

   a. A debt collector raises his collection fees when it takes longer to collect debts.

   consumer   debt collector   creditor

   b. A creditor decides to impose stricter standards for granting credit in response to the higher cost of debt collection.

   consumer   debt collector   creditor

   c. A creditor raises the interest rate charged on new loans to cover the higher price of debt collection.

   consumer   debt collector   creditor

   d. A consumer pays for legal advice to find out whether or not an action threatened by a debt collector can legally be taken.

   consumer   debt collector   creditor

   e. Due to the increased costs of using debt collection services, a creditor decides to collect her own debts.

   consumer   debt collector   creditor

   f. A consumer spends 30 minutes writing a letter to a debt collector requesting communications to cease regarding an unpaid bill.

   consumer   debt collector   creditor

   g. A debt collector sends a debt validation notice to a consumer who has been notified about the debt.

   consumer   debt collector   creditor

   h. Because the costs of debt collection have increased, a creditor provides less credit to his customers.

   consumer   debt collector   creditor

(Reprinted courtesy of the Office of Public Information, Federal Reserve Bank of Minneapolis)

5. Decide whether the debt collection activities described below are legal or illegal, or whether the legality cannot be determined on the basis of the information give. Circle your answers.

   a. A debt collector uses a post card to notify a consumer about a debt.

       legal   illegal   cannot be determined

   b. A creditor telephones a customer at work and tells the person who answers the phone the name of his company.

       legal   illegal   cannot be determined

   c. An employee of Northland Bank calls one of the bank's customers at 11 p.m. about late payments.

       legal   illegal   cannot be determined

   d. A debt collection agency telephones a consumer about a debt at 11 p.m.

       legal   illegal   cannot be determined

   e. ABC Stores, using the name ABC Collections, Inc., telephones a delinquent customer at 6 a.m.

       legal   illegal   cannot be determined

   f. A department store's collection division calls a customer repeatedly during a 12-hour period.

       legal   illegal   cannot be determined

   g. A credit union calls a member at his place of employment about a late payment.

       legal   illegal   cannot be determined

   h. A debt collection agency telephones a consumer at work even though that person's employer does not allow personal calls.

       legal   illegal   cannot be determined

   i. A person who collects debts for others threatens to "throw in jail" a consumer who refuses to pay.

       legal   illegal   cannot be determined

   j. A debt collector hired by a furniture store tells a customer that furniture purchased on credit will be repossessed if payment is not received.

       legal   illegal   cannot be determined

(Reprinted courtesy of Office of Public Information, Federal Reserve Bank of Minneapolis)

6. What is the cost of credit (finance charge) and the annual percentage rate for the following loans?

	Amount financed	Payments per year	Length of loan (in months)	Monthly payment	Cost of credit	APR
A	$2,000	12	24	$93.00	$_____	_____%
B	$900	12	12	$84.50	$_____	_____%
C	$3,400	12	30	$130.00	$_____	_____%

7. Steve borrows $100 from a friend and repays the $100 a year later in one lump sum. What is the nominal rate of interest on the loan?

8. If prices increased 7 percent during the year Steve had the loan, what would be the real rate of interest on the loan?

Supplementary Case 7-1

Topic: **Calculating the Cost of Credit**

Text Reference: pp. 213-216

After visiting several automobile dealerships, Richard Welch selects the car he wants. He likes its $10,000 price, but financing through the dealer is no bargain. He has $2,000 cash for a down payment, so he needs an $8,000 loan. In shopping at several banks for an installment loan, he learns that interest on most automobile loans is quoted at add-on rates. That is, during the life of the loan, interest is paid on the full amount borrowed even though a portion of the principle has been paid back. Richard borrows $8,000 for a period of four years at an add-on rate of 11 percent.

Case Questions

1. What is the total interest on Richard's loan?
2. What is the total cost of the car?
3. What is the monthly payment?
4. What is the annual percentage rate (APR)?

Supplementary Case 7-2

Topic: Buying Now vs. Later

Text Reference: pp. 212-214

Shirley Watson wishes to buy a freezer that now costs $600. Since the current inflation rate is 5 percent, she expects the freezer to cost $630 if she postpones the purchase for a year. If she buys it now, she estimates that it would save her $150 in food costs during the next year. It would enable her to purchase food at special sales and in larger quantities and to preserve vegetables from her garden. However, operating the freezer would increase her electricity bill. Shirley can use one of the following options in purchasing the freezer:

Option 1 Buy the freezer now, using $600 she has in a savings account that earns interest at an annual rate of 6 percent.

Option 2 Buy the freezer now, using credit at an annual rate of 10 percent. She would make 12 monthly payments of $52.50 each.

Option 3 Postpone the purchase until she saves an additional $600. Her savings earn interest at an annual rate of 6 percent.

Case Questions

1. What trade-offs should Shirley consider in deciding whether to buy the freezer now or later?

2. If Shirley wants to buy the freezer now, what trade-offs should she consider in deciding whether to use credit or pay cash from her savings?

Supplementary Reading 7-1

IRS, FTC and State Regulators Urge Care When Seeking Help from Credit Counseling Organizations, Source: http://www.irs.gov/newsroom/article/0,,id=114574,00.html, July 26, 2005.

IRS, FTC and State Regulators Urge Care When Seeking Help From Credit Counseling Organizations

WASHINGTON—The Internal Revenue Service, the Federal Trade Commission and state regulators today issued a consumer alert for those seeking assistance from tax-exempt credit counseling organizations.

Paying bills is never easy, but job loss, divorce or unexpected medical bills can be devastating to a consumer. Many consumers seek help from non-profit credit counseling organizations in managing their debt or "repairing" damaged credit. The IRS, FTC and state agencies urge consumers to be cautious when choosing a credit counseling organization.

Many credit counseling organizations provide valuable advice, education and assistance to those seeking to better manage their debt. But an increasing number of complaints to federal and state agencies indicates that some organizations are engaging in questionable activities.

Federal and state regulators are concerned that some credit counseling organizations using questionable practices may seek tax-exempt status in order to circumvent state and federal consumer protection laws. State and federal statutes regulating credit counseling agencies often do not apply to Section 501(c)(3) tax-exempt organizations.

Many of these groups provide a valuable service to consumers, but some use the tax code to skirt consumer-protection laws," said IRA Commissioner Mark W. Everson. "The IRS will work to protect the integrity of the tax law to ensure that tax-exempt organizations understand and comply with the rules. We will work with other federal agencies and state regulators to combat abuse in this area. It is not fair to taxpayers struggling with financial problems to be taken advantage of by credit counseling groups exploiting gaps in the law."

Consumers need to be wary of the "quick fixes" offered by some organizations.

"Consumers who are struggling financially need to be careful not to lose even more money to someone offering a quick and easy way to fix credit problems," said Timothy J. Muris, Chairman of the FTC. "We want all consumers seeking help to take some common sense precautions."

Consumers can help protect themselves from deceptive credit counseling practices by following these tips:
- Check that the organization will help you manage your finances better through counseling and education.
- Carefully read through any written agreement that a credit counseling organization offers. It should describe in detail the services to be performed; the payment terms for these services, including their total cost; how long it will take to achieve results; any guarantees offered; and the organization's business name and address.
- Beware of high fees or required "voluntary contributions" that, with high monthly service charges, may add to your debt and defeat your efforts to pay your bills. It is illegal to represent that negative information, such as bankruptcy, can be removed from your credit report. Promises to "help you get out of debt easily" are a red flag.
- Make sure that your creditors are willing to work with the agency you choose. If they are, follow up with those creditors regularly to make sure your debt is being paid off.
- Check with state agencies and your local Better Business Bureau to find out about a specific credit counseling organization's record.

Source:
http://www.irs.gov/newsroom/article/0,,id=114574,00.html

Study Questions

1. Why did IRS, FTC and other regulatory agencies issue a consumer alert?

2. Why should consumers be wary of the "quick fixes" offered by some organizations?

3. What can consumers do to protect themselves from deceptive credit counseling practices?

Supplementary Reading 7-2

Fiscal Fitness, http://www.ftc.gov/bcp/conline/pubs/credit/fiscal.htm, July 20, 2005.

Fiscal Fitness

Choosing a Credit Counselor

Living paycheck to paycheck? Worried about debt collectors? Can't seem to develop a workable budget, let alone save money for retirement? If this sounds familiar, you may want to consider the services of a credit counselor. Many credit counseling organizations are nonprofit and work with you to solve your financial problems. But beware—just because an organization says it is "nonprofit" doesn't guarantee that its services are free or affordable, or that its services are legitimate. In fact, some credit counseling organizations charge high fees, some of which may be hidden, or urge consumers to make "voluntary" contributions that cause them to fall deeper into debt.

Most credit counselors offer services through local offices, the Internet, or on the telephone. If possible, find an organization that offers in-person counseling. Many universities, military bases, credit unions, housing authorities, and branches of the U.S. Cooperative Extension Service operate nonprofit credit counseling programs. Your financial institution, local consumer protection agency, and friends and family also may be good sources of information and referrals.

Choosing a Credit Counseling Organization

Reputable credit counseling organizations advise you on managing your money and debts, help you develop a budget, and usually offer free educational materials and workshops. Their counselors are certified and trained in the areas of consumer credit, money and debt management, and budgeting. Counselors discuss your entire financial situation with you, and help you develop a personalized plan to solve your money problems. An initial counseling session typically lasts an hour, with an offer of follow-up sessions.

A reputable credit counseling agency should send you free information about itself and the services it provides without requiring you to provide any details about your situation. If a firm doesn't do that, consider it a red flag and go elsewhere for help.

Once you've developed a list of potential counseling agencies, check them out with your state Attorney General, local consumer protection agency, and Better Business Bureau. They can tell you if consumers have

Copyright © 2007 The McGraw-Hill Companies, Inc. All rights reserved.

filed complaints about them. (If they don't have complaints about them, it's not a guarantee that they're legitimate.) Then, it's time for you to interview the final "candidates."

Questions to Ask

Here are some questions to ask to help you find the best counselor for you.

What services do you offer?

Look for an organization that offers a range of services, including budget counseling, and savings and debt management classes. Avoid organizations that push a debt management plan (DMP) as your only option before they spend a significant amount of time analyzing your financial situation.

Do you offer information? Are educational materials available for free?

Avoid organizations that charge for information.

In addition to helping me solve my immediate problem, will you help me develop a plan for avoiding problems in the future?

What are your fees? Are there set-up and/or monthly fees?

Get a specific price quote in writing.

What if I can't afford to pay your fees or make contributions?

If an organization won't help you because you can't afford to pay, look elsewhere for help.

Will I have a formal written agreement or contract with you?

Don't sign anything without reading it first. Make sure all verbal promises are in writing.

Are you licensed to offer your services in my state?

What are the qualifications of your counselors? Are they accredited or certified by an outside organization? If so, by whom? If not, how are they trained?

Try to use an organization whose counselors are trained by a non-affiliated party.

What assurance do I have that information about me (including my address, phone number, and financial information) will be kept confidential and secure?

How are your employees compensated? Are they paid more if I sign up for certain services, if I pay a fee, or if I make a contribution to your organization?

If the answer is yes, consider it a red flag and go elsewhere for help.

Study Questions

1. When should one consider the services of a credit counselor?

2. What types of organizations provide consumer credit counseling services?

3. What are some questions you must ask to help you find the best counselor?

8 CONSUMER PURCHASING STRATEGIES AND LEGAL PROTECTION

Chapter Overview

While making consumer purchases may not be considered in most financial plans, these choices affect financial resources available for other purposes. This chapter starts with a discussion of the factors that influence buying habits. Selected purchasing strategies are then covered, including types of retail stores, brands, and comparison shopping methods. Next, a systematic approach to making purchase decisions is presented related to buying, leasing, and operating motor vehicles. The chapter concludes with a discussion of consumer protection actions and legal alternatives available to individuals.

Learning Objectives

After studying this chapter, you will be able to:

Obj. 1 Identify strategies for effective consumer buying..

Obj. 2 Implement a process for making consumer purchases..

Obj. 3 Identify the steps people can take to resolve consumer problems.

Obj. 4 Evaluate the legal alternatives available to consumers.

Key Terms

arbitration	legal aid society	small claims court
class action suit	mediation	unit pricing
cooperative	open dating	warranty
generic item	rebate	
impulse buying	service contract	

Pretest

True-False

1. (Obj. 2) Consumer information from business organizations is considered the most reliable source available when making buying decisions.

2. (Obj. 2) Consumer Reports publishes a listing of recommended companies in an area from which to purchase goods and services.

3. (Obj. 1) A cooperative is organized to benefit its members by saving them Money on various products.

4. (Obj. 1) Brand name products usually offer the least consistency of quality.

5. (Obj. 1) Even without a written warranty, consumers will have some guarantee that a product will perform in an expected manner.

6. (Obj. 1) Service contracts are designed to cover expensive repair costs on appliances or automobiles.

7. (Obj. 3) Most consumer complaints are solved with assistance from state and local government agencies.

8. (Obj. 3) Arbitration provides a legally binding solution to a dispute without your having to appear in court.

9. (Obj. 4) Small claims courts allow individuals to present a case without the use of a lawyer.

10. (Obj. 4) Class action suits usually involve complaints of less than $1,000.

Self-Guided Study Questions

Obj. 1

Consumer Buying Activities (p. 242)

1. What factors influence daily buying decisions?

2. What trade-offs are associated with daily buying decisions?

Practical Purchasing Strategies (p. 243)

3. How can the time at which you buy certain items be an effective buying strategy?

4. What factors influence a person's decision to shop at a certain store?

5. What is a consumer cooperative?

6. How do brand name, store brand, and generic items differ?

7. What is open dating?

8. What guidelines are helpful when comparing prices?

Warranties (p. 246)

9. What are examples of implied warranties?

10. What actions has the FTC taken to regulate used car sales?

11. What are the common advantages and disadvantages of a service contract?

Obj. 2

Major Consumer Purchases: Buying Motor Vehicles (p. 247)

Phase 1: Preshopping Activities (p. 248)

12. Why is problem identification a vital component of consumer purchasing decisions?

13. What are some of the different approaches to using consumer information?

14. What are the main sources of consumer information?

15. How do independent testing organizations assist consumers?

Phase 2: Evaluation of Alternatives (p. 249)

16. What attributes are commonly considered when assessing consumer goods and services?

17. To what extent is price an indication of product quality?

18. In what types of situation is comparison shopping most beneficial?

19. What are the common types of optional equipment offered on motor vehicles?

20. What are the sources from which people buy used cars?

21. What factors should a person consider when conducting an inspection of a used car?

22. What are the main benefits of leasing an automobile or other motor vehicle?

23. What financial factors should be considered when selecting a lease?

Phase 3: Determining Purchase Price (p. 253)

24. How can a person be better prepared to negotiate in a consumer buying situation?

25. How can a person determine if a fair price is being charged for a used car?

26. What factors affect the price of a used car?

27. Where can a consumer find information on the invoice price of a motor vehicle?

28. What actions should be taken to negotiate a fair price for a new car?

29. What is the purpose of a car buying service?

30. What financial institutions offer financing for buying an automobile?

31. What information is most helpful when comparing various financing alternatives?

Phase 4: Postpurchase Activities (p. 255)

32. What common efforts are necessary after a purchase is made?

33. What is a "lemon" law?

34. Which automobile costs are considered fixed costs? Which ones are usually variable costs?

35. What are common maintenance activities that can extend the life of a vehicle?

36. What factors should a person consider when selecting a source of automobile servicing?

Obj. 3

Resolving Consumer Complaints (p. 256)

37. What are the common causes of consumer complaints?

38. What are the steps suggested when attempting to resolve a consumer complaint?

39. How are most consumer complaints resolved?

40. How does mediation differ from arbitration?

Obj. 4

Legal Options for Consumers (p. 261)

Small Claims Court (p. 261)

41. What is the purpose of small claims court?

Class-Action Suits (p. 261)

42. When can a class-action suit be of benefit to consumers?

Using a Lawyer (p. 262)

43. What factors should be considered when selecting a lawyer?

Other Legal Alternatives (p. 262)

44. What is a legal aid society?

Post Test

Completion

1. (Obj. 1) _____ _____ uses a standard unit of measurement to compare the prices of packages of different sizes.

2. (Obj. 4) _____ _____ _____ is used to settle minor legal differences.

3. (Obj. 3) Suggested solutions by a third party to settle differences is _____.

4. (Obj. 1) _____ _____ is unplanned purchasing.

5. (Obj. 4) Publicly supported community law offices that provide legal assistance to consumers who cannot afford their own attorney are a(n) _____ _____ _____.

6. (Obj. 3) _____ is the settlement of a disagreement with a legally binding decision by a third party.

7. (Obj. 1) An agreement between a business and a consumer to cover the repair costs of a product is a(n) _____ _____.

8. (Obj. 4) A(n) _____ _____ _____ is legal action taken by a few individuals on behalf of many who have suffered the same alleged injustice.

9. (Obj. 1) A nonprofit organization created so that its members can save money on certain products and services is a(n) _____.

10. (Obj. 1) A(n) _____ is a written guarantee from the manufacturer or distributor of a product that specifies the conditions under which a product can be returned, replaced, or repaired.

Multiple Choice

_____ 1. (Obj. 1) An example of a social buying influence would be
   A. taxes.
   B. interest rates.
   C. advertising.
   D. government regulations.

_____ 2. (Obj. 2) The least reliable source of consumer information is likely to be from
   A. a consumer testing organization.
   B. a store salesperson.
   C. a newspaper advertisement.
   D. the label on a package of food.

3. (Obj. 1) Prices of food and personal care products are likely to be highest at a
   A. cooperative store.
   B. hypermarket.
   C. convenience store.
   D. supermarket.

4. (Obj. 1) Which of the following information is required to be on a food package?
   A. Brand name
   B. Freshness date
   C. Unit pricing information
   D. The address of the manufacturer or distributor

5. (Obj. 1) An unwritten guarantee that a product will perform its intended purpose
   is called a(n)
   A. express warranty.
   B. service contract.
   C. implied warranty.
   D. limited warranty.

6. (Obj. 2) A "cooling-off" law is designed to help consumers
   A. reduce unit prices.
   B. cancel a contract.
   C. hire a lawyer.
   D. improve product safety.

7. (Obj. 3) Most common complaints are resolved by
   A. returning to the place of purchase.
   B. contacting a government agency.
   C. taking legal action.
   D. contacting the company's main office.

8. (Obj. 3) Arbitration differs from mediation in that arbitration
   A. involves a third party.
   B. is legally binding.
   C. requires the use of a lawyer.
   D. includes involvement of federal government consumer agencies.

9. (Obj. 4) The purpose of small claims court is to
   A. settle difference between state and local government agencies.
   B. handle legal problems involving severe injuries.
   C. resolve minor legal differences.
   D. assist lawyers with settling common legal problems.

_____ 10. (Obj. 4) Which of the following could qualify as a class-action suit?
   A. A disagreement between a tenant and landlord
   B. Injuries to several people caused by a defective product
   C. An incorrect amount billed to your monthly charge account
   D. Your attempt to obtain a refund of $37 for a product that was neverdelivered

Problems, Applications, and Cases

1. Conduct a study of an item you are planning to purchase or may consider purchasing in the future. Refer to text pages to review material on sources of consumer information.

2. John Blanchard is planning to purchase a compact disc player and is considering three brands. In his buying matrix (see text page 250), he has assigned performance a weight of 0.4, warranty a weight of 0.3, store service a weight of 0.2, and product design a weight of 0.1. The following is a list of prices and ratings for the attributes:

	Price	Performance	Warranty	Store service	Product design
Brand A	$650	5	6	4	7
Brand B	$525	7	6	5	6
Brand C	$610	6	5	7	6

   Based on this analysis, which brand would John buy? What other factors need to be considered in this buying decision?

3. Conduct a survey to determine the types of products (food, health care, clothing, and others) that are most likely to be purchased on brand name form, store brand form, and generic form. What factors influence people's decisions to select a specific brand?

4. For each of the following consumer problems, indicate the federal government agency (see Appendix B) that is most likely to provide assistance for the situation presented:

Situation	Government Agency
a. You desire information on whether certain used cars you are considering for purchase have had recalls.	
b. You have received some offers in the mail that appear to be deceptive and perhaps illegal.	

c. You have an allergic reaction to a soap that is supposed to medically cleanse your skin.

d. A local company is offering an opportunity to invest in a stock that promises an unusually high rate of return.

Supplementary Case 8-1: Buyer Beware

Topic: Buying Decisions

Text Reference: pp. 242-247; 255-262

Each month, John and Tina Harper had difficulty making ends meet. They had three children, and their housing, food, and other living expenses were constantly increasing. One day at work, a friend told John about a food-buying plan that would help the Harpers save money. For a monthly payment of $165, all the food they needed would be delivered, and they would also qualify for a new refrigerator. Since the Harpers viewed this plan as a way to save money and since they also needed a new refrigerator, they signed up for the plan.

After making two payments, the Harpers were notified by the company with which they had signed up that delivery of their refrigerator had been delayed due to production problems. Meanwhile, they had received less food than they needed, so they still had to spend money for groceries.

Two months later, the refrigerator still hadn't arrived, and the Harpers were paying more for food than they had paid before they joined the plan. Two weeks later, the Harpers stopped receiving goods from the company. "Well, I guess we won't have to make any more payments," commented John, "since we aren't receiving any of the services we were paying for." He attempted to notify the company of his intention to stop making payments, but its phone had been disconnected, and its office was empty. He sighed, saying, "Now our food expenses can return to the amount they were before we got involved in this deal."

But the Harpers' problems weren't over. A few months later, a collection agency notified them that they still owed $495 for several months of service. The contract they had signed obligated them to pay for a minimum of eight months.

Such consumer problems occur frequently. People get involved in expensive situations that they could have avoided if they had known all the facts when they were making their purchasing choices.

Case Questions

1. What actions should the Harpers have taken before joining the food-buying plan?
2. How can the Harpers avoid paying the additional $495?
3. In what ways could effective financial planning help the Harpers cope with their situations?

Supplementary Case 8-2: Double Deception

Topic: Consumer Fraud

Text Reference: pp. 255-262

Melvin Hooper recently invested $8,000 in a land partnership that advertised an expected annual rate of return of 17 percent. He had read that the real estate company was responsible for some of the most successful housing developments and shopping centers in the southeastern United States. However, after four months, Melvin was no longer receiving the monthly statements that reported the value of his investment.

A couple of weeks later, Melvin saw a newspaper article stating that the company was being sued for deceptive sales practices. This was followed a few days later by a phone call from an organization who said they could help him get his money back. The organization would require a $250 fee, in advance, to help Melvin get his money back. However, this time Melvin was cautious since he had heard about "fraud recovery" services. Instead, he reported the organization to the state consumer protection office.

Case Questions

1. What actions might have helped Melvin avoid the land fraud?
2. Why are fraud recovery services able to take advantage of consumers who are recent victims of scams?
3. What legal action may be appropriate in this situation?

Supplementary Case 8-3: Used Trouble

Topic: Buying a Used Vehicle

Text Reference: pp. 249-256

Blake and Ellen Kenton recently purchased a used car for their daughter and for use by Blake's mother when she works in community programs for children and elderly citizens. The vehicle was purchased from a car rental company for $6,700. Most other sources were charging $8,200 for comparable vehicles.

After buying the car, the Kentons discovered the car need some minor repairs costing $600. They decided to have the work done at an auto repair shop a few miles away. The business, recently changed owners, but had been operating in the community for 15 years.

After the repair work was complete, the car ran well for two months. Then real trouble started; new problems arose. An oil leak was followed by a need for new brakes, which happened at the time the transmission needed major work. So ended the Kentons' used car bargain!

Case Questions

1. What actions should the Kentons have taken before buying the car?
2. How could the Kentons have made sure they were getting capable and cost-efficient repair service?
3. What additional actions might be recommended to the Kentons?

Supplementary Reading 8

Karen E. Klein, "Company Cars: To Buy or to Lease?", Smart Answers, June 8, 2005.

Company Cars: To Buy or to Lease?

Experts say the decision depends on various factors, including how long you plan to keep the vehicle and how much mileage you'll put on it

Q: I own an event- and destination-management company and am interested in buying or leasing a company car for one of our employees to use. I need any advice you can give me on buying vs. leasing, and what taxes this move will incur.
-- P.L., Gloucester, Mass.

A: Whether to lease or purchase typically depends upon how long you plan to keep the car and how much mileage it will accumulate. Other considerations you should take into account, obviously, are the monthly payments and the buyout price at the end of the lease. When you visit a dealership, the sales staff should be able to do a lease-vs.-purchase calculation that will be helpful.

As a general rule, experts say, if you will keep the car for five years or more, it's smarter to buy. If you expect to change it every three or four years, you're better off with a lease. Likewise, if you anticipate that your employee will put major mileage on the car, leasing is the way to go. Just pay attention to the mileage limit in your lease agreement: If you go over it, or the car incurs any damage, you'll be hit with an extra charge at turn-in time.

ACCIDENT INSURANCE? Tim Jacobs, owner of Design Group (www.thedesigngroup.com), a Minneapolis special-event company, prefers to lease. "If I want to provide an employee with a vehicle and want less upfront costs and a lower down payment, then a lease is perfect," he says. "It also maintains smaller monthly expenses and I would likely change the vehicle every three years [anyway]. The payments are charged as expenses and there are fewer accounting impediments."

Regardless of whether you lease or buy, a car can be a headache: You face potential liability if your employee has a traffic accident, and your company will have to purchase automobile insurance. Also, if you buy, you'll have to sell or otherwise dispose of the car when you no longer want it.

"My advice would be to have your employee buy or lease the car, and then reimburse that employee for costs," says Alan Weiner, a CPA and partner at Holtz Rubenstein Reminick, an accounting firm based in Melville, N.Y.

"But if the employee owns or leases the car, there's less likelihood of employer responsibility in the case of an accident. (This may depend on whether the car was being used for business at the time of the accident.) Also, if the employee resigns or is fired, you won't be left with having to dispose of the vehicle."

KEEPING TABS. If you decide to lease or own, as opposed to having your employee do so, you should become acquainted with the depreciation rules for luxury and nonluxury automobiles. You can read up on the rules in IRS Publication 463 and IRS Form 4562.

You should also buy a mileage log that you keep in the car, and have your employee do the record-keeping necessary to account for business use of the vehicle. When the car is used for business purposes, the miles should be logged and the destination and purpose of the trip noted. If the record-keeping is insufficient or nonexistent, the IRS could decide that business use of the car hasn't been substantiated, which would invalidate your auto expense deduction -- and leave you spinning your wheels.

Karen E. Klein

Study Questions

1. What factors should be considered when leasing a motor vehicle?

2. How can a company that leases automobiles for its employees reduce its potential legal concerns?

9 THE FINANCES OF HOUSING

Chapter Overview

This chapter provides a complete discussion of selecting housing based on life situation, needs, and personal values along with the related financial aspects of this major expenditure. First presented is material regarding factors related to renting a residence. This is followed by a discussion of buying alternatives and the home buying process, including determining housing needs, evaluating potential homes, and pricing the property. Finally, suggestions for selling a home are offered.

Learning Objectives

After studying this chapter, you will be able to:

Obj. 1 Evaluate available housing alternatives.

Obj. 2 Analyze the costs and benefits associated with renting.

Obj. 3 Implement the home-buying process.

Obj. 4 Calculate the costs associated with purchasing a home.

Obj. 5 Develop a strategy for selling a home.

Key Terms

adjustable rate mortgage (ARM)	deed	rate cap
amortization	earnest money	refinance
appraisal	escrow account	reverse mortgage
balloon mortgage	graduated payment mortgage	second mortgage
buy down	growing equity mortgage	shared appreciation mortgage (SAM)
closing costs	lease	title insurance
condominium	manufactured home	zoning laws
conventional mortgage	mortgage	
cooperative housing	payment cap	
	points	

Pretest

True-False

_____ 1. (Obj. 1) Renting tends to be less costly in the short run than buying your place of residence.

_____ 2. (Obj. 2) A lease is the legal document that sets forth the conditions of a rental agreement.

_____ 3. (Obj. 2) A security deposit is designed to cover the costs of property taxes when renting a house.

_____ 4. (Obj. 3) In a condominium, the owner only has title to the individual living unit.

_____ 5. (Obj. 3) Location is frequently mentioned as the most important factor when selecting a house to purchase.

_____ 6. (Obj. 4) A high down payment will reduce the amount of the mortgage a person needs to buy a house.

_____ 7. (Obj. 4) Qualifying for a mortgage is similar to obtaining other types of credit.

_____ 8. (Obj. 4) As interest rates rise, people are usually able to afford a higher-priced home.

_____ 9. (Obj. 4) Negative amortization is the result of an increase in the amount owed on a mortgage.

_____ 10. (Obj. 4) A deed is a document that transfers ownership of property from one party to another.

Self-Guided Study Questions

Obj. 1

Housing Alternatives (p. 272)

1. What are the main factors that influence housing selection?

Your Lifestyle and Your Choice of Housing (p. 272)
2. How do personal preferences and financial factors affect housing choice?

Opportunity Costs of Housing Choices (p. 272)
3. What are common trade-offs associated with housing decisions?

Renting versus Buying Housing (p. 273)
4. What personal and financial factors influence a person's choice of renting or buying?

5. When would renting be preferred to buying a home?

Housing Information Sources (p. 273)
6. What information is available to help a person with housing selection?

Obj. 2
Renting Your Residence (p. 274)
7. Why do most people rent their housing at some point in their life?

Selecting a Rental Unit (p. 276)
8. What are the housing types commonly available to rent?

Advantages of Renting (p. 276)
9. What are viewed as the main advantages of renting your place of residence?

Disadvantages of Renting (p. 277)
10. What are common drawbacks of renting?

11. What is the purpose of a lease?

Costs of Renting (p. 278)
12. What costs are commonly associated with renting?

13. What is the purpose of a security deposit?

Obj. 3
The Home-Buying Process (p. 279)

Step 1: Determine Homeownership Needs (p. 279)
14. What are common advantages of owning your own home?

15. What disadvantages are associated with owning your own home?

16. What options are available to a person who wants to purchase housing?

17. How does a condominium differ from cooperative housing?

18. What are the positive and negative aspects of a manufactured (mobile) home?

19. What factors need to be considered before selecting a contractor for building a home?

20. What factors influence the amount a person can spend when buying a home?

21. What features are most commonly desired in a home?

Step 2: Find and Evaluate a Property to Purchase (p. 283)

22. What is the purpose of zoning laws?

23. How does the quality of schools affect the value of all homes in an area?

24. What services can a real estate agent provide?

Step 3: Price the Property (p. 284)

25. What factors influence the price a person might offer for a home for sale?

26. How does a "buyer's" market differ from a "seller's" market when negotiating a price?

Obj. 4

The Finances of Home Buying (p. 286)

Step 4: Obtain Financing (p. 286)

27. How does the amount of money a person has available for a down payment affect financing availability?

28. What qualifications must be met to obtain a mortgage?

29. What factors affect the amount of mortgage a person can afford?

30. How do points affect the cost of a mortgage?

Fixed-Rate, Fixed-Payment Mortgages (p. 289)

31. What is a conventional mortgage?

32. How do government financing programs assist homebuyers?

Adjustable-Rate, Variable-Payment Mortgages (p. 290)

33. What are the positive and negative aspects of an adjustable rate mortgage?

34. How do a buy down and a shared appreciation mortgage assist a person when buying a home?

35. What is a second mortgage?

Step 5: Close the Purchase Transaction (p. 294)

36. What are common closing costs associated with finalizing a real estate transaction?

37. What is the purpose of title insurance?

38. What is an escrow account?

Obj. 5

Selling Your Home (p. 296)

Preparing Your Home for Selling (p. 296)

39. What should a person consider doing when preparing a home for selling?

Determining the Selling Price (p. 296)

40. What factors will influence the selling price of a home?

Sale by Owner (p. 297)

41. What are the advantages and disadvantages of selling your own home?

Listing with a Real Estate Agent (p. 298)

42. How can a real estate agent assist you when selling a home?

Post Test

Completion

1. (Obj. 4) _____ refers to the reduction of a loan balance through payments made over a period of time.

2. (Obj. 3) A(n) _____ is an individually owned housing unit in a building with a number of such units.

3. (Obj. 4) A(n) _____ mortgage has fixed monthly payments and a very large final payment.

4. (Obj. 4) The document that transfers ownership or property from one party to another is the _____.

5. (Obj. 2) The legal document that defines the conditions of a rental agreement is a(n) _____.

6. (Obj. 4) _____ are prepaid interest charged by a lender.

7. (Obj. 4) A(n) _____ _____ is an interest rate subsidy from a builder or real estate developer that reduces the mortgage payments in the first few years of the loan.

8. (Obj. 4) Money deposited with a financial institution for the payment of property taxes and home insurance is the _____ _____.

9. (Obj. 3) _____ _____ is a portion of the purchase price that the buyer deposits as evidence of good faith to show the purchase offer is serious.

10. (Obj. 4) _____ _____ are the fees and charges paid when a real estate transaction is completed.

Multiple Choice

_____ 1. (Obj. 2) A common advantage of renting a place to live is
   A. the tax advantage.
   B. equity.
   C. mobility.
   D. community pride.

_____ 2. (Obj. 2) The legal document that defines the conditions of a rental agreement is a
   A. mortgage.
   B. lease.
   C. title.
   D. deed.

_____ 3. (Obj. 3) Which of the following is a housing arrangement involving membership in a nonprofit organization in which a person may rent a living unit?
   A. Cooperative
   B. Condominium
   C. Conventional mortgage
   D. Contingency clause

_____ 4. (Obj. 3) A common disadvantage of home ownership is
   A. limited responsibility.
   B. few financial benefits.
   C. low initial costs.
   D. limited mobility.

_____ 5. (Obj. 3) The most frequently mentioned factor considered when selecting a home to buy is
   A. quality of schools.
   B. zoning restrictions.
   C. location.
   D. condition of the home.

_____ 6. (Obj. 3) The purpose of zoning laws is to
   A. reduce housing costs.
   B. improve the quality of schools.
   C. maintain public services in a community.
   D. restrict how property is used.

7. (Obj. 4) Which of the following would increase the amount of mortgage a person could afford?
   A. Increased interest rates
   B. Decreased interest rates
   C. A low down payment
   D. A large amount of other debts

8. (Obj. 4) A mortgage with a constant interest rate is commonly referred to as a(n) _____ mortgage.
   A. government-guaranteed
   B. conventional
   C. equity
   D. amortized

9. (Obj. 4) A home equity loan is also referred to as a
   A. buy-down.
   B. shared appreciation mortgage.
   C. second mortgage.
   D. conventional mortgage.

10. (Obj. 4) Which of the following items is commonly paid out of an escrow account?
    A. Title insurance
    B. Property insurance
    C. Closing costs
    D. Credit report fee

Problems, Applications, and Cases

1. Based on the following information for George and Alicia Peters, would you recommend that they continue to rent an apartment or buy a house?

    monthly rent $650

    monthly mortgage payment $790

    approximate annual mortgage interest $8,900

    annual property taxes $1,575

    estimated annual maintenance $420

    federal income tax rate 28%

    In addition to this analysis, what other factors should George and Alicia consider when deciding whether to rent or buy their housing?

2. Conduct an assessment of two or more apartments that you would consider renting. Refer to text pages 275-278 for additional information on this topic.

3. In an effort to compare different alternatives for purchasing a home, review text pages 280-282. Compare the features of three different types of housing.

4. With the use of Exhibit 9-6 on page 284, conduct an inspection of a home you or a friend might consider buying.

5. For each of the following situations, which type of mortgage discussed on pages 289-294 of the text would be most appropriate?

Situation	Type of mortgage
a. A moderate income family with limited funds available for a down payment	
b. An individual who believes interest rates are quite high and believes he will be able to refinance at a lower rate in three to five years	
c. A person who wishes to use current equity in her home to finance a son's college education	
d. A family desires a fixed-rate loan with a constant level of payments	
e. A person desires low mortgage payments at present, but will be able to afford higher payments in future years	

Supplementary Case 9-1: Hunting for a Home

Topic: Housing Choices

Text Reference: pp. 272-282

Dan and Lia Schultz were recently married and are looking for a permanent residence. Dan, a computer operator, is learning programming as a part-time student. Lia works part-time as a receptionist and is taking courses toward a degree in health care administration. They have $2,000 in a savings account.

Dan and Lia are considering renting an apartment that has a monthly rent of $575 and requires a $600 security deposit. They are also looking into a condominium that they can buy with a $2,300 down payment and monthly mortgage payments of $730.

Case Questions

1. What personal and household factors should Dan and Lia consider before choosing their housing?
2. What positive and negative aspects of the two housing alternatives mentioned above should Dan and Lia consider?
3. Besides the two housing alternatives mentioned above, what other alternatives might be available to Dan and Lia?
4. What future events might affect the current choice made by Dan and Lia?
5. What should Dan and Lia do?

Supplementary Case 9-2: Move or Remodel?

Topic: Changing Homes

Text Reference: pp. 279-285

Pat and Marci Koswall have lived in their current home for three years. The house is located within a half hour of each of their places of employment. With declining interest rates, the Koswalls are considering a larger home.

Most of the available homes they like are located in a different area, farther from work. However, these homes provide many features that appeal to Pat and Marci.

To keep the conveniences of their current location, the Koswalls are considering a major upgrade of their current home. This work would include a new kitchen floor and cabinets, a remodeled bathroom, and the addition of a bedroom (which could be used as an office).

Case Questions

1. How might Pat and Marci assess their alternatives about buying a different house or remodeling their current one?
2. What financial factors should they consider?
3. What action would you recommend for the Koswalls?

Supplementary Case 9-3: Refinance versus Home-Equity Loan

Topic: *Mortgages*

Text Reference: pp. 286-294

Ben and Jan Wooden recently encountered some unexpected medical bills and need to obtain cash for that purpose. Since interest rates have recently declined, they could refinance their mortgage. By taking out a slightly larger mortgage, the Woodens could obtain the needed cash and their monthly payments would stay at the same level.

Several financial institutions are offering home-equity loans with no closing costs. This would allow the Woodens to borrow against the equity in their home. The rates for these loans are slightly higher than the rate for refinancing—however, remember there are no closing costs.

Case Questions

1. What factors should be considered before selecting one of the two alternatives?
2. How can the Woodens evaluate the financial benefits and cost of each situation?
3. What action would you recommend for the Woodens?

Supplementary Reading 9

Peter Coy, "What The Mortgage Next Door Can Tell You", News: Analysis & Commentary, June 27, 2005.

What The Mortgage Next Door Can Tell You

You've hunted for a new house for months, and now you're ready to bid. But before you do, check one more indicator to see whether you're making a smart purchase: the types of mortgages home buyers in your market are choosing.

If lots of your prospective neighbors are taking out loans with low initial payments but much higher costs down the road, it could mean that they're stretching to buy houses they otherwise couldn't afford. That's a sign of an overpriced market.

The red lights are flashing in San Diego, Atlanta, San Francisco, Denver, and Oakland. Last year, they had the highest share of single-family-home mortgage loans that require just interest payments -- no principal -- in the early years. San Diego led overall with 47.6% of home buyers taking out interest only mortgages, up from 1.9% as recently as 2001.

Providence, Indianapolis, Houston, Pittsburgh, and Milwaukee are at the other extreme, with fewer than 8% of buyers going for interest-only mortgages last year. The data, which appeared first on BusinessWeek Online, were supplied by LoanPerformance, a San Francisco real estate information service. On a national basis, the LoanPerformance numbers closely track those of Fannie Mae Corp. and Freddie Mac Corp., even though those companies buy standard mortgages while LoanPerformance's numbers cover only big-ticket "jumbo" loans and subprime mortgages.

Why are interest-only mortgages a warning sign of a possible bubble? They tend to be most popular in overheated markets, where buyers are looking for every trick to make their monthly payments affordable. Initial payments on an interest-only mortgage are low because borrowers aren't required to pay any principal. But after a period of time -- from 2 to 10 years -- principal payments begin, and the monthly payment jumps by as much as 50%.

Be especially cautious of markets in which option adjustable-rate mortgages are hot. These loans offer borrowers extremely low teaser rates -- typically, just 1% for the first month -- and allow the option of making a minimum payment that may not even cover all of the interest owed for the month. The unpaid interest gets added to the principal, so the total owed can swell like a credit-card bill. Borrowers may be enticed by the introductory rate but unprepared for later payments on the swollen principal. Keith M. Schemm, a mortgage broker in Santa Clara, Calif., says option ARMs are "pretty dangerous loans to do" for many families. "The problem is there's such a frenzy in the marketplace to buy a home."

In assessing a market, also look at whether house prices are high relative to local incomes and relative to rental rates on equivalent properties, and at the health of the local economy. If major employers have recently closed, home prices are likely to head down. But if you're worried about buying at the top of the market, knowing what kind of mortgages your neighbors are choosing should help you make a more informed decision.

Peter Coy in New York

Study Questions

1. What are some recent trends in the types of mortgages being offered homebuyers?

2. What actions might be taken before choosing a mortgage?

10 HOME AND AUTOMOBILE INSURANCE

Chapter Overview

Adequate financial protection of property is a vital component of financial planning. This chapter covers the fundamental aspects of risk management, along with home and auto insurance. Discussed are coverages available to homeowners and renters, along with information on the types of policies and the factors that affect the cost of home insurance. The second major aspect of the chapter involves a presentation of the importance, types of coverages, and cost factors of automobile insurance.

Learning Objectives

After studying this chapter, you will be able to:

Obj. 1 Develop risk management plan using insurance.

Obj. 2 Discuss the importance of property and liability insurance.

Obj. 3 Explain the insurance coverages and policy types available to homeowners and renters.

Obj. 4 Analyze the factors that influence the coverage amount and cost of home insurance.

Obj. 5 Identify the important types of automobile insurance coverages.

Obj. 6 Evaluate the factors that affect the cost of automobile insurance.

Key Terms

actual cash value (ACV)	insurance	property damage liability
assigned risk pool	insurance company	pure risk
bodily injury liability	insured	rating territory
coinsurance clause	insurer	replacement value
collision	liability	risk
comprehensive physical damage	medical payments coverage	self-insured
	negligence	speculative risk
driver classification	no-fault system	strict liability
endorsement	peril	umbrella policy
financial responsibility laws	personal property floater	uninsured motorists protection
hazard	policy	
homeowners insurance	policyholder	vicarious liability
household inventory	premium	

Pretest

True-False

_____ 1. (Obj. 2) Vicarious liability refers to a failure to take ordinary or reasonable care in a situation.

_____ 2. (Obj. 3) Personal property refers to furniture, appliances, clothing, and other personal belongings.

_____ 3. (Obj. 3) An umbrella policy provides additional liability coverage for an individual or family.

_____ 4. (Obj. 3) Flood insurance is included in the broad form of homeowners policy.

_____ 5. (Obj. 4) A coinsurance clause requires the insured to pay the first $50 or $100 of a claim.

_____ 6. (Obj. 4) The actual cash value claim method is based on current replacement cost.

_____ 7. (Obj. 5) Financial responsibility laws require that drivers have comprehensive physical damage insurance coverage.

_____ 8. (Obj. 5) People injured in your car in an accident would be covered by medical payments coverage.

_____ 9. (Obj. 5) Comprehensive physical damage provides coverage from losses from fire, theft, or vandalism to your vehicle.

_____ 10. (Obj. 6) Most automobile insurance companies charge the same amount for coverage regardless of your place of residence.

Self-Guided Study Questions

Obj. 1

Insurance and Risk Management: An Introduction (p. 306)

What Is Insurance? (p. 306)

1. What is insurance?

2. What is an insurance company?

3. What are the financial trade-offs of not obtaining the right amount and type of insurance?

Types of Risk (p. 306)

4. What are the three types of risks?

5. What is pure risk?

6. What is a speculative risk?

Risk Management Methods (p. 307)

7. What is risk management?

8. What are the various methods of managing risk?

9. What is self-insurance?

Planning an Insurance Program (p. 308)

10. What personal factors are important in setting your insurance goals?

11. What questions must you ask when planning to reach your insurance goals?

12. How do you carry out your plan?

13. What questions must you answer when evaluating your insurance plan?

Obj. 2

Property and Liability Insurance (p. 311)

Potential Property Losses (p. 311)

14. What are the two main risks faced by property owners?

Liability Protection (p. 312)

15. What is meant by the term liability?

16. How does negligence differ from vicarious liability?

Obj. 3

Home and Property Insurance (p. 312)

Homeowners Insurance Coverage (p. 312)

17. What are the basic coverages of a homeowner's insurance policy?

18. What is the purpose of additional living expenses?

19. What is a personal property floater?

20. Why is a home inventory important to a homeowner or renter?

21. What types of potential losses are covered by the personal liability component of home insurance?

22. What is the purpose of medical payments coverage?

23. What types of natural disasters require special insurance coverage?

Renter's Insurance (p. 316)

24. What coverages are provided in a renter's property insurance policy?

Home Insurance Policy Forms (p. 317)

25. What are the main differences between the different forms of home insurance policies?

26. What is the main purpose of a modified coverage form home insurance policy?

Obj. 4

Home Insurance Cost Factors (p. 318)

How Much Coverage Do You Need? (p. 318)

27. What factors affect the amount of home insurance coverage a person needs?

28. What is the purpose of a coinsurance clause in home insurance policies?

29. How do the two methods used to settle claims differ?

Factors That Affect Home Insurance Costs (p. 319)

30. What influences the amount paid for home insurance?

31. What are common home insurance discounts?

Obj. 5

Automobile Insurance Coverages (p. 320)

32. What is the purpose of financial responsibility laws?

Motor Vehicle Bodily Injury Coverages (p. 322)

33. How does bodily injury coverage differ from medical payments coverage?

34. What is the purpose of uninsured motorists protection?

35. Why have no-fault insurance systems not been as successful as expected?

Motor Vehicle Property Damage Coverages (p. 323)

36. What is the main purpose of property damage liability insurance?

37. How does collision coverage differ from comprehensive physical damage?

Other Automobile Insurance Coverages (p. 324)

38. What is the purpose of wage loss insurance?

Obj. 6
Automobile Insurance Costs (p. 325)

Amount of Coverage (p. 325)

39. What factors should a person consider when determining the amount of automobile insurance?

Automobile Insurance Premium Factors (p. 326)

40. What factors influence the cost of automobile insurance?

41. What factors are used to create driver classification categories?

42. What is an assigned risk pool?

Reducing Automobile Insurance Premiums (p. 327)
43. What actions can a person take to lower the cost of auto insurance?

Post Test

Completion

1. (Obj. 5) _____ _____ _____ protects an automobile owner from financial loss from such risks as fire, theft, glass breakage, falling objects, and vandalism.

2. (Obj. 4) Under the _____ _____ _____ method of settling claims, the payment you receive is based on the current replacement cost of a damaged or lost item, less depreciation.

3. (Obj. 5) _____ _____ _____ protects you against financial loss when your car damages the property of others.

4. (Obj. 2) _____ liability is present when a person is held responsible for the actions of another person.

5. (Obj. 6) _____ _____ is a category based on the driver's age, sex, marital status, driving record, and driving habits used to determine automobile insurance premiums.

6. (Obj. 4) _____ _____ _____ is state legislation that requires drivers to prove their ability to cover the cost of damage or injury caused by an automobile accident.

7. (Obj. 2) Failure to take ordinary or reasonable care is referred to as _____.

8. (Obj. 5) _____ insurance pays for damage to your automobile when it is involved in an accident, regardless of who is at fault.

9. (Obj. 3) A(n) _____ policy supplements your basic personal liability coverage.

10. (Obj. 5) _____ _____ covers the costs of health care for people who were injured in your automobile, including yourself.

Multiple Choice

1. (Obj. 2) Vicarious liability refers to
   A. vandalism.
   B. failure to take ordinary and reasonable care.
   C. a person being held responsible for the actions of another.
   D. property damage caused by natural disasters.

2. (Obj. 3) Which of the following would be an example of personal property?
   A. Trees and shrubs
   B. A garage
   C. Furniture
   D. A house

3. (Obj. 3) The purpose of an umbrella policy is to
   A. provide coverage against loss from earthquakes.
   B. supplement personal liability coverage.
   C. provide insurance coverage while on vacation.
   D. reduce the cost of amounts paid for home insurance.

4. (Obj. 3) The _____ form of home insurance provides the most extensive coverage.
   A. special
   B. basic
   C. tenants
   D. broad

5. (Obj. 4) The _____ value method of settling claims involves receiving the full cost of repairing or replacing a damaged or lost item; depreciation is not considered.
   A. actual cash
   B. full cost
   C. replacement
   D. coinsurance

6. (Obj. 5) People Injured in another car in an accident for which you were at fault would be covered by
   A. medical payments.
   B. bodily injury liability.
   C. wage loss insurance.
   D. collision insurance.

_____ 7. (Obj. 5) The 50 in 100/300/50 refers to _____ coverage.
   A. collision
   B. comprehensive physical damage
   C. bodily injury liability
   D. property damage liability

_____ 8. (Obj. 5) Damage to your car caused by wind or hail would be covered by
   A. property damage liability.
   B. collision.
   C. comprehensive physical damage.
   D. no-fault insurance.

_____ 9. (Obj. 6) Rating territory for a driver is based on
   A. age.
   B. driving record.
   C. place of residence.
   D. year, make, and model of vehicle.

_____ 10. (Obj. 6) What is the purpose of an assigned risk pool?
   A. To help people with poor driving records to get insurance
   B. To obtain insurance for young drivers
   C. To offer discounts to safe drivers
   D. To implement a no-fault insurance program

Problems, Applications, and Cases

1. Prepare an inventory of your belongings that could serve as proof of value in case of damage or loss. Refer to text pages 313-314 for information.

2. Talk to an insurance agent to determine the types and amounts of automobile insurance coverages that he or she would recommend.

3. For each of the following situations, indicate the type of auto insurance coverage that would be involved.

   a. A friend is injured while riding in your car. _____

   b. You damage a neighbor's mailbox while driving in a snowstorm. _____

c. A person in another vehicle is holding you responsible for injuries.

d. Your automobile is damaged by a large tree branch in a snowstorm.

e. Members of your family are injured in an accident with another driver who doesn't have insurance.

f. You need to have your car repaired after accidentally hitting a tree.

Supplementary Case 10-1: The Importance of Planning Ahead

Topic: Developing an Insurance Plan

Text Reference: pp. 306-311

Michael Beale works in a gift shop in the city where his take-home pay is about $1,600 a month. He has a four-year old son, and he and his wife are expecting another child. Last year, during a review of his policy, Michael told his insurance agent that he felt his family was sufficiently protected with a $40,000 life insurance policy and a hospital expense health insurance policy.

Michael's shop is successful, so he feels that additional protection is not necessary. Besides, he knows that he will have plenty of time to save for his children's education.

Two weeks ago, however, Michael was injured when he fell from a ladder, leaving him disabled and unable to work. Now, Michael is concerned that his family will not have enough income to meet their monthly living expenses.

Case Questions

1. Did Michael have the right kind of insurance protection for his family? How will his disability affect the welfare of his growing children?

2. What are some ways in which Michael's insurance program could have been improved?

3. Should Michael have considered loss of income insurance? Why or why not?

Supplementary Case 10-2: Household Insurance Decisions

Topic: Home and Auto Insurance Coverages

Text Reference: pp. 312-325

Doug and Brenda Patterson have two children, Heidi, 22, and Chuck, 17. They have basic home insurance coverage on their house, and they are considering additional coverage since they collect antiques and have four rare items as well as a number of other pieces.

The Patterson's dog, Ruffy, is one of the most popular pets in the neighborhood. Ruffy can be seen playing with children almost every day.

Heidi shares an apartment with a friend, Ruth Bowman. Since Heidi and Ruth don't have much furniture or other belongings, they decided not to get insurance. Although they are assuming some risks, they are also saving the cost of insurance.

Chuck Patterson drives to school each morning, then to his part-time job. He also uses his car for social trips on evenings and weekends. He has the minimum amount of automobile liability insurance required by the state.

As you can see, the Pattersons have some financial risks that they could reduce with insurance. Damage to their home and property, harm done by their pet, injuries to people in their dwelling, and automobile accidents causing property damage and injuries are a few of the areas in which the Pattersons might consider purchasing additional insurance. Striking the proper balance between too much insurance and not enough insurance is a difficult financial decision. Knowing the risks and the available coverages related to your home and your automobile can help you make your property and liability insurance choices.

Case Questions

1. What additional insurance coverages might the Pattersons consider obtaining?

2. What factors should the Pattersons consider in deciding whether they require additional coverages?

3. How could the Pattersons' home and auto insurance coverages affect other aspects of their financial planning?

4. What efforts can the Pattersons make to reduce the amount they pay for property and liability insurance?

Supplementary Case 10-3: Can You Prove It?

Topic: Home Insurance Claim

Text Reference: pp. 312-318

Barry Kendall lives in an apartment with his seven-year-old daughter. While they were gone for the day, burglars stole a television, a portable CD player, a notebook computer, and some rare coins.

Fortunately, Barry had renters insurance for his personal property. However, Barry's insurance agent told him that the company would only pay a portion of what Barry thought the items were worth. The items were several years old and his policy included actual cash value coverage. In addition, the insurance company would not pay for any of the rare coins since Barry could not prove he had owned these items.

Case Questions

1. What action did Barry take to protect his personal property from financial loss?
2. What weakness did Barry have in his renters insurance coverage?

Supplementary Case 10-4: So You Claim!

Topic: Auto Insurance Coverage

Text Reference: pp. 320-328

Catharine Wood was driving home one evening during a rainstorm. As a result of oil on the pavement, her automobile skidded into a cement barrier on the side of the highway. Catharine was not hurt, but the accident caused extensive damage to her three-year-old car.

Auto repair experts estimated it would cost more than $10,000 to get the vehicle back in proper running condition. Since the insurance company estimated the car was worth only $8,500, that was the amount Catharine was offered to settle the claim. However, to buy a comparable car, Catharine would have to spend of $10,000.

Case Questions

1. What actions might Catharine have taken before buying auto insurance to prevent this situation?
2. Should Catharine accept the claim settlement from the insurance company? What additional actions may be appropriate for Catharine to take?

Supplementary Reading 10

Adrienne Carter, "Telling The Risky From The Reliable", The Corporation, August 1, 2005.

Telling The Risky From The Reliable

Will Allstate's detailed customer analysis keep the profits rolling in a price war?

It's a good time to shop for car insurance. Just ask Mike and Kimberly Read of Aurora, Colo. They have a pristine driving record, rarely file a claim, and have two young daughters who won't be behind the wheel for years. Still, premiums on their Chevy Beretta and Chevy Blazer had been rising steadily. After comparing rates at 11 insurers, they found a policy from Allstate Corp. (ALL) with more liability coverage that was $500 cheaper than their existing one with State Farm Mutual Automobile Insurance Co.

What's good news for the Reads may be a bit unsettling for insurance execs. In the late '90s, a rush to grab market share sparked intense price competition. That pushed the industry's combined ratio to 110% in 2000, meaning auto insurers paid out $1.10 in claims and expenses for every $1 they earned in premiums, according to research firm A.M. Best Co. Now, another price war may be under way: State Farm, the market share leader, cut its rates by an average of 4.8% last year. USAA, which primarily serves military families, has lowered prices by 8% over the past year and a half. Overall, after five consecutive years of rate increases, premiums across the group are likely to remain flat or even decline in 2005.

This time, the No. 2 auto insurer, Allstate, is determined not to get sucked into another race to the bottom. Taking a page from fast-growing rival Progressive Corp. (PGR) (No. 3 by market share), Allstate has gotten smarter about what to charge which drivers, using a technology-intensive "tiered pricing" system. Now, Allstate considers previously overlooked data such as a driver's credit history, takes a deeper look at traditional information like demographics, and better matches the premium to the risk of the customer. The new pricing discipline, combined with an industry-wide drop in the number of claims filed, has helped drive profits. In 2004, Allstate's operating income rose 16%, to $3.1 billion. Return on equity hit 15%, up from 6.5% in 2002.

For decades, Allstate had lumped customers into three main pricing categories, based on basic details such as a customer's age and place of residence. It now has more than 1,500 price levels. Agents used to simply refer to a manual to give customers a price; now they log on to a computer that uses complex algorithms to analyze 16 credit report variables, such as late payments and card balances, as well as data such as claims history for specific car models. Thus, safe bets such as the Reads are rewarded, saving up to 20% over the old system, and high-risk drivers are penalized, paying up to 20% more. It has worked well enough that Allstate now applies it to other lines, such as homeowners' insurance. "With tiered pricing, you're charging the right rate for the customers," says Jay Gelb, an insurance analyst with Lehman Brothers Inc. (LEH)

There's plenty at stake for Northbrook (Ill.)-based Allstate, the largest publicly traded auto insurer, where memories of the last price war are still fresh. Earnings at the company fell from $2.6 billion in 1998 to $1.5 billion in 2001, as Allstate got slammed by an unexpected rise in both auto and homeowners' claims. Progressive, the first to implement a more sophisticated pricing system, has increased its share of the auto insurance business from 5.5% to 7.5%, while Allstate's share has eroded from 15% to 12%. State Farm claims 22%, down from 28%.

Allstate execs promise they'll stick to their pricing system, regardless of how low competitors slash policy rates. Chairman and Chief Executive Edward M. Liddy, at the helm since 1999, figures any losses will be marginal, since Allstate will still be very competitive among low-risk, high-profit drivers, while rate-slashing insurers will likely attract less-profitable, higher-risk drivers.

Analysts say Allstate, which started to introduce some aspects of the tiered-pricing model back in the late '90s, right behind Progressive, will have an early-mover advantage -- having had time to collect reams of data and fine-tune pattern recognition. That's crucial, since "the industry is engaged in what amounts to a technological arms race," says Robert P. Hartwig, chief economist for the Insurance Information Institute, a trade group.

Of course, a new pricing scheme is no guarantee of lasting success. For one thing, more insurers are catching on: State Farm revealed in May that it would start using more sophisticated pricing techniques. Plus, Allstate has to keep up with service innovations, such as Progressive's "concierge" claim centers, which will arrange for a loaner if your car is in the shop. Most important, no matter how Liddy tries to insulate Allstate from a price war, downward pressure on prices could put the squeeze on underwriting margins. Alain Karaoglan, an equity analyst with Deutsche Bank (**DB**), estimates that Allstate's combined ratio will jump from 88.8% this year to 91.3% in 2006. Even though the nature of the business is cyclical, Allstate's new pricing discipline means it should be able to avoid any major accidents.

Adrienne Carter in Northbrook, Ill.

Study Questions

1. What factors are commonly considered by auto insurance companies when setting premium rates?

2. What actions can consumer take to obtain the best value when buying auto insurance?

11 HEALTH AND DISABILITY INSURANCE

Chapter Overview

Planning a health insurance program needs careful study, because the protection should be shaped to the needs of the individual or the family. However, the task is simplified for many families because a foundation for their coverage is already provided by group health insurance at work. We begin the chapter explaining why the costs of health insurance and health care have been increasing. Then we define health insurance and disability income insurance, and explain their importance in financial planning. Next, we explore the sources of the disability income insurance requirement. Then we analyze the benefits and limitations of the various types of health insurance coverages. Private sources of health insurance and health care are presented next, with a complete coverage of health maintenance organizations (HMOs). Finally, we discuss the sources of government health programs, such as Medicare and Medicaid.

Learning Objectives

After studying this chapter, you will be able to:

Obj. 1 Explain why the costs of health insurance and health care have been increasing.

Obj. 2 Define health insurance and disability income insurance and explain their importance in financial planning.

Obj. 3 Analyze the benefits and limitations of the various types of health care coverage.

Obj. 4 Evaluate private sources of health insurance and health care.

Obj. 5 Appraise the sources of government health programs.

Obj. 6 Recognize the need for disability income insurance.

Key Terms

basic health insurance coverage	coinsurance	copayment
Blue Cross	comprehensive major medical insurance	deductible
Blue Shield	coordination of benefits (COB)	disability income insurance
		exclusive provider

organization
health maintenance organization (HMO)
hospital expense insurance
hospital indemnity policy
long-term care insurance

major medical expense insurance
managed care
Medigap insurance
physician expense insurance
point-of-service plan

preferred provider organization
stop-loss
surgical expense insurance

Pretest

True-False

_____ 1. (Obj. 1) The United States has the highest per capita medical expenditures of any country in the world.

_____ 2. (Obj. 1) The best way to avoid the high cost of sickness is to stay well.

_____ 3. (Obj. 2) Almost all people in the United States have health insurance.

_____ 4. (Obj. 2) The coordination of benefits (COB) is a method of integrating the benefits payable under more than one insurance plan.

_____ 5. (Obj. 3) Major medical expense insurance protects against the large expenses of a serious injury or a long illness.

_____ 6. (Obj. 3) Dread disease and cancer policies are usually good values.

_____ 7. (Obj. 4) Managed care refers to prepaid health plans that provide comprehensive health care to members.

_____ 8. (Obj. 5) Medicaid is a federal health insurance program for people 65 or older.

_____ 9. (Obj. 6) There is a standard definition of disability.

_____ 10. (Obj. 6) Like Social Security benefits, workers' compensation benefits are determined by your earnings and your work history.

Self-Guided Study Questions
Obj. 1
Health Care Costs (p. 336)
1. What are the four sources of health insurance available to individuals?

High Medical Costs (p. 336)
2. What was the average per capita spending on health care in 1999?

3. How do administrative costs in the United States compare with those in Canada?

4. Currently how many Americans are uninsured or underinsured?

Why Does Health Care Cost So Much? (p. 336)
5. What factors have contributed to the high and rising costs of health care?

6. Why do hospitals, doctors, and patients often lack the incentive to make the most economical use of health care services?

What Is Being Done About the High Costs of Health Care? (p. 338)
7. How is the private sector coping with the cost of health care?

What Can You do to Reduce Health Care Costs? (p. 339)

8. What steps can you take to reduce your health care costs?

Obj. 2

Health Insurance and Financial Planning (p. 339)

9. Why have a growing number of college students been uninsured?

What Is Health Insurance? (p. 339)

10. What is the purpose of health insurance?

Group Health Insurance (p. 340)

11. What is group health insurance?

12. What is the Health Insurance Portability and Accountability Act of 1996?

13. What are Medical Savings Accounts (MSAs)?

Individual Health Insurance (p. 340)

14. What is individual health insurance?

Supplementing Your Group Insurance (p. 341)

15. What are some reasons to supplement your group insurance?

16. What is a coordination of benefits (COB) provision?

Medical Coverage and Divorce (p. 341)

17. What is the importance of discussing medical coverage of nonworking spouses when couples divorce?

18. What is the purpose of the Consolidated Omnibus Budget Reconciliation Act of 1986?

Obj. 3

Types of Health Insurance Coverages (p. 341)

19. What should a good health insurance plan cover?

Hospital Expense Insurance (p. 342)

20. What is hospital expense insurance?

Surgical Expense Insurance (p. 342)

21. What is surgical expense insurance?

Physician Expense Insurance (p. 342)

22. What is physician expense insurance?

Major Medical Expense Insurance (p. 342)

23. What is major medical expense insurance?

24. What is a deductible provision in a health insurance policy?

25. What is a coinsurance clause?

26. What is a stop-loss provision in a health insurance policy?

27. Why do some major medical policies contain a stop-loss provision?

Comprehensive Major Medical Insurance (p. 342)

28. How does major medical expense insurance differ from comprehensive major medical insurance?

Hospital Indemnity Policies (p. 343)

29. Why do some people buy a hospital indemnity policy?

30. Is a hospital indemnity policy a good buy?

Dental Expense Insurance (p. 343)

31. What is dental expense insurance?

Vision Care Insurance (p. 343)

32. What should good vision care insurance cover?

Other Insurance Policies (p. 343)

33. What are dread disease and cancer insurance policies?

34. Who should buy dread disease and cancer insurance policies?

Long-Term Care Insurance (p. 343)

35. What is long-term care insurance?

Major Provisions in a Health Insurance Policy (p. 345)

36. What are major provisions in a health insurance policy?

37. What is a copayment?

Which Coverage Should You Choose? (p. 348)
38. How do you decide which health insurance coverage you should choose?

Health Insurance Trade-Offs (p. 348)
39. How do you tackle the trade-offs between the costs and benefits of health insurance coverages?

40. What is the difference between a reimbursement policy and an indemnity policy?

Health Information Online (p. 348)
41. What are a few good sources of healthcare Web sites on the Internet?

Obj. 4
Private Sources of Health Insurance and Health Care (p. 350)

Private Insurance Companies (p. 350)
42. How many private insurance companies sell health insurance?

Hospital and Medical Service Plans (p. 351)
43. What benefits are provided by Blue Cross/Blue Shield?

44. What is the meaning of managed care?

45. Who provides managed care?

Health Maintenance Organizations (HMOs) (p. 351)
46. How do health maintenance organizations (HMOs) operate?

47. What services should be included with your membership in a typical HMO?

Preferred Provider Organizations (PPOs) (p. 353)
48. What are preferred provider organizations (PPOs)?

49. What is an exclusive provider organization (EPO)?

50. What are point-of-service plans?

51. How do PPOs and HMOs differ?

Home Health Care Agencies (p. 353)
52. How does a health association differ from a home health agency?

Employer Self-Funded Health Plans (p. 354)

53. What is an employer self-funded health plan?

54. What are the new health care accounts? (p. 354)

Obj. 5

Government Health Care Programs (p. 354)

Medicare (p. 355)

55. What are the two sources of government health insurance?

56. What hospital insurance benefits are provided through Medicare?

57. What medical insurance benefits are provided through Medicare?

58. What services are not covered by Medicare?

Medigap (p. 358)

59. What is Medigap or MedSup insurance?

60. Who needs Medigap insurance?

Medicaid (p. 358)

61. What is Medicaid?

62. Who administers Medicaid programs?

63. How is Medicaid financed?

64. Should people who have Medicaid coverage purchase supplemental insurance?

Fight Against Medicare/Medicaid Fraud and Abuse (p. 358)

65. What is the Medicare/Medicaid Anti-Waste, Fraud, and Abuse Act?

Government Consumer Health Information Web Sites (p. 359)

66. What are major Health and Human Services (HHS) Web sites?

Obj. 6

Disability Income Insurance (p. 360)

67. Why is disability often called the living death?

Definition of Disability (p. 361)

68. Why are there different definitions of disability?

69. What are the features of a good disability plan?

Disability Insurance Trade-Offs (p. 361)

70. What trade-offs should you consider when purchasing disability income insurance?

71. Why should you ask for non-cancelable and guaranteed renewable disability income insurance?

Sources of Disability Income (p. 362)

72. What are the various sources of disability income?

73. How are worker's compensation benefits determined?

Determining Your Disability Income Insurance Requirement (p. 363)

74. How do you calculate your disability income insurance requirement?

Post Test

Completion

1. (Obj. 1) The best way to avoid the high cost of sickness is to _____ _____.

2. (Obj. 2) The purpose of _____ _____ is to alleviate the financial burdens suffered by individuals because of illness or injury.

3. (Obj. 3) _____ _____ _____ pays part or all of hospital bills for room, board and other charges.

4. (Obj. 3) _____ _____ _____ pays part or all of a surgeon's fee for an operation.

5. (Obj. 3) _____ _____ _____ helps pay for physician's care that does not involve surgery.

6. (Obj. 4) _____ _____ plans provide hospital care benefits on essentially a "service-type" basis.

7. (Obj. 4) _____ _____ plans provide benefits for surgical and medical services performed by physicians.

8. (Obj. 5) _____ is a federal health insurance program for people 65 and older.

9. (Obj. 5) _____ is administered by each state within certain broad federal requirements and guidelines.

10. (Obj. 6) _____ _____ _____ benefits provide regular cash income lost by employees as the result of accident or illness.

Multiple Choice

_____ 1. (Obj. 1) In 2005, the health care costs were estimated at _____.
   A. $0.5 trillion
   B. $1.0 trillion
   C. $1.5 trillion
   D. $1.9 trillion

_____ 2. (Obj. 2) Group health insurance plans comprise more than _____ percent of all the health insurance issued by life insurance companies.
   A. 25
   B. 45
   C. 65
   D. 90

Copyright © 2007 The McGraw-Hill Companies, Inc. All rights reserved.

_____ 3. (Obj. 3) Which type of health insurance pays part or all of hospital bills for room, board, and other charges?
   A. Physician expense
   B. Surgical expense
   C. Hospital expense
   D. Major medical expense

_____ 4. (Obj. 3) Which type of health insurance helps pay for a physician's care that does not involve surgery?
   A. Physician expense
   B. Surgical expense
   C. Hospital expense
   D. Major medical expense

_____ 5. (Obj. 3) Which type of health insurance pays part or all of the surgeon's fee for an operation?
   A. physician expense
   B. surgical expense
   C. hospital expense
   D. major medical expense

_____ 6. (Obj. 4) What statewide hospital and medical service plan provides health care benefits on essentially a "service-type" basis?
   A. Blue Cross
   B. Blue Shield
   C. HMO
   D. Home Health Agency

_____ 7. (Obj. 4) What statewide hospital and medical service plan provides benefits for surgical and medical services provided by physicians?
   A. Blue Cross
   B. Blue Shield
   C. HMO
   D. Home Health Agency

_____ 8. (Obj. 5) The Social Security Act provides for a program of medical assistance to certain low-income individuals and families. The program is called
   A. Blue Cross.
   B. Blue Shield.
   C. Medicare.
   D. Medicaid.

_____ 9. (Obj. 6) Which type of insurance protects your most valuable asset—your ability to earn income?
   A. Disability income
   B. Life
   C. Liability
   D. Dread disease

_____ 10. (Obj. 6) If your take-home pay is $500 a week, you could be eligible for disability insurance of about _____ a week.
   A. $600-$650
   B. $500-$600
   C. $350-$400
   D. $200-$300

Problems, Applications, and Cases

1. The protection provided by individual and group insurance varies from plan to plan. List advantages and disadvantages of each plan.

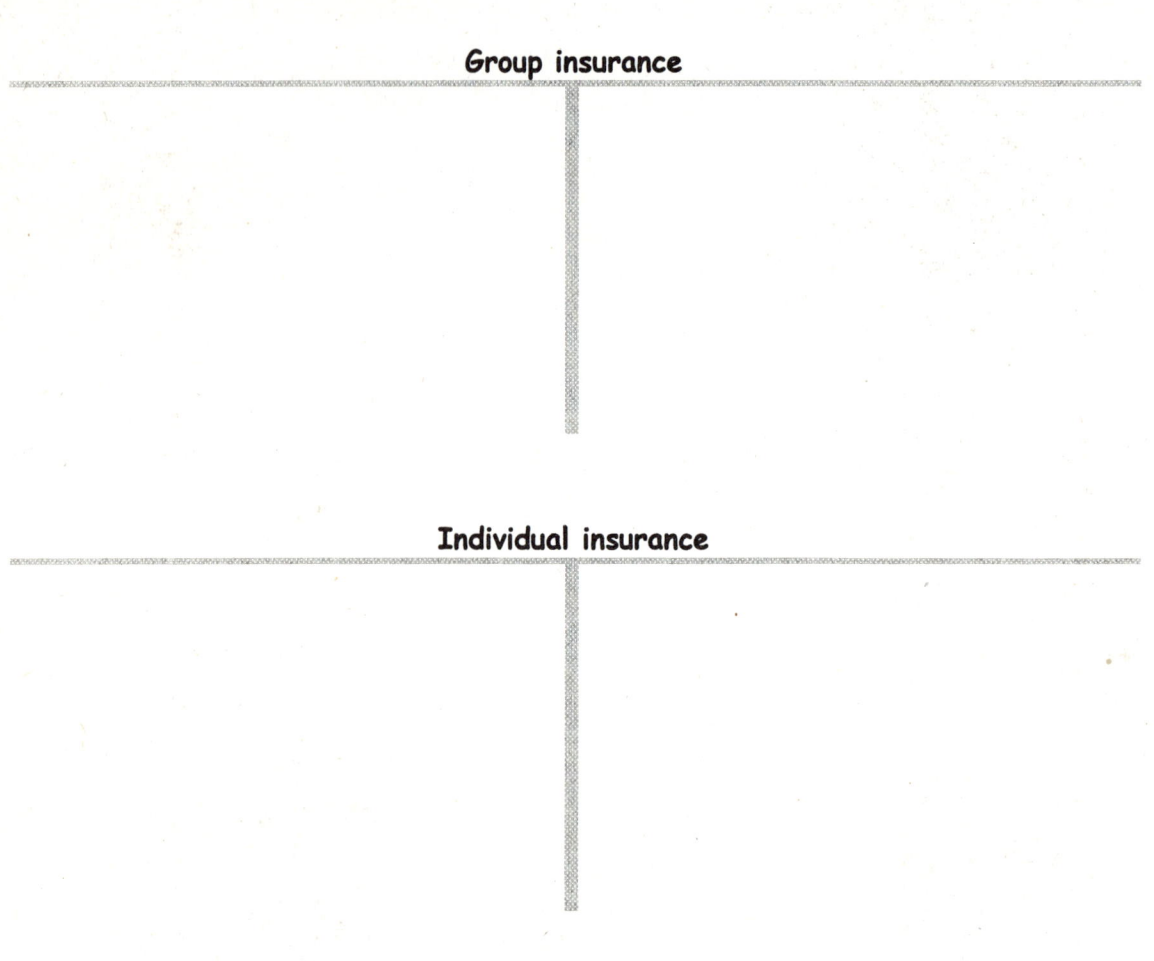

2. Whether you want to evaluate your present policies or purchase new insurance, there are some key points to explore in any health insurance. Based on what you have learned so far, decide what kinds of benefits and costs you would look for in purchasing a policy. Put this sheet aside to use in the next part of this section.

Services I would want in a health insurance policy

3 = essential   2 = not important   1 = don't need

	Now	In 5 years	In 10 years
Hospital services			
Diagnostic tests			
Prescription drugs			
Out-patient care			
Private nursing			
No limit on consecutive days hospitalization			
No limit on total number of days per year			
Small deductible			
Large percentage of major medical coverage			

No exclusions for:
    private nursing homes
    Medicare
    occupational hazards			

Non-cancelable			
Premium can't be increased			
Maternity benefits			
Short waiting period for pre-existing conditions			
Home health care			
Second opinion surgery			
Pre-admission testing			

Courtesy of Health Insurance Association of American, Washington, D.C.

3. There are many considerations in meeting cost containment objectives. If containing costs was your responsibility, which of the following ideas would you select?

Yes   No   Not sure

- reduce benefits so premiums would be lower
- provide benefits for medical care outside of the hospital
- provide benefits for medical care in the home
- develop a mechanism toward keeping doctors' charges reasonable
- cancel policies where large amounts have been paid in claims
- provide benefits for physical examinations to encourage prevention of medical care, disability, and premature death
- discourage benefits for other than hospital confinement and doctor expense, so that the number of claims would be reduced
- set specific rates for surgical procedures
- work to have all insurers—private and government—reimburse for actual expenses
- encourage the development of wellness programs (exercise, nutrition, weight control)

Courtesy of Health Insurance Association of America, Washington, D.C.

4. For each of the following situations, select the type of health insurance coverage that would be involved.

   Basic protection   Disability income

   Major medical protection Supplemental policies

   a. coronary artery by-pass surgery   _____
   b. emergency appendectomy   _____
   c. stroke that demands rehabilitation _____
   d. broken arm   _____
   e. removal of impacted wisdom tooth _____
   f. birth of a baby   _____

5. Larry and Liz are a young couple both working full time and earning about $60,000 a year. They recently purchased a house and have taken out a large mortgage. Since both of them work, they own two cars and are still making payments on them. Liz has major medical health insurance through her employer, but Larry's coverage is inadequate. Currently they do not have any children, but they hope to start a family in about three years. Liz's employer provides disability income insurance, but Larry's employer does not.

   Analyze the need for health and disability insurance for Liz and Larry.

6. Pam is 31 and recently divorced, with children ages 3 and 6. She earns $30,000 a year as a secretary. Her employer provides her with basic health insurance coverage. She receives child support from the children's father, but he misses payments often and is always behind in payments. Her ex-husband, however, is responsible for the children's medical bills.

   Analyze the need for health and disability insurance for Pam.

Supplementary Case 11-1

Topic: Buying Adequate Health Insurance Coverage

Text Reference: pp. 339-341

Kathy Jones was a junior at Glenbard High School. She had two younger brothers. Her father, the manager of a local supermarket, had take-home pay of $4,000 a month. He had a small group health insurance policy and a $40,000 life insurance policy. He said that he could not afford to buy additional insurance. All of his monthly salary was used to meet current expenses, including car and house payments, food, clothing, transportation, children's allowances, recreation and entertainment, and vacation trips.

One evening, Kathy was talking with her father about insurance, which she was studying in an economics course. She asked what kind of insurance program her father had for their family. This question started Mr. Jones thinking about how well he was planning for his wife and children. Since the family had always been in good health, Mr. Jones felt that additional health and life insurance was not essential. Maybe after he received a raise in his salary and after his daughter was out of high school, he could afford to buy more insurance.

Case Questions

1. Do you think Kathy's father was planning wisely for the welfare of his family? Can you suggest ways in which this family could have cut monthly expenses and thus set aside some money for more insurance?

2. Although Mr. Jones's salary was not big enough to buy insurance for all possible risks, what protection do you think he should have had at this time?

3. Suppose Mr. Jones had been seriously injured and unable to work for at least one year. What would his family have done? How might this situation have affected his children?

Supplementary Case 11-2

Topic: Health Care Benefits for Live-In Mates

Employers are starting to consider providing benefits to unmarried mates of employees, but the practice faces financial, tax, and insurance problems. Moreover, the employers face political opposition from conservative groups that see homosexuals as the main beneficiaries.

Still evolving, partner benefits and policies have been adopted in recent years by hundreds of employers. Such cities as Madison, Wisconsin, and Berkeley, California, have led the way in awarding sick and bereavement leave to workers with unmarried mates.

The impetus behind the drive is simple. Of an average worker's total annual compensation, 40 percent will be paid out in benefits next year, according to Hewitt Associates, a benefits consulting firm. And with health care costs surging, health coverage is an especially coveted benefit for unmarried partners who don't already have it.

The lack of health care benefits is nettlesome to Alix Olson and Martha Popp. Ms. Olson, a city police detective, can't get health coverage for Ms. Popp, her companion of 13 years, or Ms. Popp's two children. "We take our kids to school, we pay our taxes," says Ms. Popp, a substitute teacher without health coverage. "Then to turn around and not be allowed to have benefits—it wears away on you."

Case Questions

1. Do you think employers should provide health care benefits to live-in mates? Why or why not?
2. Why are health care benefits especially coveted by employees?
3. Why is the lack of health care benefits nettlesome to Alix Olson and Martha Popp?

Supplementary Case 11-3

Topic: Disability Income Insurance

Text Reference: pp. 360-364

Gene and Dixie are parents of a two-year-old girl. They live in an apartment in a small city in Illinois, where Gene, 24, earns $36,000 a year as a salesman. His monthly take-home pay is $2,400. Dixie has given up her job as a secretary to take care of their daughter. Gene has no prior military or civil service that might qualify him for government disability programs. Since Gene and Dixie rent an apartment, they have no mortgage disability insurance to cover basic housing costs in case of a disability. Unexpectedly, Gene suffers increasingly serious emotional and mental crises. He is unable to function at his job, and a psychiatrist declares him totally disabled.

Gene's employer provides a long-term disability benefit that pays 50 percent of the average earnings of the prior three years. Since Gene did not work long enough to qualify for full coverage, his benefit is based on an assumed average salary of only $20,000, rather than the $36,000 he actually earned. He is ineligible for Social Security disability benefits because he hadn't been working in covered employment long enough. He is also ineligible for worker's compensation because the disability is not job-related.

The long-term disability policy provided by his employer will pay Gene $835 a month. But Gene and Dixie now have to pay monthly premiums of $200 to continue their group life and medical insurance. While Gene was working, these premiums were paid by his employer. Therefore, Gene, Dixie, and their daughter must now live on a monthly replacement income of only $635

If Gene and Dixie had realized the inadequacies of Gene's disability income coverage, due partly to the fact that he was relatively new in his job, they could have purchased an individual policy for a nominal fee. A consultation with their agent would have helped them build the income coverage they needed to protect them against the financial disaster they now face.

Case Questions

1. What, if anything, can Gene and Dixie do to alleviate their present problems?

2. Why do you think Gene did not take advantage of the additional disability insurance that he could have purchased at work?

3. What advice would you offer to someone in Gene's situation? Why?

Supplementary Case 11-4

Topic: Health Insurance: You Can Take It With You

Text Reference: p. 340

Hadiya had been experiencing chronic back pain for the past year-and-a-half at her job as an assembly line worker in a microchip plant. She was receiving treatment that was covered by her health insurance and had decided to look for a new career. A friend told her about a new employer in her area that offered retraining for office positions; this seemed ideal because the work would be less physical.

Unfortunately, Hadiya heard that if she changed jobs, her new insurance would not cover her pre-existing medical condition. A pre-existing condition is an illness or injury you had before you switched jobs, that you are receiving treatment for at the time you switch, or that you have been treated for in the past but that might recur. This meant she would not be able to continue her current treatment or get the back surgery her doctor recommended. She felt helpless and forced to stay with a job that was actually exacerbating her back problem.

Hadiya is not alone, but thanks to a law that took effect July 1, 1997, her health insurance is now "portable." In other words, when she moves from one company to another, Hadiya will continue to receive coverage or will eventually be able to get coverage for her back problem even though it is a pre-existing medical condition.

The Health Insurance Portability and Accountability Act (HIPA) works like this: If you or your family were covered under a former employer's health plan for at least 12 months, without an interruption of 63 or more days, a new plan will have to provide coverage with no limitation on pre-existing conditions. Hadiya just needs to request a certificate of insurance coverage from her former employer to prove her eligibility under the new plan.

Under HIPAA, Hadiya's new plan can refuse to cover her condition if it was diagnosed within six months before the date she enrolled. However, since her back problems began 18 months before she decided to change jobs, she cannot be refused coverage. Even people who fall within the six-month date will be able to get coverage for a pre-existing condition if they stay with the new plan for 12 months.

Case Questions

1. What is portability?
2. How does the HIPA work?
3. What does Hadiya need to do to prove she had insurance coverage?

Supplementary Reading 11-1

"How Technology is Transforming Your Hospital—Finally", *Business Week*, March 28, 2005, p. 81.

How Technology is Transforming Your Hospital—Finally

Wiring hospitals will change the quality and business of health care by tracking patients and costs more efficiently. Here's what leading-edge hospitals like Hackensack University Medical Center are doing:

1. INVESTING IN TECHNOLOGY

Health care was so slow to adopt Net technologies that output per worker in the sector fell in the 1990s. Now spending is beginning to rise. Take Hackensack: Since 1998 the New Jersey hospital has spent $72 million to upgrade its tech infrastructure, automate its pharmacy, and roll out electronic medical records.

2. SELLING DOCS ON GOING DIGITAL

Doctor resistance is a major hurdle to e-health. To get past this obstacle, in 2002 Hackensack hired a trauma surgeon as its tech evangelist. He's making progress: The hospital's internal Web portal had 344,000 visits last year, up from 3,000 in 2000. Yet hurdles remain: Only 10% of tests and drugs are ordered electronically.

3. USING DATA TO BOOST QUALITY

The real payoff is finding errors and improving care. Hackensack halved the time between when a drug is prescribed and when it reaches the patient. It also redesigned its congestive heart failure and orthopedics procedures, improving to the top 10% of hospitals treating those diseases in a Medicare program.

4. GETTING DEALS FROM INSURERS

Insurers are paying more for better care, since it leads to fewer repeat visits. Medicare is testing a program that pays an extra 2% per case to hospitals with treatment scores in the top 10% for illnesses such as pneumonia, heart attacks, or hip replacements. Since Medicare pays for about 30% of U.S. hospital care, that's enough to double profits at some hospitals.

5. USING QUALITY TO LURE CUSTOMERS AND BUY MORE TECH

Insurers and big employers are trying to push consumers to tech-savvy, high-quality hospitals. How? They reduce co-payments if patients use preferred providers and post care-quality info on insurers' sites. Horizon Blue Cross is pushing cardiac patients to Hackensack because of the improvements it has made using tech.

Study Questions

1. What are leading-edge hospitals doing to change the quality and business of health care?

2. Why did output per worker in the health care sector fall in the 1990s?

3. What is a major hurdle to e-health?

4. Why are insurers paying more for better health care?

Supplementary Reading 11-2

Christopher Farrell, "This Could Keep You in the Pink", *Business Week*, June 13, 2005, p. 88.

This Could Keep You in the Pink

EMPLOYEES FORTUNATE enough to have a health plan have had to swallow double-digit percentage price hikes in premiums for the past five years. But they could always take comfort in knowing that their insurance was a bargain compared with what they might have to pay on their own. Indeed, the price of health insurance has long deterred budding entrepreneurs who might otherwise leave the corporate cocoon to strike out on their own.

That calculation is changing, in part thanks to the new health savings accounts (HSA) that were authorized in the 2003 Medicare prescription drug legislation. The HSA plan comes in two parts. First, you must buy a health insurance policy with a high deductible. Then you open an HSA, a tax-sheltered account much like an individual retirement account. The account is funded with pretax contributions, up to $2,650 for individuals and $5,250 for families (table). The account's earnings are not taxed—nor are withdrawals when used to pay for qualified medical expenses.

Anyone can use HSAs, but experts believe they are particularly well-suited for the self-employed. "Entrepreneurs trade off the risk of paying out a couple of thousand dollars in tax-sheltered money in order to protect themselves from catastrophic costs," says Leon Rousso, a certified financial planner in Ventura, Calif. Brad Rosley, who has a wife and three children, also a financial planner in Glen Ellyn, Ill., made the switch. His previous health insurance policy to cover his family cost him $660 a month, or nearly $8,000 a year, with a deductible of $1,000.

Rosley replaced that plan with an HSA. He went for a policy with a $5,100 deductible and put that much into the tax-sheltered account for a family. His premium for the policy is $260 a month, or $3,120 annually. He uses the $400 a month he's saving over the previous policy to fund his HSA. Rosley figures he could well end up with a six figure account, since any money left in the HSA can be rolled over from year to year. That money can pay for everything from long-term care insurance to a new hip during his golden years.

OUT-OF-POCKET COSTS

ROSLEY'S EXPERIENCE appears typical. The average yearly premium on a family policy for an HSA is $3,550 for those aged 30 to 54, according to America's Health Insurance Plans, a Washington trade group. In contrast, private sector employees with a family plan through work pay between $2,100 and $2,400 a year, according to John Ascensio, senior vice-president at Segal Co., a New York benefits consulting firm.

But the cost gap is narrowing even as companies prepare to hike employees' out-of-pocket costs during the upcoming benefits season, a number of major insurers are cutting premiums for their HSA products. Indeed, sales of HSA policies more than doubled, to 1 million, in the six months ended Mar. 31. One reason for that is the tax break. The maximum contribution to an HSA for a family in the 35% tax bracket generates a tax savings of over $1,800 a year. Plus, any earnings in the account compound tax-free, assuming the money does go for medical expenses.

To be sure, HSA plans are controversial. Advocates argue that this type of consumer-controlled health care is the main solution to braking the nation's spiraling medical costs. Opponents fret that HSAs siphon off the healthiest and wealthiest consumers, leaving traditional plans with a sicker pool of people to insure. Public policy concerns aside, anyone contemplating these policies needs to address more mundane concerns. For one, you need to have the cash to fund the HSA. Also, these plans are inhospitable for anyone with preexisting conditions such as cancer or diabetes.

The HSA market is evolving. Health insurance is regulated by the states, and these plans aren't available everywhere. Benefits and prices vary, even within the same region. But the Internet is making it easier to evaluate benefits and compare prices. "The consumer can lower costs by shopping," says Robert Hurley, who heads up HSA products for eHealth-Insurance Services, which markets health coverage online.

HSAs are complex, and many consumers rebel against paying several thousand dollars out-of-pocket, even with tax-free money. "HSAs aren't a solution to all our health-care ills," says David Dranove, an economist at Northwestern University. "But they're terrific for the entrepreneur." For this group in particular, HSAs may be the best way to obtain a safety net against catastrophic medical expense at a reasonable cost.

A Health Savings Account Primer
DECIDE which catastrophic health insurance policy you're going to buy. Price is determined by the ages of those insured, residence, and the size of the deductible, among other factors.

MALE, 45

	DEDUCTIBLE	COST/MO.
Atlanta	$1,800	$232.20
Chicago	2,000	175.22
Dallas	2,000	238.43

TWO ADULTS, 45
TWO CHILDREN, 12 & 10

	DEDUCTIBLE	COST/MO.
Atlanta	$5,000	$374.83
Chicago	5,000	375.00
Dallas	5,000	364.00

OPEN a Health Savings Account with a financial institution. Be sure to fund at least 100% of your deductible, which you do with pretax dollars. For 2005, individuals can put in $1,000 to $2,650; families, $2,000 to $5,250. The limits adjust to annual cost-of-living changes. People aged 55 to 65 can put away an extra $600 for 2005, and the bonus for that cohort grows to $1,000 in 2009. Earnings grow sheltered from taxes.

USE the HSA to pay any medical expenses incurred in meeting the deductible and any required co-insurance payments. The withdrawals to pay for qualified medical expenses are tax-free.

OTHER FEATURES:
- Unused savings remain in the account to pay future charges.
- Funds withdrawn before age 65 for nonmedical expenses are subject to a 10% penalty and income taxes. After 65, such withdrawals are no longer subject to penalty.
- A spouse can inherit an HSA free of taxes.

Christopher Farrell

Study Questions

1. What are the two parts of an HSA plan?

2. How is an HSA account funded?

3. What is the average yearly premium on a family policy for an HSA?

4. Why are HSA plans controversial?

Supplementary Reading 11-3

"Medicare Prescription Drug Plans"

Medicare Prescription Drug Plans

Coming in 2006—Medicare Prescription Drug Plans
On January 1, 2006, Medicare-approved drug discount cards will begin to phase out. The new Medicare prescription drug plans will begin.

Medicare will contract with private companies to offer this drug coverage. These companies will most likely offer a variety of option, with different covered prescriptions, and different costs. Medicare prescription drug plans are voluntary. If you want to participate, **you must choose a plan offering the coverage that best meets your needs and then enroll.** In most cases, there is no automatic enrollment to get a Medicare prescription drug plan.

How to Enroll in a Medicare Prescription Drug Plan
To enroll, you must have Medicare Part A or Part B. You can first enroll from November 15, 2005 through May 15, 2006. This is called the "initial open enrollment period." Enrolling is your choice.

Note: After this initial open enrollment period, you can change your plan during the open enrollment period, which will be from November 15 through December 31 each year. Your Medicare prescription drug plan will begin January 1 of the following year.

To join, you will need to decide how you want to get your prescriptions. You can
- get all your health care benefits and prescriptions through a Medicare Advantage Managed Care Plan that offers optional coverage for prescription drugs,
- get your health care benefits through the Original Medicare Plan and choose a Medicare prescription drug plan, or
- get your health care benefits through another type of Medicare Advantage health plan or a Medicare Managed Care Plan that isn't a Medicare Advantage Plan. In these kinds of plans, you may be able to choose a Medicare prescription drug plan.

How Plans Work
Medicare prescription drug plans might vary, but in general, this is how they will work. When you join, you will pay a **monthly** premium (varies depending on the plan you choose, but estimated at about $35) in addition to any premiums for Medicare Part A and Part B. You will pay the first $250 per year for your prescriptions. This is called your "deductible."

After you pay the $250 yearly deductible, **here's how the costs work:**

- You pay 25% of your yearly drug costs from $250 to $2,250, and your plan pays the other 75% of these costs, then
- You pay 100% of your drug costs from $2,251 until your out-of-pocket costs reach $3,600, then
- You pay 5% of your drug costs (or a small copayment) for the rest of the calendar year after you have spent $3,600 out-of-pocket and your plan pays the rest.

Medicare prescription drug plans can offer coverage like this or more generous coverage for higher premiums. Joining is your choice. However, **if you don't join when you are first eligible, you may have to pay a higher premium if you choose to join later.** You will have to pay this higher premium for as long as you have a Medicare prescription drug plan.

Note: If you already have prescription coverage from other insurance, you can keep that coverage. If that coverage offers the same or better benefits as described above, you won't have to pay a higher premium if you decide to join later. Check with your other insurance to see how your coverage compares.

Study Questions

1. How will Medicare offer Prescription Drug Plans?

2. What is the "initial open enrollment period"?

3. How will prescription drug plans work?

4. What are the premiums and other costs?

12 LIFE INSURANCE

Chapter Overview

In this chapter, we explain the meaning of life insurance, outline its history, and describe its purpose. We show how the principle of home insurance discussed in Chapter 12 can be applied to the lives of persons. We also stress the importance of determining life insurance needs and estimating life insurance requirements. Next, we identify the two types of life insurance companies—mutual and stock—and distinguish between participating and non-participating life insurance policies. Then we describe types of life insurance policies: Term life, whole life, modified life, variable life, adjustable life, and endowment policies are discussed in detail. In addition, newer types of life insurance policies such as universal life, group life, home service life, and credit life insurance are also covered. Next, we focus on major and important provisions contained in a life insurance contract. We emphasize the need for comparing insurance policy costs and examining a policy before and after the purchase. Various settlement options are also presented in this section. Finally, we conclude the chapter with a discussion on how annuities provide security to individuals.

Learning Objectives

After studying this chapter, you will be able to:

Obj. 1 Define life insurance and describe its purpose and principle.

Obj. 2 Determine your life insurance needs.

Obj. 3 Distinguish between the two types of insurance companies and analyze the various types of life insurance policies issued by these companies.

Obj. 4 Select important provisions in life insurance contracts.

Obj. 5 Create a plan to buy your life insurance.

Obj. 6 Recognize how annuities provide financial security.

Key Terms

annuity
beneficiary
cash value
chartered life underwriter
double indemnity

incontestability clause
interest-adjusted index
nonforfeiture clause
nonparticipating policy
participating policy

rider
suicide clause
term insurance
universal life
whole life policy

Pretest

True-False

_____ 1. (Obj. 1) Life insurance is mysterious and difficult to understand.

_____ 2. (Obj. 1) Life expectancy tables do not indicate the age at which a person has the highest probability of dying.

_____ 3. (Obj. 2) Everyone needs life insurance.

_____ 4. (Obj. 2) The easy method of determining life insurance is almost useless.

_____ 5. (Obj. 3) Term insurance is protection for a specified period of time.

_____ 6. (Obj. 3) Whole life insurance does not have a cash value.

_____ 7. (Obj. 4) A beneficiary is a person who is designated to receive something, such as life insurance proceeds, from the insured.

_____ 8. (Obj. 4) The accidental death benefit is often called double indemnity.

_____ 9. (Obj. 5) The price of life insurance policies does not vary among life insurance companies.

_____ 10. (Obj. 6) A prime reason for buying an annuity is to give you retirement income for the rest of your life.

Self-Guided Study Questions
Obj. 1
Life Insurance: An Introduction (p. 372)
1. How has consumer awareness of life insurance changed over the years?

What Is Life Insurance? (p. 372)
2. What is the meaning of life insurance?

The Purpose of Life Insurance (p. 372)
3. What is the purpose of life insurance?

4. How may life insurance proceeds be used?

The Principle of Life Insurance (p. 373)
5. What is the principle of life insurance? Give an example.

How Long Will You Live? (p. 373)
6. What is the purpose of the table of mortality?

Obj. 2

Determining Your Life Insurance Needs (p. 373)

7. What five factors must be considered before buying life insurance?

Do You Need Life Insurance? (p. 376)

8. How do you determine if you need life insurance?

Determining Your Life Insurance Objectives (p. 376)

9. What three factors should be considered in determining your life insurance objectives?

Estimating Your Life Insurance Requirements (p. 376)

10. How do you estimate your life insurance requirements?

11. What is the easy method of estimating your life insurance requirements?

12. What is the DINK method of estimating your life insurance requirements?

13. What is the "non-working spouse" method of estimating life insurance requirements?

14. What is the "family need" method of estimating your life insurance requirements?

Obj. 3

Types of Life Insurance Companies and Policies (p. 379)

Types of Life Insurance Companies (p. 379)

15. What are participating and nonparticipating policies?

16. What are the differences between mutual and stock insurance companies?

Types of Life Insurance Policies (p. 379)

17. What are two basic types of life insurance policies?

Term Life Insurance (p. 379)

18. What is term life insurance?

19. Why is term insurance sometimes called temporary life insurance?

20. What is meant by a renewability option in term insurance?

21. What is convertible term insurance?

22. What is decreasing term insurance?

23. What is return of premium (ROP) policy?

Whole Life Insurance (p. 382)

24. What is the whole life, straight life policy, or an ordinary life policy?

25. For what kind of people do cash value policies make sense?

26. What is cash value?

27. What is a nonforfeiture clause?

28. What type of policy has constant premiums throughout one's life?

29. What is a limited payment policy?

30. Why are annual premiums higher for a limited payment policy?

31. What is a variable life insurance policy?

32. Who assumes the risk of poor investment performance in a variable life policy?

33. What is an adjustable life insurance policy?

34. What is a universal life insurance policy?

35. How is universal life insurance different from whole life insurance?

36. What are the key distinguishing features of universal life policies?

Other Types of Life Insurance Policies (p. 384)

37. What is a group life insurance policy?

38. Usually, who pays the cost of group insurance premiums?

39. Is group life insurance always a good deal?

40. What is an endowment life insurance?

41. Who needs credit life insurance?

42. What might be a better alternative to credit life insurance?

43. What type of insurance is a good substitute for credit life insurance?

44. What is industrial life insurance?

45. How often should you reevaluate your insurance coverage?

Obj. 4
Important Provisions in a Life Insurance Contract (p. 386)
46. What are some of the most common provisions in a life insurance policy?

Naming Your Beneficiary (p. 387)
47. What is a beneficiary?

The Grace Period (p. 387)
48. What is the grace period?

Policy Reinstatement (p. 387)
49. What is a policy reinstatement provision?

50. What is the nonforfeiture clause?

51. Is there a time limit on policy reinstatement?

Incontestability Clause (p. 388)

52. What is the incontestability clause?

Suicide Clause (p. 388)

53. What is a suicide clause?

Automatic Premium Loans (p. 388)

54. What is an automatic premium loan option?

Misstatement of Age Provision (p. 388)

55. What is a misstatement of age provision?

Policy Loan Provision (p. 388)

56. What is a policy loan provision?

57. Does a policy loan reduce the death benefit if the loan is not repaid?

Riders to Life Insurance Policies (p. 388)

58. What is a rider?

59. What is a waiver of premium disability benefit? Is it always desirable?

60. Under what circumstance should you not buy the waiver of premium rider?

61. What is an accidental death benefit clause?

62. Why is the accidental death benefit often called double indemnity?

63. What is a guaranteed insurability option?

64. When is a guaranteed insurability option desirable?

65. What is the purpose of cost of living protection?

66. What are accelerated or living benefits?

67. What is second-to-die option? What is its purpose?

Obj. 5

Buying Life Insurance (p. 390)

68. What factors must you consider before buying life insurance?

From Whom to Buy? (p. 390)

69. Why should you choose carefully when deciding on an insurance company or an insurance agent?

70. What are several private and public sources of life insurance?

71. How are insurance companies rated for their financial strength?

72. Who rates insurance companies?

73. How do you go about choosing your insurance agent?

74. Who is a chartered life underwriter (CLU)?

75. Who is designated as a chartered property and casualty underwriter (CPCU)?

Comparing Policy Costs (p. 393)

76. How do you compare policy costs?

77. What is an interest-adjusted index?

Obtaining a Policy (p. 394)

78. What are the two parts in a life insurance policy?

79. How does an insurance company determine your insurability?

Examining a Policy (p. 395)

80. How do you examine an insurance policy before and after the purchase?

Choosing Settlement Options (p. 395)

81. How do you choose settlement options?

82. What is a lump-sum payment option?

83. What is a limited installment payment option?

84. What is a life income option?

85. What happens when you leave your proceeds with the company?

Switching Policies (p. 396)
86. Should you switch policies?

Obj. 6
Financial Planning with Annuities (p. 397)
87. What is an annuity?

88. What are the two kinds of annuities?

89. Why is an annuity described as the opposite of life insurance?

Why Buy Annuities? (p. 398)
90. Why do people buy annuities?

Tax Considerations (p. 398)
91. How are annuities taxed?

Post Test

Completion

1. (Obj. 1) Covering the financial need arising from the risk of untimely death is a function of _____ _____.

2. (Obj. 2) The _____ _____ of estimating life insurance requirements is based on the insurance agent's rule of thumb that a "typical family" will need about 70 percent of your salary for seven years before it adjusts to the financial consequences of your death.

3. (Obj. 3) A(n) _____ _____ has somewhat higher premiums than a nonparticipating policy.

4. (Obj. 3) _____ _____ is life insurance protection for a specified period of time.

5. (Obj. 3) The premium for the _____ _____ insurance policy stays the same for the rest of your life.

6. (Obj. 3) A(n) _____ _____ plan insures a large number of persons under the terms of a single policy without medical examinations.

7. (Obj. 4) A(n) _____ is a person who is designated to receive life insurance proceeds from the insured.

8. (Obj. 5) _____ _____ index is a method of evaluating the cost of life insurance by taking into account the time value of money.

9. (Obj. 6) A(n) _____ is a financial contract written by an insurance company to provide you with a regular income.

10. (Obj. 6) A fixed _____ is a contract stating that the annuitant will receive a fixed amount of income over a certain period or for life.

Multiple Choice

1. (Obj. 1) Which one of the following statements regarding life insurance is correct?
   A. Consumers eagerly purchase life insurance.
   B. Consumer awareness of life insurance has changed very little.
   C. Consumers are rebelling against life insurance companies.
   D. Consumers believe that life insurance companies are taking an unfair advantage of policyholders.

2. (Obj. 2) If you have no dependents and your spouse earns as much or more than you do, you may consider which of the following methods to estimate your life insurance needs?
   A. Easy
   B. DINK
   C. "Non-working spouse"
   D. Thorough

3. (Obj. 3) If you wish to pay exactly the same premium each year, you should choose what type of life insurance policy?
   A. Nonparticipating
   B. Participating
   C. Term
   D. Universal

4. (Obj. 3) The most common type of permanent life insurance is the _____ life policy.
   A. variable
   B. universal
   C. term
   D. whole

5. (Obj. 3) Which life insurance provision allows you not to forfeit all accrued benefits?
   A. Incontestability clause
   B. Forfeiture clause
   C. Nonforfeiture clause
   D. Suicide clause

6. (Obj. 3) Which type of life insurance plan insures a large number of persons under the terms of a single policy without medical examination?
   A. Group
   B. Whole
   C. Modified
   D. Variable

_____ 7. (Obj. 4) Which life insurance provision permits the owner of the policy to borrow any amount up to the cash value of the policy?
   A. Double indemnity
   B. Policy loan provision
   C. Incontestability clause
   D. Nonforfeiture clause

_____ 8. (Obj. 4) Which life insurance provision allows you to buy specified additional amounts of life insurance at stated intervals without the proof of insurability?
   A. Double indemnity
   B. Policy loan
   C. Guaranteed insurability option
   D. Incontestability

_____ 9. (Obj. 5) Which is a method of evaluating the cost of life insurance by taking into account the time value of money?
   A. Consumer price index
   B. Cash value index
   C. Insurance cost index
   D. Interest-adjusted index

_____ 10. (Obj. 6) Some of the recent growth in the use of annuities can be attributed to the passage of the
   A. Employment Retirement Income Security Act.
   B. Occupational Safety and Health Act.
   C. Fair Labor Standards Act.
   D. National Labor Relations Act.

Problems, Applications, and Cases

1. Review the sources of life insurance. Investigate the sources of life insurance available in your community for you and your family. Make a list of the pros and cons of each.

2. Contact your State Insurance Department to get information about whether interest-adjusted-cost disclosure is required in your state. Obtain any appropriate literature for your use.

3. Each of the three basic types of life insurance policies (term, straight life, and limited payment) has special features designed to serve specific purposes. For each situation described below, indicate which basic type would be most suitable.

   a. A high school student who has no insurance

   b. The head of a family who has borrowed a large sum of money which must be repaid over the next five years

   c. A professional man, age 45, whose children are grown and who earns a large income and who is more interested in protection for his wife than in retirement for himself

   d. A man, age 30, who already has $20,000 of straight life and who has just bought a home with a $10,000 mortgage on it

4. Examine your (or your parents') life insurance policy. Prepare an outline for a report describing the purposes and provisions of the policy. Consider the following questions when preparing your report. The questions are not listed in any logical order. Some questions may not apply and you will undoubtedly think of other questions that are important.

   a. What is the general title of the policy?

   b. What type or types of protection does the policy provide?

   c. How long does the policy continue?

   d. Is the policy renewable? Explain.

   e. Specifically, what is not covered by the policy?

   f. What happens if the premiums are not paid?

   g. How should claims be presented?

   h. What are the maximum benefits?

   i. What are the premium rates for this policy?

   j. Is it a participating or nonparticipating policy?

   k. What are your options if you decide not to continue paying premiums?

   l. Who is the beneficiary?

   m. What is the grace period?

   n. Is there a suicide clause?

   o. Is there an automatic premium loan provision?

   p. Is there a waiver of premium disability benefit?

   q. Is there an accidental death benefit?

   r. Do you have a guaranteed insurability option?

5. Mike is single, 21, and a college senior. He has no dependents and does not plan to marry soon. He is working part-time to supplement his college grant in order to meet school and living expenses. He is independent and does not receive any financial support from his widowed mother, who works and just meets her own living costs.

   Analyze Mike's need for life insurance.

6. Mary and Barry have two children, ages 2 and 4. Mary does not work outside the home and has no marketable job skills. Mary and Barry are planning to buy their first house. They have discussed the fact that if something happens to either of them (death or disability), the surviving spouse will stay in the house to rear the children. Barry has $30,000 worth of term insurance through his employer. Barry has been earning about $30,000 per year. His employer provides basic health insurance with an option of HMO or fee-for-service.

   Analyze the need for life insurance for this family.

Supplementary Case 12-1

Topic: Identifying the Need for and Amount of Life Insurance

Text Reference: pp. 373-377

Joanne Kitsos was a 27-year-old single parent. She and her four-year-old son, Brad, lived in a small two-bedroom apartment. Since graduating from high school, Joanne had been employed as a secretary for an insurance company. Brad stayed at a day-care center while Joanne worked.

Joanne found it very difficult to maintain a home for herself and her son on her $26,000 salary. She was often forced to borrow money from her parents. She had a small Christmas savings account in her company's credit union, a $10,000 term life insurance policy, and a $4,000 debt with a local furniture store.

Joanne's two major goals were: (1) to increase her income and (2) to protect her income should she become unable to work. She approached her employer to find out how she could progress in her company. She learned that the company had an upward mobility program for employees with at least five years seniority. Interested employees were given company-paid, on-the-job training and college courses to learn one of several jobs. Joanne quickly applied for admission to the program. Within several months, she was able to secure an entry-level position as a computer operator and an accompanying salary raise.

Joanne then turned her attention toward protecting her income and providing for Brad's future education. She bought a $50,000 term life insurance policy on herself; the policy had a disability rider under which she would be paid if she became disabled and could not work. Joanne had always been unable to stick to a savings plan—withdrawing money as quickly as she deposited it. So she took out a $10,000 endowment policy on Brad that would come due when he was 18 and contribute to his college education. The policy also gave him life insurance protection as long as the premiums were paid.

Case Questions

1. Was purchasing term insurance and an endowment policy the right decision for Joanne? Why?

2. Did Joanne need additional life insurance? Why?

Supplementary Case 12-2

Topic: A "Free Look" in Variable Annuities Contracts

Text Reference: p. 397-399

Variable annuity contracts typically have a "free look" period of ten or more days, during which you can terminate the contract without paying any surrender charges and get back your purchase payments (which may be adjusted to reflect charges and the performance of your investment). You can continue to ask questions in this period to make sure you understand your variable annuity before the "free look" period ends.

Before you decide to buy a variable annuity, consider the following questions:

- Will you use the variable annuity primarily to save for retirement or a similar long-term goal?

- Are you investing in the variable annuity through a retirement plan or IRA (which would mean that you are not receiving any additional tax-deferral benefit from the variable annuity)?

- Are you willing to take the risk that your account value may decrease if the underlying mutual fund investment options perform badly?

- Do you understand the features of the variable annuity?

- Do you understand all of the fees and expenses that the variable annuity charges?

- Do you intend to remain in the variable annuity long enough to avoid paying any surrender charges if you have to withdraw money?

- If a variable annuity offers a bonus credit, will the bonus outweigh any higher fees and charges that the product may charge?

- Are there features of the variable annuity, such as long-term care insurance, that you could purchase more cheaply separately?

- Have you consulted with a tax adviser and considered all the tax consequences of purchasing an annuity, including the effect of annuity payments on your tax status in retirement?

- If you are exchanging one annuity for another one, do the benefits of the exchange outweigh the costs, such as any surrender charges you will have to pay if you withdraw your money before the end of the surrender charge period for the new annuity?

Case Questions

1. What is the purpose of a "free look" period?
2. Why should you consult with a tax adviser before purchasing an annuity?

Supplementary Reading 12-1

"How Variable Annuities Work", Source: www.sec.gov/investor/pubs/varannty.htm, February 28, 2005.

How Variable Annuities Work

A variable annuity has two phases: an **accumulation phase** and a **payout phase.**

During the **accumulation phase,** you make purchase payments, which you can allocate to a number of investment options. For example, you could designate 40% of your purchase payments to a bond fund, 40% to a U.S. stock fund, and 20% to an international stock fund. The money you have allocated to each mutual fund investment option will increase or decrease over time, depending on the fund's performance. In addition, variable annuities often allow you to allocate part of your purchase payments to a fixed account. A fixed account, unlike a mutual fund, pays a fixed rate of interest. The insurance company may reset this interest rate periodically, but it will usually provide a guaranteed minimum (e.g., 3% per year).

Example: You purchase a variable annuity with an initial purchase payment of $10,000. You allocate 50% of that purchase payment ($5,000) to a bond fund, and 50% ($5,000) to a stock fund. Over the following year, the stock fund has a 10% return, and the bond fund has a 5% return. At the end of the year, your account has a value of $10,750 ($5,500 in the stock fund and $5,250 in the bond fund), minus fees and charges (discussed below).

Your most important source of information about a variable annuity's investment options is the prospectus. Request the prospectuses for the mutual fund investment options. Read them carefully before you allocate your purchase payments among the investment options offered. You should consider a variety of factors with respect to each fund option, including the fund's investment objectives and policies, management fees and other expenses that the fund charges, the risks and volatility of the fund, and whether the fund contributes to the diversification of your overall investment portfolio. The SEC's online publication, *Mutual Fund Investing: Look at More Than a Fund's Past Performance*, provides information about these factors. Another SEC online publication, *Invest Wisely: An Introduction to Mutual Funds*, provides general information about the types of mutual funds and the expenses they charge.

During the accumulation phase, you can typically transfer your money from one investment option to another without paying tax on your investment income and gains, although you may be charged by the insurance company for transfers. However, if you withdraw money from your account during the early years of the accumulation phase, you may have to pay "surrender charges," which are discussed below. In addition, you may have to pay a 10% federal tax penalty if you withdraw money before the age of 59½.

At the beginning of the **payout phase**, you may receive your purchase payments plus investment income and gains (if any) as a lump-sum payment, or you may choose to receive them as a stream of payments at regular intervals (generally monthly).

If you choose to receive a stream of payments, you may have a number of choices of how long the payments will last. Under most annuity contracts, you can choose to have your annuity payments last for a period that you set (such as 20 years) or for an indefinite period (such as your lifetime or the lifetime of you and your spouse or other beneficiary). During the payout phase, your annuity contract may permit you to choose between receiving payments that are fixed in amount or payments that vary based on the performance of mutual fund investment options.

The amount of each periodic payment will depend, in part, on the time period that you select for receiving payments. Be aware that some annuities do not allow you to withdraw money from your account once you have started receiving regular annuity payments.

In addition, some annuity contracts are structured as **immediate annuities**, which means that there is no accumulation phase and you will start receiving annuity payments right after you purchase the annuity.

Study Questions

1. Describe the two phases of a variable annuity?

2. What is the most important source of information about a variable annuity's investment options?

3. What is an immediate annuity?

Supplementary Reading 12-2

Tax-Free "1035" Exchanges

Tax-Free "1035" Exchanges

Section 1035 of the U.S. tax code allows you to exchange an existing variable annuity contract for a new annuity contract without paying any tax on the income and investment gains in your current variable annuity account. These tax-free exchanges, known as 1035 exchanges, can be useful if another annuity has features that you prefer, such as a larger death benefit, different annuity payout options, or a wider selection of investment choices.

You may, however, be required to pay surrender charges on the old annuity if you are still in the surrender charge period. In addition, a new surrender charge period generally begins when you exchange into the new annuity. This means that, for a significant number of years (as many as 10 years), you typically will have to pay a surrender charge (which can be as high as 9% of your purchase payments) if you withdraw funds from the new annuity. Further, the new annuity may have higher annual fees and charges than the old annuity, which will reduce your returns.

Caution!

If you are thinking about a 1035 exchange, you should compare both annuities carefully. Unless you plan to hold the new annuity for a significant amount of time, you may be better off keeping the old annuity because the new annuity typically will impose a new surrender charge period. Also, if you decide to do a 1035 exchange, you should talk to your financial professional or tax adviser to make sure the exchange will be tax-free. If you surrender the old annuity for cash and then buy a new annuity, you will have to pay tax on the surrender.

Study Questions

1. What is a "1035" exchange? Under what circumstances can it be useful?

2. What might be some drawbacks of the new annuity?

3. When might you be better off keeping the old annuity?

13 INVESTING FUNDAMENTALS

Chapter Overview

This chapter is the first chapter in Part Five—Investing Your Financial Resources. We begin our discussion by stressing the importance of preparing for an investment program. Next, we examine how the factors of safety, risk, income, growth, and liquidity affect investment programs. Then, we provide an overview of asset allocation and different investment alternatives available to individuals. We also study methods that investors can use to reduce investment risk. Included in this section on reducing risks is material on the importance of the individual's role in the investment process. Finally, we discuss sources of investment information, which include the Internet, newspapers and news programs, business periodicals and government publications, corporate reports, and investor services and newsletters.

Learning Objectives

After studying this chapter, you will be able to:

Obj. 1 Describe why you should establish an investment program.

Obj. 2 Describe how the factors of safety, risk, income, growth, and liquidity affect your investment decisions.

Obj. 3 Explain how asset allocation and different investment alternatives affect your investment plan.

Obj. 4 Recognize the importance of your role in a personal investment program.

Obj. 5 Use the various sources of financial information that can reduce investment risks and increase investment returns.

Key Terms

asset allocation	equity capital	mutual fund
corporate bond	government bond	rate of return
dividend	line of credit	speculative investment
emergency fund	liquidity	

Pretest

True-False

_____ 1. (Obj. 1) Investment goals must be specific, measurable, and tailored to your particular financial needs.

_____ 2. (Obj. 1) A good rule of thumb is to limit installment payments to 30 to 40 percent of your net monthly pay after taxes.

_____ 3. (Obj. 1) The amount of money that should be salted away in an emergency fund varies from person to person.

_____ 4. (Obj. 2) The safety and risk factors are unrelated to each other.

_____ 5. (Obj. 2) The ease with which an asset can be converted to cash without substantial loss in dollar value is called the income factor.

_____ 6. (Obj. 3) Asset allocation is the process of spreading your assets among different types of investments to lessen risk.

_____ 7. (Obj. 3) A corporation is obligated to repay equity capital sometime in the future.

_____ 8. (Obj. 3) A corporate bond is a corporation's written pledge that it will repay a specified amount of money, with interest.

_____ 9. (Obj. 3) Professional management and diversification are the two primary reasons why investors choose mutual funds.

_____ 10. (Obj. 5) The fees for investor services generally range from $5 to $30 per year.

Self-Guided Study Questions

Obj. 1

Preparing for an Investment Program (p. 408)

1. Why is the decision to start an investment program important?

Establishing Investment Goals (p. 408)

2. Why should investment objectives be specific and measurable?

3. What kinds of questions can be used by individuals to establish valid investment objectives?

4. What is the difference between a short-term objective, an intermediate objective, and a long-term objective?

Performing a Financial Checkup (p. 409)

5. Why is it necessary for an individual to make sure that his or her personal financial affairs are in order before beginning an investment program?

6. How can individuals spend more than they make on a regular basis?

7. What steps should be taken to reduce installment purchases and the resulting installment payments?

8. What types of insurance coverage do individuals need to examine before beginning an investment program?

9. What is an emergency fund?

10. Why is it a good idea to establish a line of credit at a commercial bank, savings and loan association, credit union, or credit card company?

Getting the Money Needed to Start an Investment Program (p. 410)

11. What are five specific suggestions that were presented in this chapter that may help you obtain the money needed for a successful investment program?

The Value of Long-Term Investment Programs (p. 410)

12. How does the time value of money affect a long-term investment program?

Obj. 2

Factors Affecting the Choice of Investments (p. 412)

Safety and Risk (p. 423)

13. What is the relationship between safety and risk when choosing an investment?

14. What investments fall into the conservative category? What investments fall into the speculative category?

15. How would you define the risk-return tradeoff?

16. What factors affect your tolerance for risk?

17. Describe how you would calculate return on an investment.

18. Why is rate of return on an investment important?

Components of the Risk Factor (p. 416)

19. What are the five component factors that make up the risk factor?

Investment Income (p. 418)

20. What types of investments provide a steady flow of predictable income?

21. What investments offer little, if any, potential for regular income?

Investment Growth (p. 418)

22. What sacrifice must investors make when purchasing growth stocks?

23. What types of investments offer growth potential?

24. What types of investments offer less predictable growth potential?

Investment Liquidity (p. 419)

25. How would you define liquidity?

26. How does the concept of liquidity affect an individual's investment decision?

Obj. 3

Asset Allocation and Investment Alternatives (p. 419)

27. Which investment alternative has provided the largest return since 1900?

28. Which investment alternative is projected to earn about 10 percent between now and the year 2025?

Asset Allocation and Diversification (p. 419)

29. In your own words, define asset allocation.

30. What are some typical asset classes?

31. Why do financial experts suggest that asset allocation is a valued tool that can reduce the risk associated with long-term investment programs?

32. What factors determine how much of your investment ddlars should be placed in each asset class?

33. How does the amount of time that your investments have to work and your age affect your choice of investments?

An Overview of Investment Alternatives (p. 421)

Stock of Equity Financing (p. 421)

34. What are the two factors an investor should consider before investing in stock?

35. What is the difference between common stock and preferred stock?

Corporate and Government Bonds (p. 423)

36. How would you define a corporate bond? How would you define a government bond?

37. What two major questions should an investor consider before investing in corporate or government bonds?

Mutual Funds (p. 423)

38. What is a mutual fund?

39. What are two major reasons why investors choose mutual funds?

40. What are two specific problems for mutual fund investors?

Real Estate (p. 423)

41. What questions should an investor ask before investing in real estate?

42. What are the disadvantages of real estate investments?

Other Investment Alternatives (p. 424)

43. In your own words, what is a speculative investment?

44. What types of investments are included in the speculative category?

A Personal Plan for Investing (p. 424)

45. What are the steps required for an effective personal investment plan of action?

46. Under what circumstances would an investor need to change investment goals?

Obj. 4

Factors that Reduce Investment Risk (p. 426)

Your Role in the Investment Process (p. 426)

47. Why should an investor evaluate potential investments?

48. Why is it necessary for investors to monitor the value of their investments?

49. Why is maintaining accurate and current records related to an investment extremely important?

Other Factors That Improve Investment Decisions (p. 427)

50. What type of professional help is available to help investors make informed investment decisions?

51. How do taxes affect investment decisions?

Obj. 5

Sources of Investment Information (p. 428)

The Internet (p. 428)

52. What type of investment information is available to investors who use the Internet?

53. How would you access information about investments on the Internet?

54. Name five Internet sites that provide investors with information that can be used to establish a financial plan and begin an investment program.

Newspapers and News Programs (p. 429)

55. What types of financial information is contained in newspapers?

56. What types of financial information is contained on financial news programs?

Business Periodicals and Government Publications (p. 430)

57. What are four business periodicals that would contain information that could be used by an investor to investigate investment alternatives?

58. Name four magazines that provide information on personal finance topics.

59. What type of publications are available from the federal government?

Corporate Reports (p. 431)

60. What type of information is contained in corporate reports?

Investor Services and Newsletters (p. 431)

61. What type of fees do investor services charge?

62. What are the three widely accepted services for investors who specialize in stocks?

63. What are two widely accepted services for investors who specialize in mutual funds?

Post Test

Completion

1. (Obj. 1) Before beginning an investment program, most financial planners recommend establishing an emergency fund that is equal to at least _____ month's of living expenses.

2. (Obj. 2) _____ and _____ are two sides of the same coin.

3. (Obj. 2) To calculate _____ of _____, the total income you receive on an investment over a specific period of time is divided by the original investment.

4. (Obj. 2) The _____ _____ risk associated with a fixed return investment in a preferred stock or a government or corporate bond is the result of changes in the interest rates in the economy.

5. (Obj. 3) A share of _____ _____ represents the most basic form of corporate ownership.

6. (Obj. 3) The most important priority an investor in _____ _____ enjoys is receiving cash dividends before common stockholders are paid any cash dividends.

7. (Obj. 3) The maturity dates for bonds range between _____ and _____ years.

8. (Obj. 3) A(n) _____ _____ is an investment alternative available to individuals who pool their money to buy stocks, bonds, and other securities selected by professional managers who work for an investment company.

9. (Obj. 4) Accurate _____ can help you spot opportunities to maximize profits or reduce dollar losses when you sell your investments.

10. (Obj. 5) One of the best ways to use the Internet to access investment information is to use a _____ _____.

Multiple Choice

____ 1. (Obj. 1) A short-term loan that is approved before the money is actually needed is called a(n)
   A. emergency fund.
   B. line of credit.
   C. corporate obligation.
   D. equity capital.

____ 2. (Obj. 2) Which of the following investments would offer the greatest potential for predictable income?
   A. Negotiable accounts
   B. Municipal bonds
   C. Antique collectibles
   D. Stocks

____ 3. (Obj. 2) Which of the following investments would offer the greatest potential for growth?
   A. Government bonds
   B. Stocks
   C. Gemstones
   D. Commodities
   E. Options

____ 4. (Obj. 2) Which of the following investments would be considered the most liquid?
   A. Gemstones
   B. Commodities
   C. Corporate bonds
   D. Savings accounts

____ 5. (Obj. 3) Asset allocation is
   A. not a concern for small investors.
   B. the process of spreading your assets among several types of investments.
   C. only practical for investors who choose speculative investments.
   D. the ease with which an investment can be converted to cash.

____ 6. (Obj. 3) Money obtained from the owners of a business is called
   A. corporate obligations.
   B. certificates of deposit.
   C. NOW financing.
   D. equity capital.

7. (Obj. 3) Which of the following statements is not true?
   A. As a rule, real estate increases in value, but there are no guarantees.
   B. Real estate investments, like all investments, must be carefully evaluated.
   C. Location is not important when selecting a piece of real estate in a metropolitan area.
   D. Finding a buyer can be difficult if loan money is scarce.

8. (Obj. 3) Which of the following is not classified as a speculative investment?
   A. Commodities
   B. Savings accounts
   C. Options
   D. Collectibles

9. (Obj. 4) Which of the following statements is false?
   A. Successful investors continually monitor the value of their investments.
   B. Accurate recordkeeping can help you spot opportunities.
   C. Professional assistance is too expensive for small investors with limited resources.
   D. Federal taxation may affect your decision to sell an investment.

10. (Obj. 5) A(n) _____ is a requirement for corporations selling a new issue of securities.
    A. prospectus
    B. annual report
    C. Form 10k
    D. Federal Investor Report

Problems, Applications, and Cases

1. Investment goals are classified as short-term, intermediate, or long-term according to the amount of time required to accomplish each type of goal. List two or three personal financial goals for each of the three categories below. Make your goals practical, measurable, and realistic in terms of what you really think you can accomplish.

Type of goal	Personal financial goals
Short-term goals (two years or less)	
Intermediate goals (two to five years)	
Long-term goals (more than five years)	

2. Complete the "Personal Plan of Action for Investing" using the steps listed in Exhibit 13-5. (Note: The form on the next page may help you establish your own plan.) Assume that you have been out of college for two years and are earning $34,000 a year. Your take-home pay is $2,125 per month. Your living expenses come to about $1,600 a month and you now have $8,000 in a savings account earning 2 percent interest. You have no family responsibilities, so you must decide what to do with the extra money.

Step 1
My investment goals are:

Step 2
By _____, 20___, I will have obtained $_____.
Signed,

Step 3
I have _____ available for investment purposes.
Date: _____

Step 8
Continued evaluation of your investment choices

Step 4
Possible investment alternatives:
a.
b.
c.
d.
e.

Step 7
Final decision based on re-evaluation of top three:
1.
2.

Step 6
Investment decision based on the top three:
1.
2.
3.

Step 5-B
Evaluation of projected return for each alternative:
a.
b.
c.
d
e.

Step 5-A
Evaluation of risk factor for each alternative:
a.
b.
c.
d.
e.

3. Using the information provided in this chapter, describe the advantages and disadvantages of each investment alternative presented below.

Investment alternative	Advantages	Disadvantages
1. Common stock		
2. Preferred stock		
3. Corporate bonds		
4. Government bonds		
5. Mutual funds		
6. Real estate		
7. Commodities, options, and precious metals		

Supplementary Case 13-1: Basic Rules for Investing

Topic: Preparing for an Investment Program

Text Reference: pp. 408-412

Bob Martin, 48 and single, had never thought much about saving money or establishing an investment program. He had always enjoyed life and spent everything he could lay his hands on. He always had a new car, bought designer clothes, enjoyed dating, and went on nice vacations. He had almost $3,000 in a savings account, which he thought should be enough to get him through any emergency. In his own words, he was looking forward to the future because he seemed to be on the right track.

But something happened last week that made Bob sit back and take a long, hard look at the track he was really on. Alex Newton, one of his best friends had decided to take their firm's early retirement option. The fact that Alex was going to retire was upsetting, but even more upsetting was the fact that Alex was only two years older than Bob. How could he afford to retire at 50?

Alex had started saving money when he graduated from college. Later, he began investing in what he referred to as quality, long-term stocks, and mutual funds. Early retirement had been one of his long-term goals. He wanted to travel now and eventually open a small ski-repair business in the Colorado Rockies.

Alex's retirement made Bob sit back and examine his own financial condition. He knew he would never be able to retire unless he changed his lifestyle. That's why he made an appointment with a financial planner who worked for Barns and Barnett Investment Consultants. After a two-hour exploratory meeting, he left the consultant's office with some basic ideas on how to get started. According to the consultant, Bob had to take some logical steps if he was going to change his current financial picture. The consultant made the following suggestions:

1. *Plan Your Financial Future.* Determine short-term and long-term financial goals that are important to you.

2. *Learn to Budget.* Most people spend money without thinking. A better approach is to determine which expenditures are important and which are unnecessary.

3. *Keep Accurate Records.* A good recordkeeping system lets you see where your money is going. Most experts believe that establishing such a system is one of the most important steps in financial planning.

4. *Take Advantage of Windfalls.* You should use unexpected inheritances, tax refunds, bonuses, and other windfalls to help achieve the long-term investment goals of your financial plan.

5. *Reevaluate Your Investment Plan.* Your financial goals may change over time. You should be able to change your investment plan to meet revised goals and objectives.

Although Bob realized that his financial planning was long overdue, he felt encouraged after his conversation with the consultant. He was excited by the prospect of achieving added financial security through an increase in his savings and of fulfilling some of his long-term financial goals through the purchase of quality investments.

Case Questions

1. Why did Bob Martin become upset when he learned that one of his friends had decided to take their firm's early retirement option?
2. Based on the information presented in this case, what type of investments would you recommend for Bob Martin?

Supplementary Case 13-2: An Obvious Need for Financial Planning

Topic: Preparing for an Investment Program

Text Reference: pp. 408-412

Mike Denton, 36, was a chemical engineer employed by Exxon/Mobil Corporation. During 2005, he earned $75,000. Julie, his wife, earned $46,000 a year as a medical technician for a local hospital. Since their marriage, three years ago, they had purchased two new BMWs and a new home in an exclusive Dallas suburb. They each had American Express and VISA credit cards, which they used to purchase almost anything they wanted. According to Mike, everything seemed to be right on track.

By January 2006, everything was off track. It all started when Mike lost his job—he simply got the boot. Since he had always taken his well-paying job for granted, he and Julie had never thought much about money. Now that he was unemployed, they were suffering because they had not done any financial planning. He was trying not only to find another job but also to pay the monthly bills on a lot less money.

When Mike lost his job, the Denton's had $2,800 in the bank, and their monthly expenses totaled more than $6,000. Until Mike found a new job, they had to find a way to live on Julie's $46,000 salary. First, they sold one of the BMWs. Next, they took out a bank loan to pay off their credit card debts. Finally, they put their home up for sale, but they were unable to sell it because of the depressed home prices in their suburb. Eventually, they lost their home when the mortgage company foreclosed on it. They then moved to a one-bedroom apartment.

Ten months after losing his job at Exxon/Mobil, Mike Denton got another engineering job and he and Julie began to rebuild their lives. They both vowed to develop a financial plan. They had learned their lesson well, and they didn't want to make the same mistakes again.

Case Questions

1. During 2005 Julie and Mike Denton earned $121,000. And yet, their financial affairs were thrown into a tailspin when Mike suddenly lost his job. What went wrong?

2. Ten months after losing his job, Mike got another engineering job. Not wanting to make the same mistakes again, Mike and Julie Denton ask for your help. What would you tell them?

Supplementary Reading 13

Ellen Hoffman, "Giving Your Plan Regular Tune-Ups", *Business Week Online,* (www.businessweek.com), May 6, 2005.

Giving Your Plan Regular Tune-Ups

Even the most thorough retirement plans need to be checked periodically and brought up to date. Here's what it involves.

About 10 years ago, Robert and Carla Teitt, now ages 60 and 54, of Salt Lake City, made a retirement plan. He, a projects manager at Northrup Grumman, and she, an occupational therapist, would retire at the same time, when he was 62 or 63, after their children completed Master's degrees in their chosen fields.

The Teitts calculated that with the children's schooling and their own work-related expenses out of the way, about 50% of their pre-retirement income would pay their basic expenses. But they set a financial goal that would enable them to spend up to 65%, so they could travel, do volunteer work, and afford some extras.

Twice a year, the Teitts meet with their financial planner, Ray Le Vitre of Salt Lake City, to review their investments and see if they're achieving the return needed to meet their goals. Changes they have made along the way include reducing the assumption of an 8% annual return on their investments to 7%, and adjusting their portfolio from 80% stocks and 20% bonds to 60% stocks and 40% bonds.

THE TOUGHEST STEP. The Teitts are an example of people who have taken all three phases of retirement planning seriously. They've completed the first two—estimating their retirement budget and creating a financial plan—and are now in the third, crucial phase: Implementing and monitoring their plan. (For my two most recent columns, on estimating budgets and creating a plan, see BW Online, 3/11/05, "Time to Abandon the 70% Solution", and 4/8/05, "So, What's the Plan.")

The third step is in some ways the most difficult because ideally, you'll work on it the rest of your life. "Most people we meet think that the implementation is all about the [financial] product selection. This is only partially true," says Tom Orecchio, a financial planner in Old Tappan, N.J. "It's more important to make sure that you have a sound process, that you have a plan in place to follow, and something against which to measure your progress."

Le Vitre gives his clients a checklist of action steps that can take up to three months to complete. Some tasks may relate to getting your retirement and other savings accounts in order. If you left a 401(k) with a previous employer, you may want to roll it over into an IRA; you may need to increase contributions to your 401(k), or you may need to rebalance the investments in all of your accounts to minimize risk.

VULNERABLE AGE. Other items that might appear on such a list: Updating insurance coverage, speeding up payments on your mortgage, and figuring out the tax implications of retiring at different ages.

But the paperwork is only part of what you need to do. Orecchio points out that because baby boomers are likely to be retired for 30 years or longer, they're more vulnerable than previous generations to unexpected changes, whether in their professional or personal life or to the tax code or economic conditions.

A case in point is a client of Orecchio's, a high-level financial-services executive, about 50, who was on track to retire very comfortable at age 60 until he realized that his job was hurting his family life. He traded his stressful New York job for a more family-friendly, lower-salaried position in Georgia.

After analyzing the impact on the client's plan, Orecchio cautioned him that because he gave up some retirement benefits—including unvested stock options—he may need to postpone his retirement from age 60 to 62. His client thinks that the trade-off is worth it.

CHECK YOURSELF. Once you've completed the check list, the next stage of implementation is periodic reviews and adjustments to your plan. "Someone can have a great plan drawn up and initially implemented, but it won't be effective unless it's reviewed regularly," says Le Vitre, who meets with clients every six months. "There's always tweaking to be done, and these meetings also keep clients focused on their strategies and keep them from wanting to chase every hot investment idea they run across.

Financial advisers can provide you with a variety of charts, graphs, and calculations, such as risk analysis of your portfolio or of changes in taxes or inflation, as well as Monte Carlo simulations—estimates of the likelihood that you'll meet your financial goals under various assumptions.

If you're a do-it-yourselfer, you can set up your own monitoring system. To succeed, you'll need an approach that makes sense for you personally—and the discipline to stick to it. Here are some tips for starting:

- Keep track of the statements from your retirement and other investment accounts, bank records, and other financial data you receive on a regular basis. Keep them as long as necessary for tax purposes. The general rule is to keep them three

years, but if you own your home, you need to keep all of those records until after you've sold it and reported the sale to the IRS. If you have electronic records, it can be easier to keep them "forever."
- Pay attention to financial news, so that you consider how changes in inflation or tax law—for example, in the dividends or capital-gains rate—might affect your long-range plans.
- Commit to reading and analyzing this information at least twice a year to see if your plan is holding up. One time might be around tax time, when you have to organize it anyhow.
- When you're faced with lifestyle or financial decisions, analyze how they would affect your retirement plan. For help with calculations, you can use and revisit online tools such as this 401(k) Calculator, which can help you adjust your contributions according to progress toward your goals.
- Consider investing in retirement-planning software for more comprehensive number crunching. To see what works for you, simply search "retirement planning software" on the Net and experiment with the online demos before choosing a system you like.
- Is all the time and trouble worth it? Le Vitre answers with a resounding yes. "Peace of mind is important because people make bad decisions with their money when they're stressed or unsure where they stand in relation to their goals." And after all, what's at stake should be pretty important to you: The potential quality of the rest of your life.

Ellen Hoffman

Study Questions

1. Many people go through the process of establishing a plan for investing their money. Then, once the plan is completed, they don't review the plan and make necessary changes. Why is this a flawed approach?

2. Assume that you are 35 years old and have established an investment/retirement plan.

    a. How often should you reexamine your plan?

    b. What types of adjustments may be needed for your plan to stay current and up-to-date?

3. According to financial planner Ray Le Vitre, all the time and trouble required to tune-up a retirement plan is worth it? Why?

14 INVESTING IN STOCKS

Chapter Overview

Initially, this chapter describes both common and preferred stock as investment alternatives. We discuss the topics of why corporations sell common stocks, and why investors purchase those stocks. Next, we examine the major differences between common stock and preferred stock. Methods that investors can use to evaluate stock investments are presented. The steps involved in buying and selling stocks are described. Then we explain the long-term techniques of buy and hold, dollar cost averaging, direct investment, and dividend reinvestment plans. Also, the speculative techniques of selling short, margin transactions, and stock options are discussed.

Learning Objectives

After studying this chapter, you will be able to:

Obj. 1 Identify the most important features of common and preferred stock.

Obj. 2 Explain how you can evaluate stock investments.

Obj. 3. Analyze the numerical measures that cause a stock to increase or decrease in value.

Obj. 4 Describe how stocks are bought and sold.

Obj. 5 Explain the traditional trading techniques used by long-term and short-term speculators.

Key Terms

account executive
annualized holding period yield
beta
blue-chip stock
book value
capitalization
churning
cumulative preferred stock
current yield

cyclical stock
day trader
defensive stock
direct investment plan
discretionary order
dividend payout
dividend reinvestment plan
dollar cost averaging
earnings per share
efficient market hypothesis

fundamental analysis
growth stock
income stock
initial public offering (IPO)
investment bank
large-cap stock
limit order
margin
market order
mid-cap stock

Nasdaq
option
over-the-counter (OTC) market
par value
penny stock
price-earnings (PE) ratio
primary market
proxy
record date
secondary market
securities exchange
selling short
small-cap stock
specialist
stock split
stop order
technical analysis
total return

Pretest

True-False

_____ 1. (Obj. 1) Corporations don't have to repay the money a stockholder pays for stock.

_____ 2. (Obj. 1) The record date is the date when a stockholder must be registered on the corporation's books in order to receive dividends.

_____ 3. (Obj. 1) Common stockholders receive cash dividends before preferred stockholders are paid cash dividends.

_____ 4. (Obj. 2) A blue-chip stock is a speculative investment.

_____ 5. (Obj. 2) An income stock is a stock that pays higher than average dividends.

_____ 6. (Obj. 3) Earnings per share is a measure of a company's profitability.

_____ 7. (Obj. 3) The current yield is the yearly income an investor receives divided by the original purchase price for a share of stock.

_____ 8. (Obj. 4) A market order is a request that a stock be bought or sold at a specified price.

_____ 9. (Obj. 5) Dollar-cost averaging is a short-term investment technique.

_____ 10. (Obj. 5) Selling short is selling stock that has been borrowed from a stockbroker and must be replaced at a later date.

Self-Guided Study Questions
Obj. 1
Common Stock (p. 442)
1. In your own words, describe why people buy and sell stocks.

2. What are two types of stock?

Why Corporations Issue Common Stock (p. 442)
3. Why do corporations sell common stock?

4. What is a proxy?

5. What do stockholders vote on?

Why Investors Purchase Common Stock (p. 443)
6. What are two reasons why investors purchase common stock?

7. Why is the record date important?

8. Describe how a stockholder makes a profit when a stock increases in value.

9. Why do corporations split their stock?

10. Does a stock split guarantee an increase in value? Explain your answer.

Preferred Stock (p. 447)

11. What is the most important priority that an investor in preferred stock enjoys?

12. How is the dividend on preferred stock determined?

13. What is the advantage for the investor of purchasing cumulative preferred stock?

14. Why would investors purchase convertible preferred stock?

Obj. 2

Evaluating a Stock Issue (p. 448)

15. Why do you think that many investors are unwilling to spend the time to become a better investor?

16. Explain the following statement: There is no substitute for a few hours of detective work when choosing an investment.

Classification of Stock Investments (p. 448)

17. What is a blue-chip stock?

18. What is an income stock?

19. What is a growth stock?

20. What is a cyclical stock?

21. What is a defensive stock?

22. What is a large-cap stock?

23. In your own words, define capitalization.

24. What is a mid-cap stock?

25. What is a small-cap stock?

26. What is a penny stock?

The Internet (p. 450)

27. What type of information is available on a corporation's home page?

28. What type of information is available on Web sites like Yahoo and other search engines?

29. Name three professional advisory services that provide information on stocks to Internet users.

Stock Advisory Services (p. 451)

30. What type of information is provided by investor services like Standard & Poor's, Value Line, Morningstar, and Mergent's?

How to Read the Financial Section of the Newspaper (p. 451)

31. How are stocks listed in the newspaper?

32. What type of information about stocks is reported in the newspaper?

33. What do the letters "pf" indicate?

Corporate News (p. 453)

34. What type of information is contained in a corporation's prospectus? In an annual report?

35. How can you obtain a corporation's annual report?

Obj. 3

Numerical Measures that Influence Investment Decisions (p. 454)

Why Corporate Earnings Are Important (p. 455)

36. Why would an investor want to know the amount for earnings per share?

37. How do you calculate earnings per share?

38. What is the price-earnings ratio?

39. Why would an investor be interested in a firm's earnings estimates?

Other Factors That Influence the Price of a Stock (p. 456)

40. In your own words, define dividend payout.

41. How is dividend payout calculated?

42. What is the formula for calculating current yield?

43. How do you calculate the total return for a stock investment?

44. What does the annualized holding period yield calculation measure?

45. Why would an investor be concerned with the beta for a specific stock?

46. How would you define book value?

Investment Theories (p. 459)
47. What is the fundamental theory of investment?

48. What is the technical analysis theory of investing in stocks?

49. What is the efficient market hypothesis?

Obj. 4

Buying and Selling Stocks (p. 460)

50. What is the difference between the primary market and the secondary market for stocks?

51. What is the role of an investment bank?

52. In your own words, define IPO.

Primary Market for Stocks (p. 460)

53. How would you sell $100 million worth of common stocks if you were a financial manager for a large corporation?

Secondary Market for Stocks (p. 461)

54. What is a securities exchange?

55. What does a specialist do?

56. Before a corporation is approved for listing on the New York Stock Exchange, what three conditions must be met?

57. How does the over-the-counter market differ from a securities exchange?

58. How is an order to buy or sell stock executed in the Nasdaq market?

Brokerage Firms and Account Executives (p. 463)
59. What services does an account executive provide?

60. What is churning?

Should You Use a Full-Service or a Discount Brokerage Firm? (p. 463)
61. If you wanted to buy or sell stocks, would you use a full-service or discount brokerage firm? Explain your answer.

Computerized Transactions (p. 464)
62. In what ways could a computer help you invest in stock?

Commission Charges (p. 464)
63. How are commissions for stock transactions determined?

64. Why does a full-service broker charge more commission than a discount broker?

A Sample Stock Transactions (p. 466)

65. What is the difference between a market order, a limit order, a stop order, and a discretionary order?

66. Describe how stocks are bought and sold on an organized exchange?

Obj. 5

Long-Term and Short-Term Investment Strategies (p. 467)

Long-Term Techniques (p. 467)

67. What is the difference between a long-term investment and a speculative investment?

68. In what two ways could an investor profit by using a buy and hold technique?

69. What usually happens to the value of a stock when a stock split occurs?

70. How would you describe dollar cost averaging?

71. What is a direct investment plan? How does it differ from a dividend reinvestment plan?

Short-Term Techniques (p. 468)

72. How does a day trader make money?

73. What are the problems associated with day trading?

Buying Stock on Margin (p. 469)

74. Why would an investor buy stock on margin?

75. When an investor purchases stock on margin, what is the danger?

Selling Short (p. 470)

76. Why would an investor use the selling short investment technique?

77. How could an investor lose money using the selling short technique?

Trading in Options (p. 471)

78. Why would an investor use options?

Post Test

Completion

1. (Obj. 1) A(n) _____ is a legal form that lists the issues to be decided in a stockholders' meeting and requests that stockholders transfer their voting rights to some individual or individuals.

2. (Obj. 1) A(n) _____ _____ is a procedure in which the shares of common stock owned by existing stockholders are divided into a larger number of shares.

3. (Obj. 1) _____ preferred stock can be exchanged, at the stockholder's option, for a specified number of shares of common stock.

4. (Obj. 2) A(n) _____ stock is a stock that remains stable during declines in the economy.

5. (Obj. 3) The _____-_____ ratio is the price of a share of stock divided by the corporation's earnings per share of stock.

6. (Obj. 3) The _____ theory is based on the assumption that a stock's intrinsic or real value is determined by the future earnings of the company.

7. (Obj. 4) A(n) _____ _____ is a marketplace where member brokers who represent investors meet to buy and sell securities.

8. (Obj. 4) A(n) _____ _____ is a licensed individual who buys or sells securities for his or her clients.

9. (Obj. 5) A(n) _____ _____ plan allows stockholders to purchase stock directly from a corporation without having to use an account executive or a brokerage firm.

10. (Obj. 5) A(n) _____ gives an investor the right to buy or sell shares of a stock at a predetermined price during a specified period of time.

Multiple Choice

1. (Obj. 1) Corporations issue common stock because
   A. it is a form of equity financing.
   B. dividends are not mandatory.
   C. the money obtained from this type of financing does not have to be repaid.
   D. All of the above.

2. (Obj. 1) A preferred stock issue whose unpaid dividends accumulate and must be paid before any cash dividend is paid to the common stockholders is called _____ preferred stock.
   A. callable
   B. cumulative
   C. convertible
   D. participating

3. (Obj. 2) A stock issued by a corporation that has the potential to earn above average profits when compared to other firms in the economy is called a(n) _____ stock.
   A. blue-chip
   B. income
   C. growth
   D. cyclical

4. (Obj. 3) ABC Corporation has after-tax earnings of $3 million. It also has 4 million shares of stock. What is its earnings per share?
   A. $1.33
   B. $0.75
   C. $7.50
   D. $75.00

5. (Obj. 3) A theory based on the assumption that stock price movements are purely random is called the _____ hypothesis.
   A. fundamental
   B. technical
   C. efficient market
   D. primary

6. (Obj. 4) A market for existing financial securities that are currently traded between investors is called the _____ market.
   A. primary
   B. secondary
   C. efficient
   D. fundamental

_____ 7. (Obj. 4) The _____ marketplace is an electronic marketplace for approximately 3,300 different stocks.
   A. American
   B. Nasdaq
   C. Boston
   D. Midwest

_____ 8. (Obj. 4) A request that a stock be purchased or sold at the current market price is called a _____ order.
   A. market
   B. limit
   C. stock
   D. restricted

_____ 9. (Obj. 5) When you purchase an equal dollar amount of the same stock at equal intervals, you are using _____.
   A. direct investments
   B. dividend investments
   C. margin
   D. dollar-cost averaging

_____ 10. (Obj. 5) An investor who thinks the market price of a stock will decrease during a short period of time may decide to use the _____ technique.
   A. buy
   B. dividend reinvestment
   C. selling short
   D. the margin

Problems, Applications, and Cases

1. Choose one stock that is listed on the New York Stock Exchange (NYSE) or Nasdaq. Then go to the library or the Internet to find the necessary information to complete the form below. Information provided by *Standard & Poor's*, *Value Line,* and *Mergent's* should be helpful.

Company Information Sheet

Name   Industry

Products and services

Location of headquarters

Is the Company paying dividends? If so, how much?

Total Sales Revenues for the most recent year   Profits for the most recent year

Subsidiaries

Would this company be a good investment at this time?

Why?

What have you learned about this company?

2. Assume that Watson Plastics pays an annual dividend of $0.72 a share. Also assume that the company earns $4 a share. What is the dividend payout?

3. Assume that you own 125 shares of common stock in American Chemical Company. You receive a copy of the firm's annual report. After examining the financial statements that were included in the annual report, you determine that the firm has reported assets of $17 million, liabilities of $6 million, after-tax earnings of $4 million, and 1,250,000 outstanding shares of common stock.

    a. Calculate the book value of a share of American Chemical.

    b. Calculate the earnings per share of American Chemical's common stock.

    c. Assuming that a share of American Chemical's common stock has a market value of $46, what is the firm's price-earnings ratio?

4. Assume that you purchased 100 shares of General Retail Store's common stock for $88 a share, that you received an annual dividend of $3 per share, and that you sold your General Retail stock for $96 a share at the end of two years. (Ignore commissions for this problem.)

    a. At the end of the two-year period, calculate the current yield for your General Retail common stock.

    b. Calculate the total return on your General Retail investment.

    c. Calculate the annualized holding period yield of your General Retail investment at the end of two years.

Supplementary Case 14-1: Choosing an Account Executive

Topic: Brokerage Firms and Account Executives

Text Reference: pp. 463-464

A good investment program should start before you choose an account executive. First of all, you must establish financial goals and objectives to meet your individual needs. Then you must accumulate enough money to get started. Most authorities suggest maintaining an emergency fund, equal to at least three months' living expenses. Once you have accumulated funds in excess of the emergency fund, it's time to decide if you want to use a full-service or discount brokerage firm or trade stocks online.

If You Choose a Full-Service Brokerage Firm, You Will Need To Choose an Account Executive

Many investors begin their search for an account executive by asking friends or business associates for recommendations. This is a logical starting point, but remember that some account executives are conservative, while others are risk oriented. It is quite common for investors to test an account executive's advice over a period of time. Then, if the account executive's track record is acceptable, his or her investment suggestions can be taken more seriously. At this point, most investors begin to rely more heavily on the account executive's advice and less on their own intuition and research. On the other hand, investors who choose a discount brokerage firm or trade securities online usually do their own research and make their own decisions.

Why You Need an Account Executive

Basically, your account executive sees that your order to buy or sell stocks, bonds, or other securities is correctly executed. Your account executive should also be able to provide you with current financial information about the stocks, bonds, mutual funds, or other securities in which you are interested. There are no guarantees that the securities you buy on the basis of your account executive's recommendations will increase in value, but he or she should help in the evaluation process.

A Final Word of Caution

Before choosing an account executive, you should ask a few questions to determine whether you and the account executive are on the same wavelength with regard to investment goals and objectives. Don't be surprised if your account executive wants to ask you a few questions too. In order to provide better service, he or she must know what type of investment program you want to establish. If, after a reasonable period of time, you become dissatisfied with your investment program, do not hesitate to discuss your dissatisfaction with the account executive. You may even find it necessary to choose another account executive if your dissatisfaction continues.

Case Questions

1. Would you use a full-service or discount brokerage firm or trade stocks online? Explain your answer.

2. Many investors "just choose an account executive" and let that person make all the decisions. Why can this approach lead to problems for the investor?

3. Assume that you are in the process of choosing an account executive. Prepare a list of ten questions that you could use to interview a stockbroker or account executive.

4. As part of the interview process, the account executive would probably want to ask you some questions before completing the first transaction. What type of information would an account executive want to know about you?

Supplementary Case 14-2: Research Information for Stock Investments

Topic: Evaluation of a Stock Issue

Text Reference: pp. 448-460

In Chapter 14, (Investing in Stocks), we have stressed the importance of evaluatng potential investments. Now it's your turn to try your skill at evaluating a potential investment in The Coca-Cola Company. Assume that you could invest $20,000 in common stock of this company. To help you evaluate this potential investment carefully examine the research reports available in your college library or public library provided in *Mergent's Handbook of Common Stock*, *Standard and Poor's Stock Guide*, *Value Line*, information available on the firm's home page on the Internet, or the Yahoo Finance website at http://finance.yahoo.com.

Case Questions

1. Based on your research, would you buy Coca-Cola common stock? Justify your answer.

2. What other investment information would you need to evaluate this company's stock? Where would you obtain this information?

3. On Wednesday, July 6, 2005, Coca-Cola's common stock was selling for $42 a share. Using a recent newspaper or the Internet, determine the current price of a share of Coca-Cola common stock. Based on this information, would your investment have been profitable if you had purchased Coca-Cola stock for $42 a share? Why or why not?

Supplementary Reading 14

Christopher Palmeri, "Hitch Your Wagon to a Wildcatter", *Business Week*, June 27, 2005, p. 120.

Hitch Your Wagon to a Wildcatter

ENERGY DEMAND IS climbing. New supplies are difficult to find. And the consensus on Wall Street is that oil and natural gas prices will remain high—above $35 a barrel and $5 per thousand cubic feet—for the foreseeable future. Given that tightening scenario, energy investors should direct their dollars to the companies that are out there feverishly looking for more oil and gas, unencumbered and undistracted by other businesses, such as refining or chemicals. These are the independents, the new wildcatters—the folks with mud on their boots.

One hungry independent is XTO Energy Inc. Since the start of 2004, this Fort Worth outfit has spent $3.2 billion buying properties in Texas, Wyoming, Utah, and New Mexico. XTO targets existing fields with oil and gas reserves that are being slowly depleted. It aggressively drills new wells in these fields, hedging its bets by selling half of the anticipated production in the futures market. XTO will spend $935 million this year developing its properties, a 45% increase from 2004's drilling budget. The company is a favorite of veteran energy investor Douglas G. Ober, who manages the Petroleum & Resources fund. He figures XTO will meet its projected 25% production jump this year and continue to grow at a better-than-15% rate beyond that. "Given the declines you're seeing in existing fields, few people are doing that," Ober says.

While XTO is out buying, Oklahoma City-based Devon Energy has sold more than $2 billion worth of high-cost properties in the U.S. and Canada in the past year. It's pumping some of that money back into deepwater exploration wells in the Gulf of Mexico, West Africa, and Brazil. As it develops these fields, Devon expects its oil and gas production to climb at least 5% annually over the next five years. The typical major oil company raises its production at about half that rate.

Other companies prefer to drill in their own backyards. In the past years Houston-based Southwestern Energy Co. has quietly been acquiring drilling rights in the Fayetteville Shale region in western Arkansas. The company's land grab, which tops 755,000 acres, now looks like it was a good bet. Southwestern has drilled 39 wells in the region, of which 27 are producing, 8 are in development, and 4 were not productive. "Some of those wells tested at 3 million cubic feet [of natural gas] per day," says Thomas P. Schindler, co-portfolio manager at Diamond Hill Small Cap fund. He thinks the new prospects alone are worth $20 per share, a little more than half of the current stock price of $37. The company has a good track record of adding new reserves. Over the past five years, Southwestern has found more than twice as much new oil and gas as it has produced. And that production has doubled over the same period, to 62 billion cubic feet of gas a year.

ROCKY MOUNTAIN HIGH

IT WON'T BE EASY for Burlington Resources to double its size. With the equivalent of 12 trillion cubic feet of natural gas reserves, the Houston-based energy company is one of the largest independents. It started out as the oil-exploration arm of Burlington Northern Railroad, a legacy that left it with choice reserves in the Rocky Mountains. Spun off from the railroad in 1998, Burlington made a number of well-timed acquisitions in Canada. That country now accounts for about one-third of Burlington's production. It has also begun exploratory drilling in China and Algeria. Mark Freeman, director of research and portfolio manager at Westwood Management Corp. in Dallas, likes the fact that Burlington is being conservative with its cash. Since 2000, the company has bought back 10% of its shares, helping to boost earnings per share. Freeman figures the company will earn $5.10 per share this year. He has a target price of $70 for the stock, about 30% above Burlington's current share price.

At today's energy prices, filling up your tank and paying your winter gas bill stings. But owning a piece of an independent oil company might soothe some of that pain.

Christopher Palmeri

Study Questions

1. As pointed out in this article, filling up your tank and paying your winter gas bill stings. Given the reality of this situation, why would investing in one of the four oil and gas exploration companies make sense?

2. Using the Internet, the *Wall Street Journal*, or a local newspaper, complete the chart below.

Company	Stock Symbol	Price 6-27-2005	P-E Ratio 6-27-2005	Current Price Date: _____	Current P-E Ratio
Burlington Resources	BR	$53.27	12		
Devon Energy	DVN	$47.57	10		
Southwestern Energy	SWN	$37.15	23		
XTO Energy	XTO	$31.79	13		

3. Based on the above information, would you want to invest in any of the four companies mentioned in this article.

4. What other information would you want to help evaluate the companies?

15 INVESTING IN BONDS

Chapter Overview

This chapter describes bonds as an investment alternative. Initially, we examine important characteristics that pertain to bond investments. Then, we discuss the topics of why corporations sell bonds and why investors buy those bonds. The differences between corporate and government bonds and the factors that investors use to evaluate bond investments are presented.

Learning Objectives

After studying this chapter, you will be able to:

Obj. 1 Describe the characteristics of corporate bonds.

Obj. 2 Discuss why corporations issue bonds.

Obj. 3 Explain why investors purchase corporate bonds.

Obj. 4 Discuss why federal, state, and local governments issue bonds and why investors purchase government bonds.

Obj. 5 Evaluate bonds when making an investment.

Key Terms

bearer bond	general obligation bond	subordinated debenture
bond indenture	maturity date	trustee
call feature	mortgage bond	yield
convertible bond	municipal bond	yield to maturity
corporate bond	registered bond	zero-coupon bond
current yield	revenue bond	
debenture	serial bonds	
face value	sinking funds	

Pretest

True-False

_____ 1. (Obj. 1) The usual face value for a corporate bond is $5,000.

_____ 2. (Obj. 1) The trustee is an independent firm that acts as the bondholder's representative.

_____ 3. (Obj. 2) A debenture bond is a bond that is secured by various assets of the issuing corporation.

_____ 4. (Obj. 2) The conversion feature of a convertible bond allows investors to enjoy the low risk of a corporate bond, but also to take advantage of the speculative nature of common stock by exercising their right of conversion.

_____ 5. (Obj. 3) If Ford Motor Company issues an 8 percent bond with a face value of $1,000, a bond owner would receive $40 a year.

_____ 6. (Obj. 3) When a bond is selling for more than its face value, it is said to be selling at a priority price.

_____ 7. (Obj. 4) Treasury bills are issued in minimum units of $10,000, with maturities that range from 4 weeks to 52 weeks.

_____ 8. (Obj. 4) Federal Agency debt issues offer slightly higher interest rates than securities issued by the Treasury Department.

_____ 9. (Obj. 5) The highest bond rating assigned by Standard & Poor's is BBB.

_____ 10. (Obj. 6) The current yield is determined by dividing the dollar amount of annual interest by its face value.

Self-Guided Study Questions

Obj. 1

Characteristics of Corporate Bonds (p. 482)

1. In your own words, how would you define a corporate bond?

2. What is the usual face value of a corporate bond?

3. What is the range of maturity dates for corporate bonds?

4. What is included in a bond indenture?

5. What does a trustee do?

Obj. 2

Why Corporations Sell Corporate Bonds (p. 483)

6. How does a corporate bond differ from common stock or preferred stock?

Types of Bonds (p. 484)

7. What is the difference between a debenture bond, a mortgage bond, and a subordinated debenture?

Convertible Bonds (p. 484)

8. How is a convertible bond different from a typical corporate bond?

9. Why would an investor purchase a convertible bond?

10. Why would a corporation issue convertible bonds?

Provisions for Repayment (p. 485)

11. Why would a corporation issue a bond that is callable?

12. How would you explain the two methods that corporations use to redeem a bond issue at maturity?

Obj. 3

Why Investors Purchase Corporate Bonds (p. 487)

13. What are the three reasons why investors purchase corporate bonds?

Interest Income (p. 487)

14. What is the annual interest amount for a corporate bond that has a face value of $1,000 and pays 7¼ percent interest a year?

15. How often are interest payments paid to bondholders?

16. What is the difference between a registered bond, a bearer bond, and a zero-coupon bond?

17. What two factors should you consider when investing in zero-coupon bonds?

Dollar Appreciation of Bond Value (p. 488)

18. Explain why a bond's market value may be more or less than its face value.

19. As related to bonds, what do the terms premium and discount mean?

20. What is the formula for determining the approximate market value for a bond?

21. In addition to interest rates, what other factors account for increases and decreases in a bond's value?

Bond Repayment at Maturity (p. 489)

22. When you purchase a bond, what two options do you have?

23. Explain the concept of "building a bond ladder".

A Typical Bond Transaction (p. 490)

24. In a bond transaction illustrated in Exhibit 15-2 on page 490, the investor experienced a total return of $1,040. In your own words, explain why the bondholder received $1,040.

25. If the company in this example—Borden Chemical, Inc.—had experienced financial problems before the bond's maturity, what would have happened to the value of this bond?

The Mechanics of a Bond Transaction (p. 491)

26. How are the steps in a bond transaction similar to the steps in a stock transaction?

27. What are the typical commissions for bond transactions?

Obj. 4

Government Bonds and Debt Securities (p. 493)

Treasury Bills, Notes, and Bonds (p. 493)

28. Why do investors purchase United States Treasury securities?

29. What is the difference between a treasury bill, a treasury note, and treasury bond?

Federal Agency Debt Issues (p. 495)

30. Which federal agencies issue bonds in order to obtain financing?

31. How do debt issues issued by Federal Agencies compare to securities issued by the Treasury Department?

State and Local Government Securities (p. 495)

32. How would you describe the difference between a general obligation bond and a revenue bond?

33. Why must an investor evaluate an investment in a specific municipal bond?

34. Why are municipal bonds attractive investments for investors in a higher income tax bracket?

35. What is the formula for determining the tax-equivalent yield on a municipal bond?

Obj. 5

The Decision to Buy or Sell Bonds (p. 497)

The Internet (p. 498)

36. How could you obtain financial information about bonds by accessing the Internet?

How to Read the Bond Section of a Newspaper (p. 498)

37. In bond quotations, prices are given as a percentage of the face value, which is usually $1,000. With this fact in mind, what is the selling price for a bond that is quoted at 90?

38. What type of information about bonds is provided in a newspaper?

39. For a government bond, what is the difference between the bid price and the asked price?

Annual Reports (p. 499)

40. Why must bondholders be concerned about the financial health of a corporation or government entity that issues bonds?

41. How can you obtain an annual report from a corporation that has issued bonds?

Bond Ratings (p. 500)

42. How important are the bond ratings provided by Moody's and Standard & Poor's?

43. As illustrated in Exhibit 15-6, what is the highest rating according to Moody's? According to Standard & Poor's?

44. According to Moody's and Standard & Poor's what are investment grade securities?

45. As illustrated in Exhibit 15-6, what is the lowest rating according to Moody's? According to Standard & Poor's?

46. What are the Moody's ratings for shorter-term municipal bonds?

Bond Yield Calculations (p. 500)

47. How do you calculate the current yield for a bond?

48. What factors does the yield to maturity take into account?

49. How do you calculate the yield to maturity?

Other Sources of Information (p. 503)

50. What two additional sources of information can you use to evaluate a bond investment?

Post Test

Completion

1. (Obj. 1) A(n) _____ _____ is a corporation's written pledge that it will repay a specified amount of money, with interest.

2. (Obj. 1) The _____ _____ of a corporate bond is the date on which the corporation is to repay the borrowed money.

3. (Obj. 2) A(n) _____ _____ is a bond that gives bondholders a claim secondary to that of other bondholders with respect to both income and assets.

4. (Obj. 2) A fund to which deposits are made each year for the purpose of redeeming a bond issue is called a(n) _____ fund.

5. (Obj. 3) Investors purchase corporate bonds for three reasons: (1) _____ income, (2) possible increase in _____, and (3) _____ at maturity.

6. (Obj. 3) A(n) _____ bond is a bond whose ownership is registered by the issuing company.

7. (Obj. 4) Treasury bills are issued in minimum units of _____ with maturities as long as one year.

8. (Obj. 4) A bond backed by the full faith, credit, and unlimited taxing power of the government that issued it is called a(n) _____ _____ bond.

9. (Obj. 5) The first price quotation, or the _____ price, is the highest price that a dealer is willing to pay for a government security.

10. (Obj. 5) A bond's current yield is determined by dividing a bond's yearly dollar amount of income by its current _____ value.

Multiple Choice

_____ 1. (Obj. 1) The legal document that details all of the conditions relating to a bond issue is called a
   A. trustee agreement.
   B. bond indenture.
   C. subordinated agreement.
   D. mortgage agreement.

_____ 2. (Obj. 2) A bond that is backed only by the reputation of the issuing corporation is called a
   A. debenture bond.
   B. mortgage bond.
   C. subordinated debenture.
   D. convertible bond.

_____ 3. (Obj. 2) Bonds of a single issue that mature on different dates are called
   A. trust bonds.
   B. convertible bonds.
   C. indentured bonds.
   D. serial bonds.

_____ 4. (Obj. 3) What is the annual interest for a $1,000 bond that pays 8½ percent?
   A. $75
   B. $85
   C. $90
   D. $117

_____ 5. (Obj. 3) Assume that you purchase a corporate bond that pays 8¼ percent interest based on a face value of $1,000. Also assume that new corporate bond issues of comparable quality are currently paying 10 percent. What is the approximate market value for the XYZ corporate bond?
   A. $750
   B. $825
   C. $875
   D. $1,000
   E. $1,100

_____ 6. (Obj. 4) A security issued by the federal government in $1,000 units with a maturity of more than 1 year but not more than 10 years is called a
   A. treasury bond.
   B. treasury note.
   C. savings note.
   D. savings bond.

7. (Obj. 4) A bond that is repaid from the income generated by the project it is designed to finance is called a
   A. general obligation bond.
   B. revenue bond.
   C. certified bond.
   D. coordinated bond.

8. (Obj. 5) A corporate bond that has a face value of $1,000 and is quoted as 85 ½ in *The Wall Street Journal* has a selling price of
   A. $85 ½
   B. $85.50
   C. $850.00
   D. $855.00
   E. $1,000

9. (Obj. 5) For municipal bonds maturing in one year or less, the highest rating given by Moody's is
   A. MIG1.
   B. MIG3.
   C. SP-3.
   D. SG.
   E. Municipal bonds with short maturities are not rated by Moody's because they are considered risk-free.

10. (Obj. 6) What is the current yield for a bond that pays $75 annual interest and has a market value of $900?
    A. 7.5 percent
    B. 7.75 percent
    C. 8.33 percent
    D. 10 percent
    E. With the above information, it is impossible to determine the current yield.

Problems, Applications, and Cases

1. To determine the quality and risk associated with bond issues, investors rely on the bond ratings provided by Moody's Investor's Service and Standard & Poor's Corporation. For each bond rating listed below, provide a brief description of the type of bonds included in that category.

	Rating	Description
Standard & Poor's	AAA	
Standard & Poor's	BBB	
Standard & Poor's	B	
Standard & Poor's	CCC	
Standard & Poor's	D	
Moody's	Aaa	
Moody's	A	
Moody's	Caa	
Moody's	C	

2. One of the most important features of municipal bonds is that they may be exempt from federal taxes. When evaluating this type of investment, it is necessary to determine the taxable equivalent yield. Using the formula presented in this chapter, determine the taxable equivalent yield for the problems below.

Tax-exempt yield	Applicable tax rate	Taxable equivalent yield
5%	25%	a. _____
6%	25%	b. _____
6.5%	25%	c. _____
7.5%	28%	d. _____
8%	28%	e. _____

3. Using a recent metropolitan newspaper, the *Wall Street Journal*, *Barrons*, or the Internet, fill in the following table for selected corporate bonds.

Company name	Interest rate	Maturity	Current yield	Current price
a. A T & T Wireless	8.125	2012		
b. Dole	8.750	2013		
c. DuPont E.I. De Nemours	4.750	2012		
d. Verizon New York	6.875	2012		

4. Choose one of the corporate bonds listed in Exercise 3. Then use Mergent's Industrial Manuals (available at your college or public library) to answer the following questions on this bond issue. (Hint: You may want to read the Financial Planning for Life's Situations on page 486 before completing this exercise.)

   a. What is Mergent's rating for this issue?
   b. What is the purpose of this issue?
   c. Does the issue have a call provision?
   d. Who is the trustee for the issue?
   e. What security, if any, has been pledged as security for the issue?
   f. Based on the information you have obtained, would the bond be a good investment for you? Why?

5. The yield to maturity is a yield calculation that takes into account the relationship among a bonds' maturity value, the time to maturity, the current price, and the dollar amount of interest. For the problems below, determine the yield to maturity.

Face value (par value)	Interest rate	Annual interest	Time to maturity	Current market value (price)	Yield to maturity
$1,000	6%	$60	5 years	$900	a. _____
$1,000	7%	$70	5 years	$1,100	b. _____
$1,000	8%	$80	8 years	$800	c. _____
$1,000	9%	$90	8 years	$900	d. _____
$1,000	10%	$100	10 years	$700	e. _____

Supplementary Case 15-1: The ABCs of Bond Ratings

Topic: Bond Ratings

Text Reference: pp. 500-501

Are bonds safer than common or preferred stock? The answer to that question depends on such factors as the conditions contained in the bond agreement and the likelihood of repayment at maturity. Most investors rely on two financial services, Standard & Poor's and Moody's, to provide ratings for bonds. Standard & Poor's bond ratings range from AAA (highest) to D (the lowest). Moody's bond ratings range from Aaa (the highest) to C (the lowest). For most investors, a bond rated A or better is probably as safe as a blue-chip stock, while a C-rated bond could be more risky than a speculative stock.

Recently, a number of corporate bond issues whose Standard & Poor's and Moody's ratings are lower than A have been sold in the bond market. The reasons for the lower ratings vary. A bond may have been assigned a low rating because the corporation that issued it has long-term debt that is too high or earnings that are too low, or because changing economic conditions may make payment of bond interest or repayment of the bond principal doubtful. Whatever the reasons, the corporations issuing the low-rated bonds had to increase the interest rate on them in order to attract purchasers. As a result, the bonds offer extremely attractive current yields to investors who are willing to take a chance. For example, a $1,000 corporate bond issued by Chiquita Brands is paying 7.5 percent interest until its maturity in 2014. The current market price of this bond is $972 which means that the current yield is 7.72 percent. The rating for this bond is B.

Case Questions

1. How important are the Moody's and Standard & Poor's bond ratings? What does the B rating mean?

2. A 7.72 percent current yield is at least 2 to 3 percent higher than the current yield of more conservative corporate bond issues. Is this additional interest worth the added risks involved in purchasing a bond with lower ratings such as the Chiquita Brands bond?

3. As the maturity date of this bond approaches, what should happen to the price of this bond? Why?

4. What other information would you need to evaluate the Chiquita Brands bond? Where would you get this information?

Supplementary Case 15-2: Are Higher Yields on Corporate Bonds Worth the Added Risk

Topic: Why Investors Purchase Corporate Bonds

Text Reference: pp. 487-492

The days of investors putting their money in a certificate of deposit and receiving 7 percent year after year are over. In fact, since the late 1990s, investors in certificates of deposit have seen their returns bottom out at between 2 and 5 percent. These low returns, the lowest in over 40 years, have forced many investors like Barbara Haynes to look for ways to squeeze additional income from their investment portfolios.

Back in 1996, Barbara, then 36 and single, was injured in an automobile accident. After a lengthy court battle with the driver of the other car and his insurance company, Barbara won a $575,000 settlement, of which she paid almost $150,000 to her attorney. She invested the remaining $425,000 in long-term certificates of deposit that earned an average of 7 percent, or about $30,000 a year. But now the highest CD interest rates she could find are around 4 percent. Faced with the prospects of lower income, she decided it was time to explore other investment options. To accomplish the goal, she made an appointment with Jim Mathis, an account executive with the brokerage firm of Paine Webber.

According to Jim, there were ways to increase the yield on Barbara's investment portfolio, but she would have to assume greater risks. After considering different alternatives, both decided that one option, investing in high-quality corporate bonds with maturities no shorter than 10 years, could increase her income with only a slight to moderate increase in risk. Jim went on to say that the bond market had many high-quality corporate bonds with current yields between 5 and 7 percent. At the conclusion of the meeting, he suggested that she might evaluate bonds issued by AT&T Broadband.

A trip to the library yielded some useful information about AT&T Broadband bonds. Barbara discovered that the company had many different bond issues, not just one. Since her goal was to increase her investment income, Barbara decided to research the bond with the highest yield. This particular bond had a maturity value of $1,000, matured in 2013, and paid 8.375 percent interest each year. Because the bond was currently selling at a premium price of $1,228, the current yield had decreased to 6.82 percent. That was still almost three percentage points higher than her bank was offering on CD renewals. Although Barbara liked the higher income the AT&T Broadband bond offered, she wanted to know more about the risks before investing her nest egg.

Case Questions

1. During the year 2005, investors were forced to look for ways to squeeze additional income form their investment portfolios. Do you think investing in corporate bonds is the best way to increase income? Why or why not?

2. What other information could Barbara Haynes use to evaluate this bond issue? Where would you get this information?

3. If you were Barbara Haynes, would you purchase AT&T Broadband bonds? If so, how much of her $425,000 nest egg would you invest in this AT&T Broadband bond?

Supplementary Reading 15

Christopher Farrell, "Tax Smart Stashes for Your Assets", *Business Week*, June 27, 2005, p. 102.

Tax Smart Stashes for Your Assets

If you want the perfect asset-allocation plan, you'll have to design it in a tax-smart way. That means carefully distributing your stocks, bonds, and other investments between taxable and tax-deferred vehicles such as 401(k)s and individual retirement accounts. "Investors can increase their returns by locating their assets optimally across taxable and tax-deferred accounts," says Clemens Sialm, assistant professor of finance at the University of Michigan Stephen M. Ross School of Business.

Asset location is tricky because of the Byzantine tax code. Taxes are deferred on contributions to and earnings from 401(k)s and IRAs, but withdrawals are taxed at ordinary income rates. But in a Roth IRA, the contribution is funded with aftertax dollars and the savings are tax-free. Taxes are owed every year in a taxable account, but Uncle Sam plays favorites. Interest earned on bonds by a high-income saver is taxed at the top federal marginal income tax rate of 35%, yet the levy on most dividends is only 15%.

You can minimize total taxes and maximize returns by putting assets that face the highest taxes into tax-sheltered retirement accounts. Here's an example from James M. Poterba, a Massachusetts Institute of Technology economist: Suppose you put $10,000 into bonds that generate a pretax return of 5% per year, and the interest is reinvested at 5%. After 30 years, the $10,000 is worth $30,800 if you are in the 25% marginal federal tax rate. If the same bonds were in an IRA, and taxed at 25% on withdrawal after the 30 years, it would be worth about 9% more.

With investments taxed at lower rates, such as the 15% maximum tax on long-term capital gains, the IRA could work against you. Had you put $10,000 in stocks, earned 5% a year, sold them in three decades, and paid only capital-gains tax, the investment would be worth nearly $40,000. Had that equity investment been made in a traditional IRA, the proceeds would be taxed at the 25% rate, leaving you with about $6,000 less (assuming tax rates stay the same).

Remember, the location choice comes after the asset allocation decision. And you should make sure you're funding your tax-deferred accounts to the max. But the more you're able to save, the more you will help boost your returns by paying attention to different tax treatments.

Location, Location, Location
BEST FOR TAX-DEFERRED ACCOUNTS
- Taxable bonds and bond funds
- Real estate investment trusts
- Any actively traded mutual, commodity, or hedge funds
- Individual equities you expect to hold less than a year

BEST FOR TAXABLE ACCOUNTS
- Tax-exempt bonds and bond funds
- Individual equities you expect to hold more than a year
- Tax-managed mutual funds
- Growth stocks with no dividend payout

THESE CAN GO IN EITHER
- Broad-based equity index funds
- High dividend-paying stocks
- Exchange-traded funds

Christopher Farrell

Study Questions

1. What is the difference between a tax-deferred account and a taxable account?

2. According to this article, taxable bonds, taxable bond funds, actively traded mutual funds, and individual equities (stocks) you expect to hold less than a year should be placed in a tax-deferred account. Why?

3. According to this article, tax-exempt bonds, tax-exempt bond funds, and individual equities (stocks) you expect to hold more than a year should be placed in a taxable account. Why?

16 INVESTING IN MUTUAL FUNDS

Chapter Overview

This chapter examines the topic of mutual funds—an investment alternative chosen by individuals who pool their money to buy stocks, bonds, and other securities selected by professional managers who work for an investment company. In this chapter, we consider why individuals invest in mutual funds. We also look at the unique characteristics of different mutual fund investments. Then, we discuss how mutual funds are classified according to the investment objective of the fund. Finally, we consider different methods that investors can use to evaluate mutual funds and the methods of buying and selling shares in a mutual fund.

Learning Objectives

After studying this chapter, you will be able to:

Obj. 1 Describe the characteristics of mutual fund investments.

Obj. 2 Classify mutual funds by investment objective.

Obj. 3 Evaluate mutual funds for investment purposes.

Obj. 4 Describe how and why mutual funds are bought and sold.

Key Terms

capital gains distribution	income dividends	no-load fund
closed-end fund	investment company	open-end fund
contingent deferred sales load	load fund	reinvestment plan
exchange-traded fund (EFT)	market timer	12b-1 fee
expense ratio	mutual fund	
family of funds	net asset value (NAV)	

Pretest

True-False

_____ 1. (Obj. 1) The major reasons why investors purchase mutual funds are professional management and diversification.

_____ 2. (Obj. 1) A closed-end fund is a mutual fund whose shares are issued and redeemed by the investment company at the request of investors.

_____ 3. (Obj. 1) Current research indicates that load funds outperform no-load funds.

_____ 4. (Obj. 1) A 12b-1 fee is charged by some investment companies to defray the costs of marketing and distributing a mutual fund.

_____ 5. (Obj. 2) A growth fund invests in common stocks of companies in the same industry.

_____ 6. (Obj. 2) A family of funds exists when one investment company manages a group of mutual funds.

_____ 7. (Obj. 3) *Kiplinger's Personal Finance Magazine* and *Business Week* provide professional advisory research reports.

_____ 8. (Obj. 3) An investment company sponsoring a mutual fund must give investors a prospectus each calendar quarter.

_____ 9. (Obj. 4) Income dividends are the earnings that a fund pays to shareholders from its dividend and interest income.

_____ 10. (Obj. 4) Because closed-end funds are listed on securities exchanges, it is possible to sell shares in such a fund to another investor.

Self-Guided Study Questions

1. In your own words, define the term mutual fund.

2. How does the Mutual Fund Education Alliance define an investment company?

Obj. 1

Why Investors Purchase Mutual Funds (p. 514)

3. What are the two major reasons why investors purchase mutual funds?

4. Since investment companies have professional portfolio managers with years of experience, is it still necessary for investors to evaluate mutual funds? Why?

5. Why does diversification of mutual funds spell safety?

Characteristics of Investment in Mutual Funds (p. 516)

6. What is the difference between a closed-end fund and an open-end fund?

7. What is an exchange-traded fund (EFT)?

8. What are the advantages of investing in an exchange-traded fund?

9. How is the net asset value (NAV) for a share in a mutual fund determined?

10. What is the difference between a load fund and a no-load fund?

11. What do several major research studies indicate about the performance of funds that charge commissions compared to funds that don't charge commissions?

12. What is the typical contingent deferred sales load?

13. What is the average management fee for a mutual fund?

14. What is the typical 12b-1 fee?

15. Why do investment companies charge 12b-1 fees?

16. What is the difference between Class A, Class B, and Class C shares?

17. What is an expense ratio and why is it important?

18. What is the purpose of a fee table?

Obj. 2
Classifications of Mutual Funds (p. 520)
19. Why is a fund's objective important?

Stock Funds (p. 520)

20. What types of securities are included in an aggressive growth fund?

21. What types of securities are included in an equity income fund?

22. What types of securities are included in a global stock fund?

23. What types of securities are included in a growth fund?

24. What types of securities are included in an index fund?

25. What types of securities are included in an international fund?

26. What type of securities are included in a large-cap fund?

27. What types of securities are included in a mid-cap fund?

28. What types of securities are included in a regional fund?

29. What types of securities are included in a sector fund?

30. What types of securities are included in a small-cap fund?

31. What type of securities are included in a socially responsible fund?

Bond Funds (p. 522)

32. What types of securities are included in a high-yield (junk) bond fund?

33. What type of securities are included in an index bond fund?

34. What types of securities are included in an intermediate corporate bond fund?

35. What types of securities are included in an intermediate U.S. bond fund?

36. What types of securities are included in a long-term corporate bond fund?

37. What types of securities are included in a long-term (U.S.) bond fund?

38. What types of securities are included in a municipal bond fund?

39. What types of securities are included in a short-term corporate bond fund?

40. What types of securities are included in a short-term (U.S.) government bond fund?

41. What types of securities are included in a world bond fund?

Other Funds (p. 522)

42. What type of securities are included in an asset allocation fund?

43. What types of securities are included in a balanced fund?

44. What types of securities are included in a money market fund?

45. In your own words, define a family of funds.

46. For the investor, what are the benefits of a family of funds?

47. What services does a market timer perform?

Obj. 3

How to Make a Decision to Buy or Sell Mutual Funds (p. 524)

48. Why is the decision to buy or sell shares in a mutual fund "too" easy?

Managed Funds Versus Indexed Funds (p. 524)

49. What is a managed fund?

50. Why is the fund manager important to a managed fund?

51. What is the difference between a managed fund and an indexed fund?

52. Why do investors often choose index funds?

53. What are the typical expense ratios that index fund investors pay?

54. How is the total return for a mutual fund calculated?

The Internet (p. 525)

55. What type of information about mutual funds can be obtained by using the Internet?

Professional Advisory Services (p. 526)

56. What type of information is provided by professional advisory services?

57. List 4 professional advisory services that were described in this chapter.

How to Read the Mutual Funds Section in the Newspaper (p. 528)

58. What type of information is provided in the mutual fund section of the newspaper?

59. In a newspaper quotation, what do the letters "p," "r," "t," and "s" mean?

Mutual Fund Prospectus (p. 529)

60. What type of information is contained in the prospectus that investors could use to evaluate a mutual fund investment?

Mutual Fund Annual Report (p. 529)

61. What type of information is contained in a mutual fund annual report?

Financial Publications (p. 529)

62. What financial publications can investors use to evaluate mutual fund investments?

Obj. 4

The Mechanics of a Mutual Fund Transaction (p. 532)

Return on Investment (p. 532)

63. What is an income dividend?

64. What is a capital gain distribution?

65. What is the difference between a capital gain distribution and a capital gain?

Taxes and Mutual Funds (p. 533)

66. What are the tax implications of investing in mutual funds?

Purchase Options (p. 535)

67. How can an investor purchase shares in a closed-end fund or exchange-traded funds?

68. What are three methods that can be used to purchase open-end load funds?

69. What are two advantages of using mutual fund supermarkets?

70. What are the four options that investors can use to purchase shares in an open-end fund?

71. All four purchase options allow investors to buy shares over a long period of time. How do these options allow investors to use the principle of dollar cost averaging?

Withdrawal Options (p. 536)

72. How can an investor sell shares in a closed-end fund or exchange-traded fund?

73. How can an investor sell shares in an open-end fund?

74. In addition to just selling shares in an open-end fund, what are four options that investors can use to systematically withdraw funds from an open-end fund?

Post Test

Completion

1. (Obj. 1) The two major reasons why investors purchase mutual funds are _____ management and _____.

2. (Obj. 1) A(n) _____-_____ fund is a mutual fund that invests in the stocks contained in a specific stock index, and whose shares are traded on a stock exchange.

3. (Obj. 1) The _____ _____ _____ per share is equal to the current market value of the mutual fund's portfolio minus the mutual fund's liabilities divided by the number of shares outstanding.

4. (Obj. 1) A(n) _____ _____ _____ _____ is a 1 to 5 percent charge that shareholders pay when they withdraw their investment from a mutual fund.

5. (Obj. 2) A(n) _____ _____ fund invests in lesser known companies that offer high growth potential.

6. (Obj. 2) A(n) _____ fund invests in stocks and bonds with the primary objective of conserving principal.

7. (Obj. 3) Morningstar is a(n) _____-_____ service.

8. (Obj. 3) Generally, a(n) _____ contains a summary of the fund and information about fees, past financial performance, and the fund's management and is given to potential investors.

9. (Obj. 4) _____ _____ distributions are payments made to a fund's shareholders that result from the sale of securities in a fund's portfolio.

10. (Obj. 4) From a tax standpoint, investors can determine when they experience a(n) _____ gain.

Multiple Choice

_____ 1. (Obj. 1) Which of the following statements is false?
   A. Investors purchase mutual funds because they offer professional management.
   B. Investors purchase mutual funds because they are diversified.
   C. Mutual Funds are often chosen by individuals for their retirement or IRA accounts.
   D. Because of professional management, there is no need for investors to evaluate a mutual fund investment.
   E. Investment companies often hire professional managers who have years of investment experience.

_____ 2. (Obj. 1) A mutual fund that charges a commission—sometimes as high as 8 ½ percent of the purchase price—is called a(n) _____ fund.
   A. open-end
   B. closed-end
   C. load
   D. redemption

_____ 3. (Obj. 1) The average yearly management fee for a mutual fund is _____ percent of the fund's assets.
   A. 0.25 to 0.50
   B. 0.5 to 1.25
   C. 1 to 1.50
   D. 1.50 to 2
   E. 2 to 3

_____ 4. (Obj. 1) A fee used to defray the costs of marketing and distributing a mutual fund is a called a _____ fee.
   A. load
   B. management
   C. redemption
   D. 12b-1
   E. 44K-3

5. (Obj. 2) A mutual fund that invests in companies expecting higher than average revenue and earnings growth is called a(n) _____ fund.
   A. balanced
   B. beta
   C. growth
   D. industry
   E. index

6. (Obj. 2) A mutual fund that invests in stocks of companies throughout the world and outside of the U.S. is called a _____ fund.
   A. balanced
   B. family
   C. growth
   D. international
   E. world

7. (Obj. 3) In a newspaper like *The Wall Street Journal*, which of the following would indicate that a 12b-1 fee is charged?
   A. r
   B. p
   C. NL
   D. Q
   E. +

8. (Obj. 4) Earnings that a fund pays to shareholders from its dividend and interest income are called
   A. capital gains.
   B. capital gain distributions.
   C. ordinary distributions.
   D. income dividends.
   E. fund dividends.

9. (Obj. 4) Contractual savings plans are sometimes referred to as _____ funds.
   A. front-end load
   B. prepaid commission
   C. no-load
   D. Securities and Exchange Commission
   E. prepaid purchase

10. (Obj. 4) Because _____ and exchange-traded funds are listed on securities exchanges, it is possible to sell shares in such a fund to another investor.
    A. closed-end
    B. load
    C. open-end
    D. redemption
    E. 12b-1

Problems, Applications, and Cases

1. Match each term with the statements that follow.
    a. closed-end fund
    b. open-end fund
    c. net asset value
    d. exchange-traded fund
    e. Class C shares
    f. no-load fund
    g. management fee
    h. contingent deferred sales load
    i. 12b-1 fee

    _____ 1. The current market value of the mutual fund's portfolio minus the mutual fund's liabilities divided by the number of shares outstanding.

    _____ 2. A fee to defray the costs of marketing and distributing a mutual fund.

    _____ 3. A mutual fund whose shares are issued and redeemed by the investment company at the request of investors.

    _____ 4. A yearly fee that usually ranges from 0.50 to 1.25 percent of the fund's total assets.

    _____ 5. A mutual fund that invests in the stocks contained in a specific stock index and whose shares are traded on a stock exchange.

    _____ 6. A mutual fund whose shares are issued by an investment company only when the fund is organized.

    _____ 7. A mutual fund in which investors pay no commission to buy or sell shares, but higher ongoing 12b-1 fees.

    _____ 8. A 1 to 5 percent charge that shareholders pay when they withdraw their investment from a mutual fund.

    _____ 9. A mutual fund in which no sales charge is paid by the individual investor.

2. The managers of mutual funds tailor their investment portfolios to the investment objectives of their customers. The major categories of mutual funds are presented below. In your own words, describe the type of securities that would be found in each type of mutual fund.

Classification of fund	Type of securities generally included
Aggressive growth fund	
Equity income fund	
Global stock fund	
Growth fund	
Index fund	
International fund	
Large-cap fund	
Mid-cap fund	
Regional fund	
Sector fund	
Small cap fund	
Socially-responsible fund	
High-yield bond fund	
Index bond fund	
Intermediate corporate bond fund	
Intermediate U.S. bond fund	
Long-term corporate bond fund	
Long-term (U.S.) bond fund	
Municipal bond fund	
Short-term corporate bond fund	

Short-term (U.S.) bond fund

World bond fund

Asset allocation fund

Balanced fund

Money market fund

3. Choose at least three different mutual funds that could help you meet your personal investment objectives. Then use the mutual fund quotations published in *The Wall Street Journal*, a local newspaper, or the Internet to monitor the value of each fund for a period of four weeks.

Mutual fund	Week 1 Net asset value Date _____	Week 2 Net asset value Date _____	Week 3 Net asset value Date _____	Week 4 Net asset value Date _____
1.				
2.				
3.				

Based on your findings, answer the following questions to complete Exercise 3.

a. Which of the above mutual funds had the largest dollar amount of change over the four-week period of time?

b. After watching each of the three mutual funds for a period of four weeks, would you want to invest in one of the funds? Why?

c. What other types of information would you use to evaluate the above mutual funds?

4. ABC Growth Fund is an aggressively managed growth fund that invests in small, rapidly growing corporations in the electronics and computer fields. According to the fund's annual report, ABC has $590 million of assets, $1.4 million of liabilities, and 40,124,200 shares outstanding.

   a. What is the net asset value per share?

   b. If this fund charges a 4 percent commission on the total amount invested, how much commission would be paid on an investment of $2,000?

5. Assume that one year ago you bought 200 shares of a mutual fund for $12.25 per share, that you received $0.60 per share income distribution during the past 12 months, and that the market value of the fund is now $10.75 per share.

   a. Calculate the current yield for this investment at the end of the 12-month period.

   b. Calculate the total return for this investment at the end of 12 months.

Supplementary Case 16-1: Are Mutual Funds for You?

Topic: Evaluation of Mutual Funds

Text Reference: pp. 524-532

Today, there are more mutual funds than ever before—all developed to meet the needs of investors like you. And while putting your money in a mutual fund may seem like a carefree method of investing, nothing can be further from the truth.

In evaluating a mutual fund, the first factor you should consider is the fund's investment objectives. Whether you want your money in conservative, long-term government bonds, or in speculative foreign stocks, there is a mutual fund for you. The key question may be, "Do the objectives of a specific mutual fund match your objectives?"

The second factor you should consider is information about the fund. It is fairly easy to obtain a comparative performance ranking for periods ranging from the last 10 years to the most recent quarter. Sources of information on mutual funds that are available at most libraries include *Business Week, Kiplinger's Personal Finance Magazine, Money,* and *Forbes.* The most comprehensive reference sources on mutual funds are Morningstar, Inc., and the reports published by Standard and Poor's Corporation, and Value Line.

The third factor you should consider is recommendations about a fund available in newsletters on mutual funds. Thanks to the great interest in mutual funds, many investment newsletters now specialize in this subject. Many of these newsletters have survived the test of time and provide investors with reliable advice for fees ranging from $20 to $300 a year.

More information on mutual funds is available from the Mutual Fund Education Alliance at www.mfea.com and the Investment Company Institute at www.ici.org.

Case Questions

1. Today, mutual funds are one of the most popular investments in the United States. Why do you think mutual funds have become so popular?

2. Since professional management and diversification are characteristics of mutual funds, why must investors still evaluate a mutual fund?

3. Assume that you are interested in mutual funds. Visit the Web site for the Mutual Fund Education Alliance (www.mfea.com) or the Investment Company Institute (www.ici.org). Then describe the type of information the site provides.

Supplementary Case 16-2: How Do You Evaluate a Mutual Fund?

Topic: Evaluation of Mutual Funds

Text Reference: pp. 524-532

In Chapter 16 (Investing in Mutual Funds), we have stressed the importance of evaluating potential investments in mutual funds. Now it's your turn to try your skill at evaluating a mutual fund investment. Assume that you have established an emergency fund and have also accumulated $4,000 that you would like to invest in mutual funds. Also, assume that you are a college graduate and have a job that pays $27,000 a year. Finally, assume that you can choose any mutual fund that is reported in *The Wall Street Journal,* your local newspaper, or the Internet.

To help you evaluate "your" mutual fund, you may want to use the Yahoo Finance website (http://finance.yahoo.com or examine issues of *Business Week, Forbes, Kiplinger's Personal Finance Magazine,* or *Money.* Also, to help guide your search for a quality investment, you may want to complete the Personal Financial Planner Sheet No. 62—Evaluation of a mutual fund.

Case Questions

1. Based on your research, would you buy shares in the mutual fund you originally chose?
2. What other investment information would you need to evaluate your mutual fund? Where would you obtain this information?

Supplementary Reading 16

Lauren Young, "Now the Real Value Is in Growth", *Business Week*, June 27, 2005, pp. 124-125.

Now the Real Value Is in Growth

With profits strong, growth stocks are leaving their value cousins behind.

After more than five years of sitting on the sidelines watching value investors bask in the market's glory, growth-stock aficionados can smell vindication in the air. In the past three months the Russell 1000 Growth Index has nosed past the Russell 1000 Value Index by a little more than a percentage point.

That may seem like small potatoes, but the shift is huge considering that growth stocks, and the mutual funds that invest in them, have been lagging their value cousins since 2000. "It's the first time we've had any kind of outperformance on a sustained basis for several years," says Larry Puglia, manager of the $8.6 billion T. Rowe Price Blue Chip Growth Fund. Adds Peggy Adams, an associate manager of the $8 billion MFS Massachusetts Investors Growth Stock Fund: "We are in the process of a rebound."

Growth mutual funds—which focus on companies with significant earnings growth—are a core holding in many portfolios, so a major switch from value to growth styles could offer a seismic boost for fund shareholders. (Value funds, by contrast, tend to invest in companies that are out of favor and undervalued.) But don't expect to see big gains in your midyear fund statements. While growth funds have closed in on value funds since March, the typical growth fund is still down 1.7% while the average value fund lost 0.1% through the year ended June 10. Fund returns are calculated by Standard & Poor's, which, like *BusinessWeek*, is a unit of The McGraw-Hill Companies.

Fund managers have a long list of reasons why growth stocks should outperform in the coming years. First, there's the valuation argument. "The top 25 companies in the S&P 500 are as cheap as they've been in several decades," says Puglia. Stocks in the T. Rowe Price manager's fund are trading at 17 times next year's earnings. In January, 2001, the typical stock in the Standard & Poor's 500-stock index was trading with a forward price-earnings ratio of 30.

One other good sign is that in the midst of an acquisition boomlet, the stocks of acquiring companies haven't tanked. They often do when a major deal is announced because shareholders think the price tax is too expensive. Since Procter & Gamble Co. unveiled plans in January to buy Gillette Co., P&G's stock has risen slightly. In addition, stock buybacks are soaring among companies. T. Rowe Price's Puglia says most of the companies in his portfolio have announced share repurchases. That is a clear signal big companies, including Citigroup, Home Depot, and Nokia, think that their stocks are a good deal. Flush with cash, more companies also are raising their dividends. And while earnings growth, which has been on a strong upward trajectory for the past year, is expected to slow down a bit, profits should continue to be strong. "[The stocks of] high-quality companies tend to perform much better when you have slowing earnings growth in the S&P 500," Puglia says.

Leading the blue-chip pack is General Electric Co. "Management has executed extraordinarily well," Puglia says, noting that GE recently posted the best quarterly results in a decade. Puglia likes the fact that GE has sold businesses that earned skimpy returns while making major acquisitions in the lucrative entertainment and health-care fields. He's also bullish on Harrah's Entertainment in the gaming sector and Nokia in the telecommunications group.

MFS's Adams, meanwhile, is betting on storage-device maker

EMC Corp. "Ask a chief technology officer what really matters, and they'll say it's storage and security," Adams says. Her fund, which is down 2%, is also nibbling selectively on large-cap drug companies such as Eli Lilly, Johnson & Johnson, and Wyeth.

Surprisingly, a similar list of drugmakers appears in the $30 million Live Oak Health Sciences fund. A standout in the health-care group with a 7.3% gain in 2005, the fund usually focuses on biotech names. But pharmaceutical giants offer a backdoor biotech play. Aside from the reasonable price tag, co-manager Brandi Allen likes Pfizer Inc. because it's deftly partnering with biotech companies like Neurocrine Biosciences, which offers Indiplon, an insomnia drug. "If I were a biotech company, it's the first door I'd knock on," she says. "Pfizer has marketing muscle and scale."

RIDING OIL'S CLIMB

With Oil prices soaring, the hot natural-resources group is the best-performing mutual-fund sector, with a 13.3% gain. Some investors are clearly chasing performance: A record $2.2 billion has poured into natural-resources funds through early June, according to fund tracker AMG Data Services. Even the normally staid Vanguard Group, which shuns market-timing shareholders, is letting investors back into its chart-topping $6.1 billion Vanguard Energy Fund. Closed to new investors at the end of last year, the fund has gained 18.8% in 2005. To curb short-term opportunists, Vanguard is imposing a minimum initial investment of $25,000.

With a mere $8 million in its coffers, Guinness Atkinson Global Energy Fund is one of the top-performing funds overall so far in 2005, with a gain of 25%. Some 20% of the portfolio is focused on established Canadian companies, including OPTI Canada, Canadian Natural Resources, and Canadian Oil Sands Trust, which are mainly in the business of extracting oil from Canadian oil sands. That usually is an unprofitable venture because it typically costs about $24 a barrel to extract oil from frozen bitumen. "But when oil is above $40 a barrel, it's a perfectly reasonable proposition," says manager Tim Guinness.

There's another nice surprise coming in the midyear statements. Bond funds remain in positive territory despite moves by the Federal Reserve to boost interest rates. The average bond fund has had a total return of 1.2% so far this year, and some fixed-income portfolios are posting even better results. High-yield municipal funds rose 3.7% while long government bonds are up 3.6%. Those certainly aren't blockbuster gains, but considering that analysts were projecting Armageddon, they look pretty good. Many pros say that the U.S. bond rally is nearing its end, though.

With rising commodity prices, emerging-markets bonds have been on a hot streak, too. Emerging-markets bonds are up 3.7%. A decade ago, investors in the U.S. had few fixed-income options abroad—they could buy only sovereign debt as well as a smattering of corporate offerings in Latin America. In the past year, it has become easier to buy debt denominated in local currencies. "There's a lot of value in local currency markets," says Kristin Ceva, co-manager of the $61 million Payden Emerging Markets Bond Fund. Ceva has been a buyer of local currency bonds in Brazil, Mexico, Peru, and Colombia.

Fund investors also have done well in Latin American stock funds (up 7.1%), since they are chock-full of raw materials companies. Plenty of Latin American names are popping up in more diversified portfolios, including the $1.2 billion UMB Scout WorldWide Fund, which holds Cemax, a Mexican cement maker, Petrobras, a Brazilian oil company, and Aracruz Celulose, a Brazilian pulp manufacturer. Manager James Moffett expects these commodities to lose momentum eventually as economies cool down worldwide, but so far he's sticking with his investments. "The horse is still running," he says.

Investors who ventured south earlier this year have been duly rewarded. But with large-cap growth stocks perking up, the best returns of the second half may be earned at home.

Rising Rates Haven't Hurt Bond Funds—Yet

Category	Total Return*
Emerging Markets Bond	3.74%
Muni. High Yield	3.65
Long Government	3.60
Long (General)	3.42
Muni. Calif. Long	2.60
Muni. New York Long	2.34
Muni. National Long	2.16
Muni. Single-State Long	2.15
Muni. New York Intermediate	1.72
Intermediate Government	1.40
Muni. Calif. Intermediate	1.37
Intermediate (General)	1.30
Muni. Single-State Intermediate	1.30
Muni. National Intermediate	1.27
Short Government	0.84
Ultrashort	0.84
Short (General)	0.60
Muni. Short	0.39
Multisector	0.15
High Yield	−0.51
International Bond	−1.40
Convertibles	−3.46
Tax-Free Bond Funds	1.81
All Bonds Funds	1.22
Taxable Bond Funds	0.74

*Appreciation plus reinvestment of dividends and capital gains before taxes, Jan. 1-June 10, 2005.
Data: Standard & Poor's

More Losses Than Gains for Equity Funds

Category	Total Return*
Natural Resources	13.28%
Utilities	7.79
Latin America	7.06
Pacific/Asia ex-Japan	4.14
Real Estate	3.91
Diversified Emerging Mkts.	3.47
Mid-cap Value	1.23
Mid-cap Blend	1.00
Large-cap Value	0.57
Domestic Hybrid	0.13
Miscellaneous	−0.08
Diversified Pacific/Asia	−0.09
International Hybrid	−0.30
Europe	−0.48
Large-cap Blend	−0.51
Health	−0.56
World	−0.71
All Cap	−1.01
Foreign	−1.09
Small-cap Value	−1.14
Mid-cap Growth	−1.20
Large-cap Growth	−1.34
Small-cap Blend	−1.62
Communications	−2.65
Small-cap Growth	−3.57
Financial	−3.83
Japan	−4.84
Technology	−5.46
Precious Metals	−8.92
International Equity Funds	0.18
S&P 500	−0.40
All Equity Funds	−0.52
U.S. Diversified Funds	−0.87

*Appreciation plus reinvestment of dividends and capital gains before taxes, Jan. 1-June 10, 2005.

Data: Standard & Poor's

The Big Equity Funds Tread Water

Fund	Assets (Billions)	Total Return*
Vanguard 500 Index Inv.	$79.3	−0.38%
Investment Company of America A	63.4	0.16
Washington Mutual Investors A	61.2	0.27
Growth Fund of America A	59.0	1.17
Fidelity Magellan	55.6	−0.47
Standard & Poor's Depositary Rcpts.	48.4	−0.38
Fidelity Contrafund	45.6	2.63
Dodge & Cox Stock	44.4	0.48
Income Fund of America	43.8	−0.56
EuroPacific Growth A	36.9	0.03

*Appreciation plus reinvestment of dividends and capital gains before taxes. Jan.1-June 10, 2005.

Data: Standard & Poor's

Lauren Young

Study Questions

1. In your own words, describe the difference between value funds and growth funds.

2. This article points out that a number of individual stocks including Citigroup, Home Depot, Nokia, and General Electric represent excellent investments at the time the article was published. Given this information, would you prefer to buy the above corporate stocks or a mutual fund that contains these stocks in its investment portfolio? Explain your answer.

3. There are a number of funds that have done well because of an increase in the cost of oil and other natural resources. Describe the relationship between rising costs for oil and other natural resources and the performance of a fund that invests in companies that specialize in developing these same natural resources.

17 REAL ESTATE AND OTHER INVESTMENT ALTERNATIVES

Chapter Overview

Traditionally, Americans have invested in real estate. We begin this chapter by classifying types of real estate as direct and indirect investments. We analyze the investment potential of commercial property and show one method that may be used to calculate the expected profitability of commercial properties. Indirect real estate investments such as real estate syndicates or limited partnerships, real estate investment trusts, first and second mortgages, and participation certificates are discussed in depth. Then we present advantages and disadvantages of real estate investments. We close the chapter with investments in precious metals, gems, and other collectibles. Investing in gold, gold bullion, gold bullion coins, gold stocks, gold futures contracts, silver, platinum, palladium, and rhodium are all discussed in this section. Lastly, collectibles such as rare coins, works of art, antiques, stamps, rare books, sports memorabilia, rugs, Chinese ceramics, paintings, and other items that appeal to collectors and investors are presented.

Learning Objectives

After studying this chapter, you will be able to:

Obj. 1 Identify types of real estate investments.

Obj. 2 Evaluate the advantages of real estate investments.

Obj. 3 Assess the disadvantages of real estate investments.

Obj. 4 Analyze the risks and rewards of investing in precious metals, gems, and other collectibles.

Key Terms

collectibles	participation certificate (PC)	(REIT)
commercial property	passive activity	syndicate
direct investment	passive loss	
indirect investment	real estate investment trust	

Pretest

True-False

_____ 1. (Obj. 1) In direct real estate investment, the investor holds legal title to the property.

_____ 2. (Obj. 1) In indirect investment, the investors appoint a trustee to hold legal title on behalf of all the investors in the group.

_____ 3. (Obj. 1) Passive loss is the total amount of losses from a passive activity minus the total income from the passive activity.

_____ 4. (Obj. 1) Investing in participation certificates is not as secure as Uncle Sam's own bonds and notes.

_____ 5. (Obj. 2) Generally speaking, real property equity investments are not a good hedge against inflation.

_____ 6. (Obj. 2) Financial leverage enables you to acquire a more expensive property than you could acquire on your own.

_____ 7. (Obj. 2) Limited financial liability is one of the biggest disadvantages of investing in limited partnerships.

_____ 8. (Obj. 3) During deflationary and recessionary periods, the value of real property may decline.

_____ 9. (Obj. 3) The Tax Reform Act of 1986 limits the ability of taxpayers to use losses generated by real estate investments to offset income gained from other sources.

_____ 10. (Obj. 4) Collectibles provide current income and they are easy to sell in a hurry.

Self-Guided Study Questions

Obj. 1

Investing in Real Estate (p. 546)

1. How are real estate investments classified?

2. What are the differences between direct and indirect real estate investments?

Direct Real Estate Investments (p. 546)

3. What are some examples of direct real estate investments?

4. What are some examples of indirect real estate investments?

5. What is the definition of commercial property?

6. How do you determine the investment potential of commercial property?

7. What does commercial property include?

8. What type of real property investment is preferred by small investors?

9. How have many investors acquired sizable commercial properties?

10. What is an example of passive activity?

11. What is a passive loss?

12. Why have some investors been favoring undeveloped land for development?

Indirect Real Estate Investments (p. 550)

13. What is a real estate syndicate?

14. How does a limited partnership work?

15. What is a real estate investment trust (REIT)?

16. Who sells indirect real estate investments?

17. What are three types of REITs?

18. What are the differences among equity REITs, mortgage REITs, and hybrid REITs?

19. What are the risks and rewards of investing in REITs?

20. Who is most likely to invest in first and second mortgages?

21. What is a participation certificate (PC)?

22. What are Ginnie Maes and Freddie Macs?

23. Why are Maes and Macs as secure as U.S. Treasury bonds and notes?

24. How can investors buy participation certificates?

Obj. 2

Advantages of Real Estate Investments (p. 552)

A Hedge Against Inflation (p. 553)

25. How do real property equity investments provide protection against purchasing power risk?

Easy Entry (p. 553)

26. How can one gain easy entry in a shopping center investment?

Limited Financial Liability (p. 554)

27. What is your financial liability as a limited partner?

28. Who must bear all financial risks in a general partnership?

No Management Concerns (p. 554)
29. Why are there no management concerns in some real estate investments?

Financial Leverage (p. 554)
30. What is financial leverage?

31. How is financial leverage an advantage in real estate investments?

Obj. 3
Disadvantages of Real Estate Investments (p. 554)

Illiquidity (p. 554)
32. What is perhaps the largest drawback of real estate investments?

Declining Property Values (p. 554)
33. How does deflation affect real estate values?

Lack of Diversification (p. 555)
34. Why is diversification in direct real estate investments difficult?

Lack of a Tax Shelter (p. 555)

35. What is the tax shelter aspect of real estate syndicates after the enactment of the 1986 tax law?

Long Depreciation Period (p. 555)

36. What are the new depreciation guidelines for depreciating real estate investments?

Management Problems (p. 555)

37. How can buying and managing individual properties create management problems?

Obj. 4

Investing in Precious Metals, Gems, and Collectibles (p. 556)

38. What are several methods for buying precious metals?

Gold (p. 556)

39. How are gold prices affected by war, political instability, and inflation?

40. What is the basic unit of gold bullion?

41. How can you avoid storage and assaying problems?

42. How can you invest in gold stocks and gold futures contracts?

Silver, Platinum, Palladium, and Rhodium (p. 557)

43. Why do some investors prefer to invest in silver, platinum, palladium, and rhodium?

Precious Stones (p. 558)

44. What should you keep in mind when you invest in precious stones?

45. Who certifies a precious stone's characteristics?

Collectibles (p. 558)

46. What are collectibles?

47. Why have forgeries become a significant problem in the world of art?

48. What rules must you follow when investing in collectibles?

49. How is collecting for investment purposes very different from collecting as a hobby?

50. What are some caveats if you invest in rare coins?

Post Test

Completion

1. (Obj. 1) With _____ _____, the investor holds legal title to the property.
2. (Obj. 1) The term _____ _____ refers to land and buildings that produce lease or rental income.
3. (Obj. 1) The _____ may be organized as a corporation, as a trust, or, more commonly, as a limited partnership.
4. (Obj. 1) There are three types of real estate investment trusts: equity REIT, mortgage REIT, and _____ REIT.
5. (Obj. 2) If you are _____ _____, you are not liable for losses beyond your initial investment.
6. (Obj. 2) _____ _____ is the use of borrowed funds for investment purposes.
7. (Obj. 3) _____ in direct real estate investments is difficult because of the large size of most real estate projects.
8. (Obj. 4) The basic unit of gold bullion is one _____.
9. (Obj. 4) _____ and other precious stones are not easily turned into cash.
10. (Obj. 4) An acknowledged industry leader in certifying a precious stone's characteristics is _____ _____ _____ _____.

Multiple Choice

_____ 1. (Obj. 1) Real estate investments are classified as
   A. pure and impure.
   B. speculative and nonspeculative.
   C. direct and indirect.
   D. liquid and illiquid.

_____ 2. (Obj. 1) Which one of the following is not an example of commercial property?
   A. your home.
   B. hotels.
   C. office buildings.
   D. stores.

3. (Obj. 1) Which one of the following statements is not correct about real estate syndicates?
   A. Syndicates provide limited financial liability.
   B. Syndicates provide professional management for their members.
   C. Syndicates provide diversification.
   D. Syndicates provide guaranteed rate of return on investment.

4. (Obj. 1) Which one of the following is not an example of a real estate investment trust?
   A. Mortgage REIT
   B. Hybrid REIT
   C. Preferred REIT
   D. Equity REIT

5. (Obj. 1) Participation certificates from the Government National Mortgage Association are called _____ Maes.
   A. Sallie
   B. Ginnie
   C. Fannie
   D. Sonny

6. (Obj. 1) If you want a relatively risk-proof real estate investment, you should invest in
   A. a participation certificate.
   B. a vacation home.
   C. land.
   D. commercial property.

7. (Obj. 2) Real property equity investments usually provide
   A. above average returns on investment.
   B. below average returns on investment.
   C. protection against purchasing power risk.
   D. protection against deflation.

8. (Obj. 2) The use of borrowed funds for investment purposes is called
   A. financial average.
   B. financial yield.
   C. rate of return on investment.
   D. financial leverage.

9. (Obj. 3) During deflationary and recessionary periods, the value of tangible assets usually
   A. increases slightly.
   B. decreases.
   C. remains unchanged.
   D. skyrockets.

_____ 10. (Obj. 4) Diamond prices can be affected by the whims of
   A. the U.S. government.
   B. the South African government.
   C. De Beers Consolidated Mines of South Africa.
   D. the Gemological Institute of America.

Problems, Applications, and Cases

1. If you are a homeowner, when did you buy the house? What price did you pay for it? What improvements did you make during your ownership? How much did the improvements cost? What is the present market value of the house? Subtract the purchase price and the improvements cost from the market value. What is the appreciation value? Divide the appreciation by the number of years you have owned the home to determine average annual appreciation. Calculate annual percentage increase in value. Has the increased value kept pace with inflation? (Use the Consumer Price Index as a guideline for the years of home ownership.)

2. You have just inherited $30,000 from Uncle Harry. Since the inheritance represents excess funds, you would like to invest the $30,000. Determine how you will invest your money using the investment objectives and alternatives given below. Outline (a) your investment objectives, (b) the investment alternatives considered, and (c) why you made particular investment decisions.

   a. What are your investment objectives?

Investment objective	Possible advantages	Possible disadvantages
Safety of capital		
Liquidity		
Steady income		
Growth of capital		
Inflation hedge		
High speculative return		
Combination		

b. What are your investment alternatives?

Investment objective	Possible advantages	Possible disadvantages
Down payment on a home		
Down payment on a rental property		
A limited partnership		
First/second mortgages		
Participation certificates		
Stocks		
Bonds		
Commodities market		
Options market		
Precious metals		

c. Investment(s) selected:

Reasons:

3. Use the following inventory sheet for your collectibles and determine percent appreciation in value since you purchased the collectible.

Item	Date purchased	Today's market value	How value was determined	Appreciation (or depreciation)	Percent appreciation	Consumer price index change
Americana 19th Cent. paintings Folk art Furniture						
Antiques						
Automobiles (antiques and classics)						
Coins: gold/silver						
Commemorative coins & medals						
Diamonds						
Fine jewelry						
Paintings						
Rare books						
Rare coins						
Rugs						
Sports memorabilia						
Stamps						
Western art						
Works of young artists						
Wine						
Other _____						
Other _____						

4. Consult "Money & Investing" section (Section C) of *The Wall Street Journal* to find the commodity futures prices for one troy ounce of

   a. gold

   b. platinum

   c. palladium

   d. silver

5. For each of the following investments, compute the current yield:

Investment	Initial cost	Value-one year later	Yield
a. rare books	$550	$625	_____ %
b. undeveloped land	$20,000	$23,500	_____ %
c. rare coins	$4,400	$3,900	_____ %

Supplementary Case 17-1

Topic: Art Fraud

Text Reference: pp. 560-562

Richard Welch, a recent community-college graduate, received a letter inviting him to participate in a drawing for a free original lithograph by a famous artist. He was asked to return a postcard with his name, address, and phone number. After he returned the postcard, he was telephoned for more information, including his credit-card number.

At some point, the caller asked Richard to buy a print, using such glowing terms as "fabulous opportunity," "onetime offer," "limited edition," and "excellent investment" to describe the purchase. Richard was told that the print was the work of a famous artist who was near death and that its value would increase after the artist's death. He was assured that when the artist died, the company that the caller represented would gladly buy back the print at two to three times what he paid for it and that he could always resell the print elsewhere at a substantial profit. He was told that he would receive a certificate testifying to the "authenticity" of the print. And he was promised a trial examination period with a 30-day money-back guarantee.

Case Questions

1. Does the offer seem genuine to you? Explain your answer.

2. How can Richard protect himself against a phony offer. List at least five suggestions that you would give him.

3. If Richard bought the work of art and discovered fraud, how should he try to resolve his dispute with the company that sold it to him? Where should he complain if the dispute is not resolved?

Supplementary Case 17-2

Topic: The Trouble in Paradise

Text Reference: pp. 550-551

To William D. Sanders, home is a parched, windswept New Mexico ranch that extends over 125 square miles beneath the Sangre de Christo mountains—a world away from the clamor of the real estate industry. The white-haired, denim-clad entrepreneur is patrolling his rugged, high-desert spread from the front seat of a white Ford pickup. "What is great about this place," says the Texas native, his drawl erased by decades spent traveling between cities such as Chicago and London, where he erected companies, "is that you can think."

These days Bill Sanders has plenty to think about. His $20 billion real estate empire, the biggest and most complex in the country, is in serious trouble. There's even a risk it might be dismembered. That would be an enormous comedown for Sanders, who is widely regarded in the industry as the foremost visionary behind the 1990s boom in real estate investment trusts. "He is the senior statesman of our industry," say Mortimre Zuckerman, CEO of REIT Boston Properties. Beyond the real estate world, though, the reclusive Sanders is little known. His extensive talk with *Business Week* over several months was the first in years. Sanders' long-time goal has been to extend his reach across the globe, building giant real estate operating companies. He wants to be the one-stop shop for real estate investors worldwide. But over the years, his empire has suffered big losses because of a bear market that has damaged most real estate equities. The major reason: With real estate at the top of the cycle, investors fear commercial real estate is headed south.

Unfortunately, investors these days hate real estate. Despite the solid cash flow of REITs, the REIT index fell by 23 percent in 1998. One thing that should not be underestimated, however, is Bill Sanders' dedication to REITs. As his pickup travels the dirt tracks of his ranch, Sanders' dream seems as dry as his parched spread.

Case Questions

1. Who is regarded as the foremost visionary in real estate investment trusts?
2. What is William Sanders' long-time goal?
3. What has happened to Sanders' empire, and why?
4. Why do today's investors hate real estate investments?

Supplementary Case 17-3

Topic: Investing in Indium, Ostrich Farming and Gemstones

Text Reference: p. 560

Fraudulent telemarketing firms are selling indium, germanium, selenium, cadmium, and other "strategic metals" at greatly inflated prices. Recently Val Archer received a telephone call from Joe Johnson, an investment adviser. Joe began by assuring Val that "No," he didn't want her to invest a single cent. "Never invest with someone you don't know," he admonished. However, Joe wanted to demonstrate his firm's "research skill" by sharing with Val the forecast that indium was about to experience a significant price increase. Sure enough, the price soon went up.

A second telephone call from Joe didn't solicit an investment either. Joe simply wanted to share with Val a prediction that the price of indium was about to plummet. "Our forecasters will help you decide whether ours is the kind of firm you might someday want to invest with," he added. As predicted, the price of indium subsequently dropped.

By the time Val received a third call, she was a believer. She not only wanted to invest but insisted on it, and with a big enough investment to make up for the opportunities she had missed.

What Val did not know was that Joe had begun with a calling list of 400 names. On the first round of calls, he told 200 prospects that the price of indium would soon go up and the other 200 that it would go down. When the price went up, Joe made a second call to each of the 200 prospects to whom he had given the "correct forecast." Of these, he told 100 that the next price of indium would move up and the other 100 that it would go down.

Once the predicted price decline occurred, Joe had a list of 100 people eager to invest. After all, how could you go wrong with such an infallible source of price forecasts?

Today scam artists like Joe Johnson are turning to the Internet to promote their schemes. They are using online computer services to promote familiar scams such as fraudulent stock offerings and exotic or high-tech investment opportunities such as ostrich farming, gold mining, gemstones, and wireless cable television.

Remember, *never* make an investment decision based solely on information obtained from a single source, whether electronic bulletin board, online chatroom, newspaper or direct-mail ad, telemarketer, or broadcast commercial. The National Fraud Information Center maintains a toll-free Consumer Assistance Service at 1-800-876-7060 to provide consumers with information about telemarketing and online scams. You may also access the Federal Trade Commission on the World Wide Web at http://www.ftc.gov.

Case Questions

1. What can you do to protect yourself from investment swindles like this one.
2. What can the federal and state governments do to stop such scams?
3. What other techniques do investment swindlers use?
4. What questions could you ask that might turn off investment swindlers?

Supplementary Reading 17-1

"Lights! Camera! Rip-Off! How to Tell When a Scam is Born", *Source:* www.ftc.gov, August, 2005.

Lights! Camera! Rip-Off!
How to Tell When a Scam is Born

So you wanna be in pictures? Opportunities for investors abound, but many of them are far less entertaining—and far more likely to fail than their promoters let on. Indeed, according to the Federal Trade Commission, investment opportunities in the entertainment industry may sound glamorous, cutting edge and can't miss, but films, infomercials and the Internet are among the most risky of ventures.

"Potential investors need to be on the alert for grifters who take their money and promise the gold, glitz and glitter we all associate with the entertainment world," said Jodie Bernstein, Director of the FTC's Bureau of Consumer Protection. "Unfortunately, titanic profits are reserved for very few investors or groups of investors—generally, people who know the industry very well and who take a very cautious and studied approach to investing."

Promoters often invite consumers into the "lucrative world of entertainment" with promises of projects that "have already generated profits for industry insiders." But many films never make it to a theater, let alone television or video distribution. Even if a film succeeds at the box office, financial backers usually are the last to recoup their investment from the project. Pitchmen also hawk the profits to be made in special interest television programming. But the success of any new network venture requires a rare combination of creative programming, an ability to get access to cable systems and an ability to draw viewers and advertisers.

In addition, fraudulent telemarketers are marketing "opportunities" to invest in Internet gambling operations and the occasionally profitable world of infomercials—part of the fast-growing direct response industry. Potential investors in cybercasinos should know that Internet gambling is not legal in any state and that fraudulent promoters traditionally overstate the profitability of casinos. As for infomercials, legitimate industry members estimate that only one infomercial in 30 is successful in generating enough sales of the featured product to make any money for investors.

Scamming telemarketers often recommend that consumers transfer their self-directed IRAs (Individual Retirement Arrangements) to finance the investment, claiming that the investment "has been approved for your IRA" and suggesting that it has been evaluated and deemed a prudent, low risk savings instrument. The fact is that the IRS does not approve or evaluate any investments for IRAs.

What's the low down on investing in supposed high-profit, low-risk entertainment-related offerings?

According to the FTC, if you want to invest in a movie, buy a ticket. If you want to invest in cable television, subscribe to a service. And if you want to invest in the Internet, sign up with an Internet service provider.

For more information about avoiding investment scams altogether, write or call the Federal Trade Commission, Consumer Response Center, 6th Street and Pennsylvania Avenue, NW, Washington, DC 20580, or contact the Securities and Exchange Commission (1-800-SEC-0330), or visit them online at www.ftc.gov or www.sec.gov.

Study Questions

1. According to the Federal Trade Commission, what are some of the riskiest investment ventures?

2. How do promoters often lure consumers into the "lucrative world of entertainment"?

3. How can you avoid investment scams?

Supplementary Reading 17-2

Thane Peterson, "Why Collectors Are Crazy For Chinese Art", *Business Week*, December 27, 2004, p. 114.

Why Collectors Are Crazy For Chinese Art

It's not only dynastic porcelain vases. Art mavens are buying contemporary works as well.

Back in the 1960s and 1970s, when Jim Eccles was working as an IBM systems engineer, he fell in love with the work of the late Chinese artist Chao Chung Hsiang, who was then living in New York. Now 69 and retired, Eccles still loves the seven colorful paintings, some abstract and others in a more traditional Chinese style, that he bought for $200 to $500 each. But lately he has thought about selling them. Based on recent auction sales, he figures they can fetch $50,000 to $100,000 each.

With the emergence of free-spending, nouveau riche collectors from mainland China, the Chinese art market is at the start of what may be an extended boom. Buyers are snatching up everything from 3,000-year-old bronze vessels to avant-garde paintings by Chinese-born artists living in China and abroad. Ever since more than 50 Asian bidders, many from China, showed up at a seminal September, 2003, sale of Chinese rarities at the Doyle auction house in New York, prices have been surpassing estimates. Some examples: At this fall's Hong Kong sales, a 1947 ink scroll by the painter Fu Baoshi, who died in 1965, sold for $1.1 million, four times as much as Sotheby's predicted. On Nov. 17, London dealer Giuseppe Eskenazi, who often buys for European and American collectors, paid a record $5.7 million for an 18-inch early Ming Dynasty dish at a Bonhams & Butterfields auction in San Francisco.

Art collecting was one of the "bourgeois" activities purged in the 1960s and '70s during the Cultural Revolution, but it has flourished under recent economic reforms. Dozens of art auction houses have sprung up in China in recent years, the most prominent of which is China Guardian in Beijing.

Experts expect prices to continue rising as China's wealth grows. "The Chinese don't understand why there's such a big price difference between Western art and the greatest Chinese art," says Henry Howard-Sneyd, Sotheby's Hong Kong-based managing director for China and Southeast Asia. For instance, while a Picasso painting sold this spring for $104 million, works by Zhang Daqian, who lived from 1899 to 1983 and is known as "China's Picasso," usually top out at about $1 million. Chinese collectors figure Zhang's paintings should eventually approach Picasso's level.

Is it too late for smaller collectors to dive in? "Oh, God, no," says David Tang, the Hong Kong entrepreneur and art collector who argues that the rise of the Chinese art market "is just beginning."

Before you make any purchases, there are a few things you should know. It's important to buy through reputable dealers. Fakes and copies are rife, particularly of classic paintings and furniture, and even the experts can be fooled. If you're buying within China, stick to recent works. It's illegal to export paintings and artifacts dating before 1949.

One way of approaching the market, says Theow Tow, New York-based deputy chairman of Christie's Americas, is by "looking for categories where mainland Chinese haven't started buying yet but probably will." For instance, Qing-era (1368-1644) and Ming-era (1644-1911) ceramics have soared, in part because Asian buyers most prize later works connected to the Chinese emperors. But experts say Song Dynasty (960-1269) ceramics remain relative bargains. A small 13th century Song Dynasty bowl went for $2,390 at Christie's in Hong Kong on Sept. 21.

CROUCHING RABBIT

Works in stone and pottery from the Han (206 B.C.-220 A.D.) and Tang (618-907) periods remain comparatively cheap. For example, Eskenazi has a small stone Tang-era sculpture of a crouching rabbit on sale for $23,000. Chinese furniture with imperial connections commands a huge premium: A Qing Dynasty bed made from exotic hardwoods went for $847,500 at a Christie's sale in New York in September. But older softwood pieces with no imperial associations sold for as little as $5,000. Some small collectors specialize in Chinese snuff bottles, which sell for $2,000 on up. Check out Christie's snuff bottle sale in March, 2005, and the selection of London dealer Robert Hall at www.snuffbottle.com.

You can also find bargains in China's far-out contemporary art. Prices for the best known artists, such as 39-year-old Zhang Huan, have soared to $40,000 and up. Zhang, who lives in New York, often uses his own body as a canvas and sells photographs of his work. But many promising artists remain affordable. A top pick of Kent Logan, a retired securities executive in Vail, Colo., who owns 120 contemporary Chinese works, is 30-year-old Zhao Bo of Chongqing, in south-central China's Sichuan province. His jazzy street scenes sell for $700 to

$9,000 or so. Julia Colman, co-owner of London's Chinese Contemporary Gallery, which sells Zhao's paintings, also likes painter and photographer Zhang Dali, 41, who documents the social stresses caused by China's modernization. His pieces start at $6,000.

If this art appeals to you, start thumbing through catalogs, visiting galleries, and studying Web sites of galleries and important shows. Dealers with expertise in Chinese art include Eskenazi Ltd. (eskenazi.co.uk) and J.J. Lally in New York for classic ceramics and pottery; Kaikodo in New York (kaikodo.com) and Alisan in Hong Kong (alisan.com.hk) for traditional paintings; and Chinese Contemporary (chinesecontemporary.com) in London, Ethan Cohen Fine Arts in New York (art-net.com/ecohen.html), and the Hanart gallery in Hong Kong (hanart.com) for avant-garde pieces. If you see something you like, don't dally. As Jim Eccles discovered, prices are rising as we speak.

By Thane Peterson

Study Questions

1. What factors are causing Chinese art prices to jump?

2. Do you think the works by Zhang Daqian eventually will approach Picasso's levels? Why or why not?

3. Before you make any art purchases, what are a few things you should know?

18 RETIREMENT PLANNING

Chapter Overview

As increasing numbers of Americans join the 65-and-over ranks, the United States faces a serious question—is this country prepared to meet the demands of a growing elderly population? The evidence that America is growing older is clear. In the last two decades, the 65-and-over population grew twice as fast as the rest of the population. Today, one of every nine Americans—a group of at least 25 million people—is 65 years of age or older. We begin this chapter by recognizing the importance of retirement planning. We show how individuals can analyze their current assets and liabilities to make sure they are suitable for retirement. Then, we suggest that individuals estimate their needs by considering changes in spending patterns and where and how they plan to live. Next, we describe various types of housing suitable for retirees. In estimating retirement expenses, we emphasize that expenses should be adjusted for inflation. Once expenses are estimated, we then turn to the importance of evaluating planned retirement income. Income from Social Security, other public pension plans, employer pension plans, personal retirement plans, and annuities are discussed in depth. Finally, we stress the need for living on retirement income and balancing the retirement budget.

Learning Objectives

After studying this chapter, you will be able to:

Obj. 1 Recognize the importance of retirement planning.

Obj. 2 Analyze your current assets and liabilities for retirement.

Obj. 3 Estimate your retirement spending needs.

Obj. 4 Identify your retirement housing needs.

Obj. 5 Determine your planned retirement income.

Obj. 6 Develop a balanced budget based on your retirement income.

Key Terms

annuity
defined-benefit plan
defined-contribution plan
401(k) (TSA) plan
individual retirement account (IRA)
Keogh plan
reverse annuity mortgage
vesting

Pretest

True-False

_____ 1. (Obj. 1) The ground rules for retirement planning don't change rapidly.

_____ 2. (Obj. 1) Saving money comes naturally to many young people.

_____ 3. (Obj. 2) If your mortgage is largely or completely paid off, you can get a reverse annuity mortgage.

_____ 4. (Obj. 2) Your pension benefits are not considered as marital property.

_____ 5. (Obj. 3) Spending patterns of retirees do not change.

_____ 6. (Obj. 3) Retirees' medical expenses tend to increase with age.

_____ 7. (Obj. 4) The housing needs of people often change as they grow older.

_____ 8. (Obj. 5) Private pension plans are the most widely used source of retirement income.

_____ 9. (Obj. 5) Social Security benefits do not increase automatically if the cost of living has increased during the preceding year.

_____ 10. (Obj. 6) Dipping into savings during your retirement years is inherently wrong.

Self-Guided Study Questions

Obj. 1

Why Retirement Planning? (p. 570)

1. Why is it important to engage in basic retirement planning throughout your working years?

Tackling the Trade-Offs (p. 570)

2. Why is the old adage "you can't have your cake and eat it too" particularly true in planning for retirement?

3. What actions taken today can ensure a comfortable retirement later?

The Importance of Starting Early (p. 570)

4. How many years can you expect to spend in retirement?

5. Why is retirement planning both emotional and financial?

6. What three reasons make financial planning for retirement critical?

The Basics of Retirement Planning (p. 571)

7. What are the four basic steps in retirement planning?

Obj. 2

Conducting a Financial Analysis (p. 572)

8. How do you calculate your net worth now and at retirement?

Review Your Assets (p. 573)

9. What factors must you consider in reviewing your assets?

10. What is a reverse annuity mortgage (RAM)?

11. How should you handle life insurance during retirement years?

Your Assets After Divorce (p. 575)

12. How are pension benefits divided when couples divorce?

Obj. 3

Retirement Living Expenses (p. 576)

13. Why is it impossible to predict the exact amount of money you will need during retirement?

14. What expenses may be lowered or eliminated during retirement?

15. What four expenses may increase during retirement?

Adjust Your Expenses for Inflation (p. 577)

16. Why must you adjust your retirement expenses for inflation?

Obj. 4

Planning Your Retirement Housing (p. 579)

17. What factors should you consider before moving to a new housing location?

Types of Housing (p. 580)

18. Why do housing needs change when people grow older and retire?

19. What housing alternative is preferred by most people approaching retirement age?

20. What is a "universal design home"?

21. Why are contractors building universal design homes from scratch?

Avoiding Retirement Housing Traps (p. 581)

22. Why is research important before making a move to a new housing location?

23. What are some tips from retirement specialists on how to uncover hidden taxes and other costs of a retirement area before moving?

Obj. 5
Planning Your Retirement Income (p. 581)

24. What are some possible sources of income for retirees?

Social Security (p. 581)

25. Is Social Security intended to provide 100 percent of retirement income?

26. When and where should you apply for Social Security benefits?

27. What information would you need to apply for Social Security benefits?

28. What effect will it have on your Social Security benefits if you decide to retire at age 62 instead of 65?

29. Why will the full retirement age be increased in gradual steps until it reaches 67?

30. How do you estimate your retirement benefits?

31. How do you qualify for Social Security retirement benefits?

32. What are the approximate monthly Social Security benefits for workers at age 65?

33. Are Social Security benefits taxable?

34. How are your Social Security benefits affected if you decide to work after you retire?

35. Are Social Security benefits adjusted for inflation?

36. What is the future of Social Security?

Other Public Pension Plans (p. 587)

37. Besides Social Security, what are other government retirement plans?

Employer Pension Plans (p. 588)

38. What is a defined-contribution plan?

39. Why are defined-contribution plans sometimes called individual account plans?

40. What four plans may be included in defined-contribution plans?

41. What is a 401(k) plan?

42. What are tax benefits of a tax-sheltered accounts (TSAs)?

43. What is vesting?

44. What is a defined-benefit plan?

45. What is a pension plan portability?

Personal Retirement Plans (p. 591)

46. What are the two most popular personal retirement plans?

47. What are Individual Retirement Accounts (IRAs)?

48. What is the Roth IRA Plus?

49. What are some advantages of the Roth IRA?

50. What is an education IRA?

51. Should you convert your traditional IRA to a Roth IRA Plus?

52. What is the biggest benefit of an IRA?

53. How do 401(k) contributions compare with IRA contributions?

54. What are Simplified Employee Pension Plans—IRA (SEP-IRA)?

55. In what kinds of investments can you put your IRA funds?

56. What kinds of investments are prohibited for IRA accounts?

57. When can you withdraw from your IRA account?

58. How are IRA withdrawals treated for federal income tax purposes?

59. What are the income tax consequences if you withdraw before age 59½?

60. What is an IRA rollover?

61. What is a Keogh plan?

62. Why should you obtain professional tax advice before using a Keogh plan?

63. When must you start withdrawing from your retirement plans?

Annuities (p. 598)

64. What is a deferred annuity?

65. Who should consider an annuity?

66. How are annuity payments taxed?

67. What are two types of annuities?

68. What are the differences between immediate and deferred annuities?

Options in Annuities (p. 599)

69. What are major settlement options in annuities?

70. Who should select a straight life annuity option?

71. What is an annuity with installments certain?

Which Annuity Is the Best? (p. 600)

72. Which annuity option is best for you?

Will You Have Enough Money During Retirement? (p. 600)

73. What can you do if your planned retirement is less than your estimated retirement expenses?

Obj. 6

Living on Your Retirement Income (p. 601)

74. What is the first step in stretching your retirement income?

Tax Advantages (p. 602)

75. What should you do if you have any questions about your taxes during retirement?

Working During Retirement (p. 602)

76. How can your part-time earnings affect Social Security benefits?

Investing for Retirement (p. 602)

77. What are some suggested investment strategies for the "35-year-olds," "50-year-olds," and "65-year-olds"?

Dipping Into Your Nest Egg (p. 602)

78. Should you draw down your savings during retirement?

Post Test

Completion

1. (Obj. 1) You can expect to spend about _____ years in retirement.
2. (Obj. 1) Retirement planning involves both emotional and _____ components.
3. (Obj. 3) The exact amount of money you will need in retirement is _____ to predict.
4. (Obj. 3) Your daily living expenses will be _____ when you retire than they were when you were working.
5. (Obj. 5) _____ _____ is the most widely used source of retirement income.
6. (Obj. 5) In employer-offered pension plans, a(n) _____ _____ _____ has an individual account for each employee.
7. (Obj. 5) In employer-offered pension plans, a(n) _____ _____ _____ specifies the benefit promised to the employee at the normal retirement age.
8. (Obj. 5) A(n) _____ _____, is a retirement plan for self-employed people and their employees.
9. (Obj. 5) _____ annuities are generally purchased by people of retirement age.
10. (Obj. 5) A(n) _____ annuity is generally purchased by younger people.

Multiple Choice

_____ 1. (Obj. 1) At age 65, what is an average life expectancy of a man?
   A. 9 years
   B. 14 years
   C. 19 years
   D. 25 years

_____ 2. (Obj. 1) At age 65, what is an average life expectancy of a woman?
   A. 9 years
   B. 14 years
   C. 19 years
   D. 25 years

3. (Obj. 1) What is considered the critical age to begin financial planning for retirement?
   A. 24
   B. 35
   C. 45
   D. 55

4. (Obj. 1) What is the first step in planning for your retirement?
   A. Analyze your current assets and liabilities.
   B. Estimate your spending needs.
   C. Evaluate your planned retirement income.
   D. Estimate the inflation rate.

5. (Obj. 3) Which of the following expenses will most likely be lower during your retirement?
   A. Medical
   B. Leisure activities
   C. Gifts and contributions
   D. Federal income tax

6. (Obj. 3) Which of the following expenses will most likely be higher during your retirement years?
   A. Work-related
   B. Clothing
   C. Medical and life insurance
   D. Housing

7. (Obj. 5) What is the most widely used source of retirement income?
   A. Social Security
   B. Employer pension plans
   C. Personal retirement plans
   D. Annuities

8. (Obj. 5) In which of the following employer pension plans must the employer set up an individual account for each employee?
   A. Undefined-benefit
   B. Undefined-contribution
   C. Defined-benefit
   D. Defined-contribution

_____ 9. (Obj. 5) Under what retirement plan does your employer make non-taxable contributions to the plan for your benefit and reduce your salary be the same amount?
   A. Keogh
   B. 401(k)
   C. Gramm-Rudman
   D. Defined-benefit

_____ 10. (Obj. 5) In what types of annuity is the money you pay invested in common stocks or other equities, with the income you receive depending on the investment results?
   A. Installment refund equity
   B. Life annuity with installments certain
   C. Variable annuity
   D. Fixed annuity

Problems, Applications, and Cases

1. Request a statement of your earnings record from the Social Security Administration. The postal cards are available at your local Social Security Administration office and at many U.S. Postal Service branches. There is no charge for this service of the federal government.

   Read the statement closely to understand how the information applies to you. When you receive your Summary Statement of Earnings, study the folder sent with it, entitled *Your Social Security Earnings Record*.

2. Write to the Housing and Urban Development (HUD) Office of Interstate Land Sales Registration (OILSR) to obtain free brochures on out-of-state land developers. Prepare a checklist of factors you will consider before purchasing land for retirement housing needs.

3. Check the want ads, talk with real estate brokers and with friends, and make your own survey of retirement housing costs in your community.

Apartments

furnished apartments are renting for:
$ _____ a month for 1 ½ rooms
$ _____ a month for 2 rooms
$ _____ a month for 3 rooms

unfurnished apartments are renting for
$ _____ a month for 1 ½ rooms
$ _____ a month for 2 rooms
$ _____ a month for 3 rooms

Houses

Four-room houses sell for:
$ _____ to $ _____
Five-room houses sell for:
$ _____ to $ _____
Six-room houses sell for:
$ _____ to $ _____

4. Conduct a survey of workers to determine the types of retirement plans in which they are involved. Request information about both company-sponsored plans and personal investment funds set aside for retirement.

5. Suppose you have $80,000 in savings that earn 5.5 percent interest, compounded quarterly.

   a. How much money could you withdraw each month for 15 years before reducing your savings to zero?

   b. How much money could you withdraw each month for 15 years so as to leave your savings intact?

6. Based on the following information, what annual deposit must a person make to achieve the desired retirement income needs?

   - expected retirement income needs: $22,000 a year
   - number of years to retirement: 37 years
   - expected rate of return on investment funds: 9%
   - expected annual inflation rate: 4%

   Required annual deposit $ _____

Supplementary Case 18-1

Topic: Determining Retirement Income Needs

Text Reference: pp. 581-601

Fred Reinero is 42 and single, and has an after-tax annual income of $30,000. His annual living expenses are $28,000, and he saves the remaining $2,000. Fred believes he needs 80 percent of his annual income, or $22,400, during his retirement years to maintain his current standard of living. Of course, this amount does not allow for increases in the cost of living. Fred plans to retire at age 62 and expects to live 18 years in retirement.

Case Questions

1. How much of a nest egg, in current dollars, will Fred need to finance his retirement?
2. Assuming a 4 percent rate of inflation, how much money will Fred need during his first year of retirement? (Use the Inflation Factor Table on page 579.)

Supplementary Case 18-2

Topic: Housing Options for Retirees

Text Reference: p. 580

Helen, 66, a resident of the suburban area of a large eastern city, lives alone in the house that she and her husband bought when they were first married. She has three adult children, all of whom live in other parts of the country. Helen's income is modest—she works as a salesclerk in a department store. She took this job soon after her husband's death because she could not support herself and her teenage son, the only child who was still living at home, on the insurance and Social Security benefits left by her husband.

Helen has found it increasingly difficult to maintain her large house. The costs of heating and cooling it have increased, and she must pay for minor repairs and yard work. Helen has spent most of her holidays and vacations with one of her children. However, she is quite lonely, and she misses her children and grandchildren.

Helen will retire soon. She has three financial goals: (1) to maintain enough income to support herself after she retires, (2) to have enough savings to meet emergencies, and (3) to eliminate some of the expense and responsibility of maintaining a large house.

Helen's daughter, Janet, had tried for several years to get her mother to move in with her and her family. Helen resisted until recently, afraid of losing her independence and becoming a burden. Now that Janet is divorced and could use day-to-day help with her two children, Helen has reconsidered. She realizes that once she moves in with Janet, she can sell her house and use the money for savings and living expenses. However, after careful thought, Helen has decided not to sell her house in case living with her daughter does not work out. Instead, she has arranged to have a real estate company find tenants, manage the property, collect the rent, and mail it to her (minus the company's fees) each month.

Helen knows that she should review and update her will so that her property will be handled according to her wishes if she dies or becomes unable to handle her own affairs. Because of the income that she expects from rent and Social Security and the decreased expenses that will result from sharing her daughter's household, Helen is looking forward to retirement.

Case Questions

1. What are some of the housing options that might be available to Helen after her retirement? What might be some advantages and disadvantages of each of these options?

2. Do you agree with Helen's decision to move in with her daughter? Why? What might be a few disadvantages of this choice?

3. Is it a sound financial idea for Helen not to sell her house? Why?

Supplementary Reading 18-1

"Do-It-Yourself Retirement; The Burden of Funding One's Later Years Has Shifted Irrevocably", *Business Week,* July 25, 2005, p. 116.

Do-It-Yourself Retirement

The Burden of Funding One's Later Years Has Shifted Irrevocably

Mention retirement, and many people dreamily imagine quiet days on the golf course or long walks on the beach. But as the burden of assuring retirement security is increasingly shifted from employers and the government onto the backs of workers, a far less tranquil picture is emerging. Millions of baby boomers are financially unprepared as they approach traditional retirement age. A staggering half of households headed by 50-to-59-year-olds have $10,000 or less in their 401 (k) accounts, for instance, even as public and employer retirement benefits are being trimmed. To avoid a crisis, government, businesses, and employees must make critical choices in the coming years.

Washington's role in all this is smaller than many people think. That's because the feds already have approved a host of tax-advantaged retirement savings products, such as individual retirement accounts, 401 (k)-type savings plans, and annuities. Across-the-board expansion of such incentives usually results in more-affluent workers shifting existing savings from taxable accounts into new tax-advantaged accounts—costing the Treasury billions in lost revenues without spurring much new saving. So federal efforts to boost retirement savings should target poor and working-class households, which have lower savings rates.

To do this the Bush Administration would be wise to note the encouraging results of a recent H & R Block-sponsored study that found IRA use skyrocketed when the contributions of low- and moderate-income taxpayers were matched at varying percentage levels. When such taxpayers were not offered matching payments, only 3% contributed to an IRA. When a 50% IRA match was offered, the participation rate jumped more than fivefold, to 17%. The cost to the Treasury would be only about $15 billion—10% of what it currently costs the government to subsidize the retirement savings accounts of mostly middle- and upper-class taxpayers—yet it could jump-start retirement saving among millions of people who need it most. The Treasury also should consider allowing income tax refunds to be split between two accounts, enabling a taxpayer to deposit a portion into a bank account and the rest directly into an IRA or other retirement savings account—a low-cost fix.

Still, government action is only part of the solution. Companies must expand the use of so-called automatic 401 (k) plans, which enroll employees in retirement savings plans unless they opt out. This approach, used by about a quarter of large companies, including J.C. Penney Corp. and IBM, typically boosts 401 (k) participation by new workers more than 50%. Participation rates and contribution amounts also jump when businesses offer more investment help for often-confused workers. Next, financial-services companies must do a better job of creating retirement and long-term care products that have cheaper fees and are easier to understand.

Finally, workers must accept that the era of employer paternalism is over—and the demise of nanny government may not be far behind. So relying solely on Social Security, Medicare, and a company pension for retirement security is risky at best. The smarter, safer approach is to plan for a future wherein retirees work longer, pay more for medical and long-term care, and receive lower Social Security and pension payments than previous generations did. This tough new retirement reality won't be a stroll down the beach. But if workers aren't prepared for the worst, their retirement years may turn out to be anything but golden.

The McGraw-Hill Companies, Inc.

Study Questions

1. What do many people imagine when you mention the word "retirement"?

2. What did a recent H & R Block-sponsored study find regarding the use of IRAs?

3. Should the U. S. Treasury consider allowing income tax refunds to be split between two accounts? Explain.

4. How can companies expand the use of automatic 401 (k) plans?

Supplementary Reading 18-2

Ellen Hoffman, "Greener Pastures for Golden Years", *Business Week Online*, Feb. 11, 2005.

Greener Pastures for Golden Years

Where you live in retirement can profoundly influence how happy and secure this time in life will be. Here's a primer on what to consider.

What's the best place to live when you retire? How you answer this question could make a big difference in your lifestyle, your budget, and maybe even your physical and mental health over a couple of decades or more.

With the baby boomers on the verge of retirement, the options for retirement living are proliferating to include everything from a golf-course community to a university town or—a popular choice—simply a different house or apartment in your current neighborhood or metropolitan area.

The 2000 Census found that of 6.2 million people age 55 to 64 who moved from 1995 to 2000, 3.6 million did so within the county where they lived, 1.3 million moved elsewhere in the same state, and 1.3 million moved to a different state. In *Retirement Migration in America*, a book to be published later this year, author Charles Longino of Wake Forest University lists the most popular destinations for people age 60 and older. Maricopa County, Arizona (Phoenix) and Palm Beach, Fla., are the top two, and 7 of the top 10 are in Florida.

UPSIZING A NEST EGG. This and other census data suggest that climate is a major factor in choosing a retirement location, but you should consider many others: proximity to family and friends, cultural offerings, financial issues, and what you plan to do in retirement—from travel to playing golf and taking classes. Ideally, your choice should take all these into consideration.

Here's an example of how it worked out for one woman in her early 60s. When she retirement from her corporate-management job, proximity to her former workplace was less important. She moved about 20 miles, downsizing from a three-bedroom townhouse to a less-expensive, two-bedroom condominium in a gated community. Now she can choose from a variety of activities, including a fitness club, photo lab, sewing class, and computer club. She feels safer—a big plus as people age—because of the gated community. Plus, she was able to pocket extra cash in her nest egg from the sale of her townhouse.

Whether you're thinking of staying nearby or moving far away, you'll need to set some criteria to identify possible locations. For state- and county-level data on areas you may be considering, start with Web sites such as the Census Bureau's Census Quick Facts, which offers snapshots on issues such as population, age of population, education level, and income. Want to know what the tax bite might be? You can find state-by-state information on income, property, sales, or estate taxes at the Retirement Living Information Center's Taxes by State site.

MANY INTANGIBLES. On some interactive Web sites, you can express preferences about climate, health-care facilities, proximity to an airport, safety and crime considerations, and cost of living. Such sites—using search terms such as "best places" and "retirement places"—help pinpoint some key criteria. However, they have their limitations. When I entered my priorities on one site, it listed my ideal retirement spots as 25 towns in New Jersey. With 25 options, I would've expected more diversity in location.

As that experience suggests, deciding where to live should also be based on additional more personal, criteria—and often more subtle. Gene D. Cohen, director of the Center on Aging, Health & Humanities at George Washington University in Washington, D.C., says the ideal retirement location should be "a vital community in terms of social interaction" and offer opportunities for intellectual and cultural challenges and stimulation. It should also provide access to "backup resources," such as good health-care services.

"Social interaction" criteria encompass proximity to family and friends. It requires you to think about whether, if you move far away, you'll be able to make new friends easily and how important it is to be near your family.

WALK THE WALK. Cohen suggests that you search for a retirement location with lots of potential for social contact and for intellectual experiences and challenges, such as taking courses or learning a new hobby. Why? Because research shows these factors are actually "associated with positive health outcomes" as we age.

What happens next, once you've done preliminary research on basics such as climate and cost of living? The best way to find a place where you might want to live in retirement: visit and spend time there—perhaps on more than one vacation—so you get a feeling for the lifestyle and the culture.

Depending on the type of environment you want, several varieties retirement-living situations could satisfy Cohen's criteria. One is to move a short distance from the suburbs where your kids grew up, into a center city, such as Washington, D.C. This would offer easy access to educational, cultural, and medical resources, and the opportunity to stay in touch with friends in the area. Alternately, you could move to a small town that's within, say, an hour's drive to a city.

BUDDING MARKET. You could also look for one of the select but growing number of "elder-friendly" neighborhoods, such as the 10 in the AdvantAge Initiative. This is a network of communities around the country that are consciously building a system of social, health-care, and other opportunities and services to enable residents to remain in their homes—even if they become frail and ill in later years.

Lastly, "retirement communities," usually restricted to people 50 or 55 or older, offer a wide range of activities to stimulate your mind and body, as well as the convenience of nearby transportation, shopping, and health care.

The prospect of millions of mobile, well-educated, economically secure baby boomers approaching retirement has stirred the real estate industry not only to build and sell homes in retirement communities but also to develop a training program and credential, the "Seniors Real Estate Specialist," for brokers and agents who want to specialize in working with older clients. You can find one of these certified agents at the Seniors Real Estate Specialists site.

THE PAYOFF. Bill Buss, a Laguna Hills (Calif.) agent who holds this certification, says he has created a network of colleagues to help him work with older clients. They include accountants, attorneys, and moving companies. He has even included an expert in antiques and collectibles who can advise downsizing clients on items to keep, toss, or sell when moving.

After all, Buss says, choosing a place to retire "isn't just about buying another house. It's a transition to another phase to life." Securing the quality you want in this phase of life deserves concerted time and attention because chances are, after all, you'll want to want to make this not only your last home, but your best.

http://www.businessweek.com/bwdaily/dnflash/feb2005/nf20050211_7492_db026.htr

Ellen Hoffman

Study Questions

1. According to the census data, what is the major factor in choosing a retirement location?

2. What other factors should you consider in choosing a retirement location?

3. What are some helpful Web sites that may help you in choosing a retirement location?

4. According to Gene D. Cohen, what is the ideal retirement location?

Supplementary Reading 18-3

Ellen Hoffman, "Time to Abandon the 70% Solution", *Business Week Online*, March 11, 2005.

Time to Abandon the 70% Solution

The one-size-fits-all approach to estimating your future retirement spending is obsolete. Try this four-step strategy instead.

Financial planning for retirement consists of three basic steps: estimating your financial needs and goals, creating a plan to meet those goals, and implementing the plan. If you don't complete the first step, your chances of succeeding at the other two diminish significantly.

For many years the rule of thumb said that to maintain your preretirement lifestyle, you needed 70% of your preretirement income. An Internet search of retirement-planning Web sites turns up this guidance over and over again.

Don't believe it. Instead, consider newer advice offered by many financial planners: Start by analyzing your preretirement expenses and then making adjustments on a line-by-line basis. That's the most effective method, says Patrick Doland, a financial planner in Northbrook, Ill. With this method, you're more likely to get a result that makes sense for you.

TOUCH CHOICES. The closer you are to retiring, the more detailed you should make your list of anticipating spending. But that doesn't mean you have to—or should—wait until retirement to start. Lauren Klein, a financial planner of Newport Beach, Calif., recommends doing your estimates now, before you're preparing to leave the workforce. Remember to update your estimates periodically.

Keeping an eye on retirement can also help you make day-to-day decisions. Take a couple in their 50s who had "marginal" financial resources for their retirement, although they were hoping to retire soon. They asked Klein to help them figure out how to pay for their third child's college education and for a new, $50,000 kitchen they "needed." After talking to Klein and calculating the impact of these other expenses on their retirement, the couple started looking into loans to pay for college, put the kitchen project on hold, and gave up on the idea of an early retirement.

Decisions like this are tough, but if you take the time to go through the following four-step process, you'll have a better idea of what you really need.

1. Itemize and add up your current expenses. Make the list as complete as possible, covering housing, utilities, health care, transportation, insurance, entertainment, vacations, taxes, and even contributions to retirement or college accounts or other savings.

Checking-account records, credit-card statements, and tax records can help you come up with a complete list. It may help to break the list down into routine monthly expenses (mortgage payments, utilities, etc.) and annual ones (income taxes, property insurance, etc.)

2. Estimate which expenses will disappear. These may include commuting costs, your "dress for success" wardrobe, lunches, and contributions to retirement accounts. Tally these disappearing expenses, then subtract that amount from your current spending total.

3. List what expenses you'll add. Be sure to consider the cost of your ideal lifestyle, which may include more travel and entertainment, or large gifts to your grandchildren. And don't forget to add on potential health-care costs. These include premiums and co-payments you'll need for Medicare. If you're retiring before age 65, include what it will cost to pay for health insurance out of your own pocket. Add this list of new retirement expenses to the total from the second step.

4. Decide what you can live without. Until you do, the dollar figure that you've come up with lacks authenticity. Separate out the essential expenses from discretionary ones. Essentials will include food and health-care, plus housing and such related costs as property taxes, utilities, and homeowner's insurance.

Travel, entertainment, and maintaining two vehicles instead of one are examples of discretionary areas you may need to reduce or eliminate.

The calculations I've described appear pretty straightforward, but experts caution that overlooking or miscalculating just one or two items can make a big difference in whether your retirement budget will succeed or fail.

A recent study by Barbara Butrica and other Urban Institute researchers found that the biggest retirement expense for most people is housing, which amounted to 37% of expenses for married couples and 42% for individuals with an aftertax income of at least $49,000. If you need to look for costs to cut, concentrate on housing.

Health care gets tricky due to the difficulty of predicting both your health and the price of medical care. Probably, the best you can do is to learn how Medicare works so that you're aware of at least the minimum costs you'll face after age 65, and include them in your budget.

The biggest remaining issue: inflation. Try this calculator for an idea of past inflation rates. It shows, for example, that if you were living on an income of $60,000 in 1990, you needed nearly $85,000 by the end of 2003. If you use a financial adviser, you can also ask him or her for software that helps calculate inflation's impact on your retirement expenses.

No amount of preretirement calculation can predict your expenses with complete accuracy. But taking the time to start now offers the best hope that you'll have adequate resources not only for what you need but also for what you want.

http://www.businessweek.com/bwdaily/dnflash/mar2005/nf20050311_5138_db026.ht

Ellen Hoffman

Study Questions

1. What are the three basic steps in financial planning for retirement?

2. What are some touch choices to make as you get closer to retirement?

3. What is the four-step process that will give you a better idea of what you will need in retirement?

4. Why is inflation the biggest remaining issue as you plan for your retirement?

19 ESTATE PLANNING

Chapter Overview

This chapter presented us with a delicate challenge. On the one hand, estate planning should be taken very seriously. On the other hand, reading about it can be, well, deadly. We begin with the importance of estate planning. Its goal is to assure that the estate's assets go to the rightful heirs, not Uncle Sam. Next, we present personal aspects of estate planning, noting that if you are married, estate planning involves the interest of at least two people. But never having been married does not eliminate the need to organize your papers. Then, we discuss the legal aspects of estate planning. Simple will, traditional marital share will, exemption trust will, and stated dollar will are described and compared. We offer tips in writing a will, selecting an executor, and altering or rewriting a will. Next, we differentiate among living trust, testamentary trust, insurance trust, and lifetime gifts and trusts. We conclude the chapter with an explanation of federal and state taxes imposed on estates. The four types of taxes—estate taxes, estate income taxes, inheritance taxes, and gift taxes, are described.

Learning Objectives

After studying this chapter, you will be able to:

Obj. 1 Analyze the personal aspects of estate planning.

Obj. 2 Assess the legal aspects of estate planning.

Obj. 3 Distinguish among various types and formats of wills.

Obj. 4 Appraise various types of trusts and estates.

Obj. 5 Evaluate the effects of federal and state taxes on estate planning.

Key Terms

adjusted gross estate	disclaimer trust	gift tax
beneficiary	estate	guardian
charitable lead trust	estate planning	holographic will
charitable remainder trust	estate tax	inheritance tax
codicil	exemption trust will	intestate
community property	formal will	irrevocable trust
credit-shelter trust	generation-skipping trust	life insurance trust

living trust
living will
marital deduction trust
power of attorney
prenuptial agreement
qualified personal residence trust (QPRT)

revocable trust
self-declaration trust
simple will
spend thrift trust
stated dollar amount will
statutory will
testamentary trust

traditional marital share will
trust
trustee
trustor
will

Pretest

True-False

_____ 1. (Obj. 1) Most people now live long lives.

_____ 2. (Obj. 1) Never having been married eliminates the need to organize your important documents.

_____ 3. (Obj. 2) In case of death, proof of claims must be produced, or the claims will not be processed.

_____ 4. (Obj. 2) The Economic Recovery Tax Act of 1981 created estate planning opportunities and problems for many people.

_____ 5. (Obj. 3) If your spouse had separate property or if the value of your estate increased, the simple will would cause lower taxation.

_____ 6. (Obj. 3) The exemption trust will has been decreasing in popularity due to its increased exemption ($675,000 in 2001).

_____ 7. (Obj. 3) A statutory will is one type of formal will.

_____ 8. (Obj. 4) A trust is a property arrangement through which your assets are held by a trustee for your benefit or for that of your beneficiaries.

_____ 9. (Obj. 5) Whatever you give your spouse is exempt from gift and estate taxes.

_____ 10. (Obj. 5) Inheritance taxes are imposed only by the federal government.

Self-Guided Study Questions

Obj. 1

Why Estate Planning? (p. 614)

What Is Estate Planning (p. 614)

1. Why is estate planning an essential part of retirement planning?

2. What is an estate?

3. What are the two components of estate planning?

If You Are Married (pp. 614-615)

4. What are some of the personal aspects of estate planning if you are married?

If You Are Never Married (p. 615)

5. What are some of the personal aspects of estate planning if you never married?

New Lifestyles (p. 616)

6. What are some unique estate planning problems for millions of non-traditional households?

The Opportunity Cost of Rationalizing (p. 616)

7. What are the consequences of not planning your estate?

8. Why is it essential to plan your estate while you are in good health?

Obj. 2

Legal Aspects of Estate Planning (pp. 617-618)

9. What are the legal aspects of estate planning?

10. What are some important necessary documents, and how can they be obtained?

Wills (p. 618)

11. What is a will?

12. What is an intestate?

13. What are the effects of marriage or divorce on a will?

14. What is the cost of preparing a standard will?

Obj. 3

Types and Formats of Wills (pp. 620-621)

15. What are the various types of wills?

16. What is a simple will?

17. What are the characteristics of a traditional marital share will?

18. What is an exemption trust will?

19. What is the main advantage of the exemption trust will?

20. What is a stated dollar amount will?

21. What is one major shortcoming of the stated dollar amount will?

22. How do you determine which type of will is best for you?

Formats of Wills (pp. 621-622)

23. What is a holographic will?

24. Is a holographic will valid in all states?

25. What is a formal will?

26. Must two witnesses sign the formal will in your presence?

27. What is a statutory will?

28. What are serious risks in leaving a statutory will?

Writing Your Will (p. 622)

29. What precautions should you take in writing a will?

30. Who is an executor or an executrix?

31. What are some guidelines in selecting an executor?

32. Who sets the fees for executors?

33. What is a guardian?

34. What is a trustee?

35. What precautions should you take in selecting a guardian?

36. What is the difference between a guardian and a trustee?

Altering or Rewriting Your Will (p. 624)
37. How do you alter an existing will?

38. What circumstances should trigger you to review your will?

39. What is a codicil?

40. What is the purpose of a prenuptial agreement?

A Living Will (pp. 624-625)
41. What is a living will?

42. Who should have a living will?

43. How can you ensure the effectiveness of a living will?

44. How can a living will become a problem?

Power of Attorney (p. 626)
45. What is a power of attorney?

Letter of Last Instruction (p. 627)
46. What is a letter of last instruction?

47. What should a letter of last instruction contain?

48. What is the purpose of a letter of last instruction?

Obj. 4
Types of Trusts and Estates (p. 628)
49. What is a trust?

50. What is the trustor or grantor?

51. What is a revocable trust?

52. What is an irrevocable trust?

53. Which trust offers tax advantages?

Benefits of Establishing Trusts (p. 628)

54. What are some common reasons for setting up a trust?

Types of Trusts (pp. 629-632)

55. What are the benefits of establishing a trust?

56. Who can provide trustee services?

57. What is a credit-shelter trust?

58. What are some other names for a credit-shelter trust?

59. What is a disclaimer trust?

60. What is a living or inter-vivos trust?

61. What are the advantages of a living trust?

62. What are the unique features of a testamentary trust?

63. What is a pourover will?

64. What is a life insurance trust?

Estates (pp. 633-634)

65. What is an estate?

66. What is meant by community property?

67. Why is joint ownership of property between spouses very common?

68. What is joint tenancy with the right of survivorship (JT/WROS)?

69. What is tenancy in common?

70. What is tenancy by entirety?

71. How are life insurance and employee benefits treated for income tax and probate purposes?

72. What are the tax consequences if lifetime gifts and trusts have strings attached to them?

73. How is the estate settled?

Settling Your Estate (pp. 634-635)

74. Who carries out your wishes if you die "intestate"?

Obj. 5

Federal and State Estate Taxes (p. 635)

75. What has happened to the maximum tax rate on estates and gifts?

Types of Taxes (pp. 635-636)

76. What are the four major taxes you should consider in estate planning?

77. What is an estate tax?

78. Who levies an estate tax?

79. What is the difference between an estate tax and an estate federal income tax?

80. Who imposes inheritance taxes?

81. What is a gift tax?

82. Who levies a gift tax?

Tax Avoidance and Tax Evasion (p. 637)

83. What is the difference between tax avoidance and tax evasion?

84. What charitable gifts and bequests are exempted from taxes?

Calculating the Tax (pp. 637-638)

85. How is estate tax calculated?

86. What is net taxable estate?

87. What are probate and administration costs?

88. How is your taxable estate determined?

Paying the Tax (p. 638)

89. How is the estate tax paid?

90. What are some ways of handling the estate tax?

Post Test

Completion

1. (Obj. 1) The need to take estate planning steps is especially great if you are only _____ or _____ years away from retirement.

2. (Obj. 2) A(n) _____ is the legal declaration of a person's mind as to disposition of his or her property after his or her death.

3. (Obj. 2) If you die without a will, you are called a(n) _____.

4. (Obj. 3) An "I love you" will is known as a(n) _____ _____.

5. (Obj. 3) A(n) _____ _____ is a handwritten will that you prepare yourself.

6. (Obj. 3) A(n) _____ is a document that explains, adds, or deletes provisions in your existing will.

7. (Obj. 3) A documentary agreement between spouses before marriage is called a(n) _____ _____.

8. (Obj. 3) A(n) _____ _____ _____ is a legal document authorizing someone to act on your behalf.

9. (Obj. 4) In a(n) _____ trust, you retain the right to end the trust or change its terms during your lifetime.

10. (Obj. 5) Your estate administration costs run between _____ and _____ percent of your estate.

Multiple Choice

1. (Obj. 1) A definite plan for the administration and disposition of one's property during one's lifetime and at one's death is called
   A. a trust.
   B. an intestate.
   C. a codicil.
   D. estate planning.

2. (Obj. 2) A legal declaration of a person's mind as to the disposition of his or her property after his or her death is called a(n)
   A. trust.
   B. estate.
   C. codicil.
   D. will.

3. (Obj. 3) An "I love you" will is sometimes called a(n) _____ will.
   A. simple
   B. compound
   C. traditional
   D. exemption trust

4. (Obj. 3) Which type of will has been gaining popularity due to the increased exemption?
   A. Simple
   B. Stated dollar amount
   C. Exemption trust
   D. Traditional marital share

5. (Obj. 3) A handwritten will that you prepare yourself is called a(n) _____ will.
   A. formal
   B. holographic
   C. beneficiary
   D. statutory

6. (Obj. 3) Which document explains, adds, or deletes provisions in your existing will?
   A. Prenuptial agreement
   B. Trust agreement
   C. Power of attorney
   D. Codicil

_____ 7. (Obj. 3) A person who assumes the responsibilities of providing the children with personal care and of managing an estate for them is called
A. trustor.
B. trustee.
C. guardian.
D. beneficiary.

_____ 8. (Obj. 3) Which legal document authorizes someone to act on your behalf?
A. Power of attorney
B. Letter of instruction
C. Trust agreement
D. Prenuptial agreement

_____ 9. (Obj. 4) A trust established by your will that becomes effective upon your death is called a _____ trust.
A. living
B. testamentary
C. revocable
D. willed

_____ 10. (Obj. 5) Probate and administration costs of your estate may run between _____ percent of your estate.
A. 2-4
B. 5-8
C. 9-12
D. 15-20

Problems, Applications, and Cases

1. Interview an employee of a bank to determine the types of trusts the financial institution has available. Use the following form to summarize your findings.

Type of trust	Features	Advantages	Disadvantages

2. Conduct a survey of lawyers to determine the costs of having a will prepared. What factors influence these fees?

3. Draft your living will based on examples shown in Exhibits 19-3 and 19-4.

4. Make a list of desirable qualities you would want in a guardian for your minor children.

5. What is a tentative unified transfer tax for a decedent who dies in 1999 and makes a gift of $1,250,000 just before dying? Use the table as shown in Exhibit 19-7.

6. Fill out this sheet and provide copies to all those individuals whom you wish to attend to these important matters.

What to do when the emergency comes

(Helpful information for others)

In case of serious illness or my death, my doctors should be called as quickly as possible. (The doctor may, in turn, suggest calling the most available ambulance or emergency service. The numbers listed here should also be listed near a telephone.)

Doctor

Telephone

Ambulance or emergency service

Telephone

Call a relative or friend who can immediately assist you in handling some of the details listed on this page.

Name

Telephone

Call a clergy member (if desired).

Name

Telephone

Call a funeral director

Name

Telephone

Newspapers in which the obituary notice should be published.

Name of newspaper

Address

Newspaper

Address

(The funeral director generally assumes this responsibility. However, check with director if out-of-town notifications of death are to be published.) After funeral arrangements and other priority matter are completed, take care of the following:

You'll need death certificates—have about 15 copies made.

Notify employer, insurance companies, associations, banks, and other institutions.

Visit or call:
The local VA office

Address

Telephone

The local Social Security office:

Address

Telephone

The information on this page conveys a sense of immediacy. Thus, it should be readily available for others.

Courtesy of Aetna Life & Casualty, 151 Farmington Ave., Hartford, CT 06156.

Supplementary Case 19-1

Topic: Retirement and Estate Planning in a High-Income Family

Rich, 48, and Mariann, 47, have a gross estate of $1,160,000 and a high family income. Last year, their combined gross income was about $175,000, most of which came from a medical clinic in which Rich and several other physicians are partners. The remaining income came from Mariann's part-time job and from interest and dividends on various stocks, bonds, mutual funds, tax-sheltered investments, and rental property that Rich holds.

Rich and Mariann also own, in joint tenancy with right of survivorship, a home, a summer home, and an undeveloped lot in another state; and Mariann will receive $100,000 from a trust fund next year. Their net worth is about $510,000.

Since their holdings are extensive, Rich and Mariann contacted an estate planner for help in determining the most advantageous way of organizing their estate. Naturally, they wanted to be sure that the estate was set up in such a way as to minimize tax and probate shrinkage when it was passed on, first to the surviving spouse and ultimately to their four children. They also wanted to accumulate additional assets and to minimize their income taxes.

Case Questions

1. Should Rich and Mariann retitle some of the assets they currently hold in joint tenancy, so as to take advantage of the unified estate and gift-tax credit? Why?

2. Should Rich and Mariann establish a gifting program to reduce their income taxes and build up education funds for their children? Why or why not?

Supplementary Case 19-2

Topic: Retirement and Estate Planning in a Middle-Income Family

Bob, 42, an account executive for a manufacturing company, makes $55,000 a year. Judy, 42, a teacher, makes $43,000 a year.

With a son and a daughter, aged 15 and 13, respectively, Bob and Judy first want to make sure that they have enough money to pay for their children's education. They also want to make sure that they can retire at about 75 percent of their current monthly income when Bob is 64. Finally, Bob and Judy want to know how these goals and the overall status of their estate would be affected if either of them became disabled or died prematurely.

Case Questions

1. Assuming a modest rate of growth in their current capital plus monthly additions by each of them, do you think that Bob and Judy will be able to finance their children's education? Would you recommend that they establish an education fund?

2. If Judy were to die prematurely, would the family face an income shortage? What if Bob died?

3. What suggestions do you have for Bob and Judy's estate planning? For example, what type of will do you recommend, and do you recommend a trust arrangement?

Supplementary Reading 19-1

"Should You Hire a Professional to Prepare and File Estate Tax Return?", August 20, 2005.

Should You Hire a Professional to Prepare and File Estate Tax Return?

The Internal Revenue Service cannot make recommendations about specific individuals, but there are several factors to consider.

1. How complex is the estate? By the time most estates reach $1,000,000, there is usually some complexity involved.
2. How large is the estate?
3. In what condition are the decedent's records?
4. How many beneficiaries are there and are they cooperative?
5. Do I need an attorney, CPA, Enrolled Agent (EA) or other professional(s)?

With these questions in mind, it is a good idea to discuss the matter with several attorneys and CPAs or EAs. Ask about how much experience they have had and ask for referrals. This process should be similar to locating a good physician. Locate other individuals that have had similar experiences and ask for recommendations. Finally, after the individual(s) are employed and begin to work on estate matters, make sure the lines of communication remain open so that there are no surprises during administration or if the estate tax return is examined.

Finally, most estates engage the services of both attorneys and CPAs or EAs. The attorney usually handles probate matters and reviews the impact of documents on the estate tax return. The CPA or EA often handles the actual return preparation and some representation of the estate in matters with the IRS. However, some attorneys handle all of the work. CPAs and EAs may also handle most of the work, but cannot take care of probate matters and other situations where a law license is required. In addition, other professionals (such as appraisers, surveyors, financial advisors and others) may need to be engaged during this time.

Source: http://www.irs,gov/businesses/small/article/0,,id=108143,00.html, August 20, 2005.

Study Questions

1. What factors should you consider before hiring an individual to prepare the estate tax return?

2. How would you select a professional to prepare the return?

3. Should you hire the services of both attorneys and CPAs? Why or why not?

Supplementary Reading 19-2

"The Importance of Estate Planning"

The Importance of Estate Planning

Waiting too long can be very costly, say the pros. Too often people either don't want to think about death and incompetency or they do not have enough information to make informed decisions. Then a problem occurs, and by then many valuable planning opportunities have been lost. Anyone with a home, savings, or minor children should consult an experienced estate planning attorney.

The term *estate planning* generally refers to the legal issues involved in planning for death, incompetency, and reducing or avoiding estate taxes. The process for settling a deceased person's affairs is called *probate*. Probate is a court process with two primary goals (1) to make sure all debts are paid, and (2) to distribute property to the proper recipients. A will is a set of your instructions to a probate court judge for settling your affairs. A will allows you to avoid some of the more expensive aspects of probate. If you have minor children, a will is an absolute necessity for naming guardians, who will raise your children if you and your spouse are deceased. If you don't have a will, your state will give you a will by statute. This is called *intestate probate*. Intestate probate usually takes much longer and is more expensive. Everyone should at least have a will or risk leaving the families with a lot of unnecessary cost and aggravation.

Planning for incompetency may be even more important than planning for death. What will happen if, because of age or illness, you are unable to make decisions for yourself? Everyone should have durable powers of attorney for health care and property management. A *durable power of attorney* is a document that authorizes the person you choose to make decisions for you if you cannot make decisions for yourself. A *living will* is a statement of intent that you do not want your life to be artificially prolonged by a life support system.

A *living trust* is a modern approach to solving many of the problems of basic estate planning. A properly established living trust avoids probate and guardianship and may reduce or eliminate estate taxes. When you create a living trust, you establish a new legal "person" that becomes the owner of your property. You do not give up any control of your affairs. Typically, you are the trustee (the manager of your property) and the beneficiary (the person entitled to the property). During your lifetime, there will be no effect on your day-to-day affairs. However, upon your death, because your trust—not you—is the legal owner of your property, there is no need for probate. Your designated successor trustee, typically your spouse or children, takes control of the trust and distributes your property according to your wishes without the cost and time of probate. If you become incompetent, a trust will empower your successor trustees to manage your affairs for you without the need for guardianship. A living trust can also be an invaluable tool to reduce or avoid estate taxes.

Study Questions

1. Who should consider consulting with an experienced estate planning attorney?

2. What is a probate and what are its two primary goals?

3. What is a durable power of attorney and why is it important to draft?

4. What is the modern approach to solving many of the problems of basic estate planning?

Chapter 1 Answers

Pretest *True-False*
1. T (p. 4)
2. F (p. 7)
3. F (p. 13)
4. T (p. 17)
5. T (p. 13)
6. F (p. 14)
7. F (p. 4)
8. T (p. 8)
9. T (p. 22)
10. F (p. 24)

Post Test *Completion*
1. personal finance planning (p.4)
2. adult life cycle (p.13)
3. goals (p.5)
4. opportunity cost (p.6)
5. Economics (p.13)
6. time value of money (p.17)
7. inflation (p.14)
8. Liquidity (p.22)
9. Values (p.13)
10. plan (p. 24)

Multiple Choice
1. C (p. 4)
2. B (p. 4)
3. A (p. 18)
4. B (p. 13)
5. B (p. 13)
6. A (p. 16)
7. D (p. 8)
8. C (p. 22)
9. D (p. 24)
10. C (p. 24)

Problems, Applications, and Cases

1. a. $501.38
   b. $1,395
   c. $310.80
   d. $1,724.10

2. Answers will vary.

3. Answers will vary.

4. a. estate planning
   b. planning
   c. managing risk
   d. borrowing (or spending)
   e. obtaining (or planning)
   f. savings (or planning)
   g. borrowing (or planning)
   h. investing (or planning)

5. Answers will vary.

6. Answers will vary.

Copyright © 2007 The McGraw-Hill Companies, Inc. All rights reserved.

Chapter 2 Answers

Pretest *True-False*
1. T (p. 44)
2. T (p. 44)
3. F (p. 45)
4. T (p. 49)
5. T (p. 53)
6. T (p. 68)
7. T (p. 68)
8. F (p. 73)
9. T (pp. 56-58)
10. T (p. 59)

Post Test *Completion*
1. screening (p. 73)
2. targeted (p. 68)
3. job (p. 44)
4. mentor (p. 60)
5. cover letter (p. 55)
6. chronological (p. 68)
7. informational (p. 53)
8. career (p. 44)
9. selection (p. 73)
10. functional (p. 68)

Multiple Choice
1. B (p. 45)
2. A (p. 53)
3. D (p. 68)
4. B (p. 68)
5. C (p. 71)
6. B (p. 71)
7. C (p. 73)
8. A (p. 73)
9. C (p. 56)
10. C (p. 56)

Problems, Applications, and Cases

1. Answers will vary.
2. Answers will vary.
3. Answers will vary.
4. Answers will vary.
5. Answers will vary.
6. Answers will vary.

Chapter 3 Answers

Pretest *True-False*
1. F (p. 79)
2. T (p. 81)
3. F (p. 82)
4. F (p. 83)
5. F (p. 84)
6. T (p. 85)
7. T (p. 84)
8. F (p. 87, 91)
9. T (p. 93)
10. T (p. 97)

Post Test *Completion*
1. Liquid (p. 82)
2. variance (p. 93)
3. balance sheet (p. 81)
4. take-home pay (p. 86)
5. liabilities (p. 83)
6. cash flow statement (p. 84)
7. Insolvency (p. 84)
8. allocations (p. 91)
9. net worth (p. 83)
10. safe-deposit box (p. 79)

Multiple Choice
1. B (p. 79)
2. A (p. 81)
3. A (p. 82)
4. D (p. 83)
5. B (p. 84)
6. C (p. 87)
7. B (p. 84)
8. B (p. 88)
9. B (p. 93)
10. A (p. 98)

Problems, Applications, and Cases

1. Student activity.

2. Balance sheet:
   Assets: $29,234
   Liabilities: $2,193
   Net Worth: $27,041

   Cash flow statement:
   Income: $2,112
   Payments: $2,102
   Surplus: $100

3. Student activity.

4. Answers will vary.

5. Answers will vary.

6. a. variable
   b. variable
   c. fixed
   d. variable
   e. variable
   f. fixed
   g. variable
   h. variable

Copyright © 2007 The McGraw-Hill Companies, Inc. All rights reserved.

Chapter 4 Answers

Pretest *True-False*
1. T (p. 107)
2. F (p. 107)
3. T (p. 106)
4. F (p. 108)
5. T (p. 109)
6. F (p. 112)
7. F (p. 113)
8. F (p. 117)
9. F (p. 125)
10. F (p. 129)

Post Test *Completion*
1. credit (p. 112)
2. excise (p. 106)
3. capital gain (p. 129)
4. tax audit (p. 125)
5. Earned (p. 108)
6. inheritance (p. 107)
7. itemized deductions (p. 109)
8. exemption (p. 111)
9. exempt (p. 128)
10. exclusion (p. 109)

Multiple Choice
1. B (p. 106)
2. D (p. 106)
3. A (p. 108)
4. C (p. 109)
5. A (p. 111)
6. D (p. 114)
7. B (p. 116)
8. A (p. 124)
9. D (p. 126)
10. C (p. 128)

Problems, Applications, and Cases

1. Taxable income $28,550
2. Student activity.
3. Answers will vary.

Chapter 5 Answers

Pretest *True-False*
1. T (p. 139)
2. T (p. 139)
3. F (p. 141)
4. T (p. 139)
5. F (p. 142)
6. F (p. 151)
7. F (p. 148)
8. F (p. 155)
9. F (p. 155)
10. F (p. 158)

Post Test *Completion*
1. savings and loan association (p. 143)
2. rate of return (p. 150)
3. Demand (p. 139)
4. share draft account (p. 156)
5. automatic teller machines (p. 140)
6. certificate of deposit (p. 148)
7. asset management account (p. 139)
8. credit union (p. 144)
9. compounding (p. 151)
10. time (p. 139)

Multiple Choice
1. B (p. 145)
2. C (p. 139)
3. D (p. 142)
4. C (p. 139)
5. A (p. 150)
6. A (p. 153)
7. D (p. 150)
8. B (p. 156)
9. C (p. 158)
10. D (p. 159)

Problems, Applications, and Cases

1. Answers will vary.

2. Answers will vary.

3. Answers will vary.

4. a. $599.20
   b. $887.60
   c. $259.21
   d. $1,453.83

5. Answers will vary.

6. Answers will vary.

7. Corrected (adjusted) checkbook balance: $230

Chapter 6 Answers

Pretest *True-False*
1. T (p. 168)
2. F (p. 169)
3. F (p. 172)
4. T (p. 173)
5. T (p. 180)
6. T (p. 180)
7. F (p. 186)
8. T (p. 191)
9. F (p. 191)
10. T (p. 196)

Post Test *Completion*
1. Credit (p. 168)
2. closed-end credit (p. 172)
3. open-end credit (p. 173)
4. Line of credit (p. 173)
5. character (p. 186)
6. capacity (p. 186)
7. Collateral (p. 187)
8. 20 percent (p. 180)
9. seven years (p. 184)
10. The Fair Credit Billing Act (p. 190)

Multiple Choice
1. C (p. 168)
2. A (p. 170)
3. D (p. 173)
4. A (p. 172)
5. B (p. 186)
6. D (p. 186)
7. C (p. 180)
8. A (p. 183)
9. B (p. 190)
10. D (p. 195)

Problems, Applications, and Cases

1. Students will find various and varying information in their credit files.

2. a. open-end
    b. incidental
    c. incidental
    d. closed-end
    e. closed-end
    f. incidental
    g. open-end
    h. open-end
    i. closed-end
    j. open-end

3. The student responses will vary. Here are possible answers:
    a. yes
    b. yes
    c. no
    d. maybe
    e. yes
    f. no
    g. maybe
    h. no
    i. no
    j. maybe

4. Answers will vary.

5. Yes. Alyssa meets all the tests of the Fair Credit Billing Act. The purchase is over $50, within her home town and home state, and she has made a good faith effort to resolve the matter.

6. No. Mark has not made a good faith effort to resolve that matter. The TV repair problem may be unrelated to the earlier service call he made to Ace TV Repair Shoppe.

7. No. Amy can't withhold the payment because the purchase was not over $50.

Chapter 7 Answers

Pretest *True-False*
1. T (p. 206)
2. F (p. 206)
3. T (p. 210)
4. T (p. 210)
5. F (p. 221)
6. T (p. 224)
7. T (p. 225)
8. F (p. 226)
9. F (p. 230)
10. F (p. 230)

Post Test *Completion*
1. cheaper (p. 206)
2. growing (p. 207)
3. consumer finance companies (p. 209)
4. Simple interest (p. 213)
5. finance charge (p. 210)
6. annual percentage rate (p. 210)
7. Fair Debt Collections Practices Act (p. 221)
8. Consumer Credit Counseling Service (p. 225)
9. Chapter 7 bankruptcy (p. 230)
10. Chapter 13 bankruptcy (p. 230)

Multiple Choice
1. B (p. 209)
2. A (p. 209)
3. A (p. 215)
4. C (p. 210)
5. D (p. 218)
6. A (p. 221)
7. C (p. 221)
8. B (p. 225)
9. B (p. 231)
10. C (p. 230)

Answers to Problems, Applications, and Cases

1. To find the interest rate on a loan, use the simple interest formula:
   I = P x R x T (PRT)
   = $2,000 x 0.10 x 1 = $200
   Total owed at the end of one year = P + I = $2,000 + $200 = $2,200

2. Over the first year, you have the full use of the $2,000 principal and, therefore, incur an interest obligation of $200 ($2,000 x 0.10 x 1). This first year's interest expense, however, is payable at the *end* of the second year.
   Over the second and last year of the loan, you again have full use of $2,000, for which another $200 interest obligation is incurred and due at the end of the second year. At the end of two full years, you must repay the two years interest ($200 + $200 = $400), in addition to the original amount borrowed ($2,000). In other words, you have to pay interest *only* on the amount borrowed and *not* on any accumulated interest charges.

   Total loan repayment = principal + interest charges on the principal only.
   = P + I or
   = P + (P x R x T)
   = $2,000 + ($2,000 x 0.10 x 2)
   = $2,000 + $400
   = $2,400

3. P = $1,500; R = 0.132 or 13.2/100; and T = 6 months or ½ year. The amount due on the loan consists of principal plus the half-year's interest on the principal:

Total loan repayment = $1,500 (1 + 0.132 × ½)
= $1,500 (1 + 0.066) = $1,500 (1.066)
= $1,599

Note: While the simple annual interest rate is 13.2%, the amount of interest charged for half the year is 6.6% or ½ of 13.2% of the principal.

Since the total amount due is $1,599 and the amount borrowed is $1,500, the difference of $99 ($1,599 - $1,500) is the total amount of interest on the six-month loan.

4. a. Creditor
    b. Consumer
    c. Consumer
    d. Consumer
    e. Debt collector (The debt collector loses business. The creditor, too, may still be incurring high collection costs as a result of the Act.)
    f. Consumer
    g. Debt collector
    h. Consumer (The creditor has shifted the higher costs of debt collection to consumers. However, the creditor may still incur costs if reducing the availability of credit also causes business to decrease.)

5. a. Illegal. A debt collector cannot use a post card to communicate with a customer.
    b. Legal. As long as the creditor does not go by a different name when collecting debts, he/she is not covered by the Fair Debt Collection Act.
    c. Legal. A bank collecting its own debts is not covered by the Act.
    d. Illegal. A debt collector cannot call at an unusual or inconvenient time (before 8 a.m. or after 9 p.m.)
    e. Illegal. ABC Stores is covered by the Act because it goes by ABC Collections, Inc., when collecting debts. (6 a.m. is generally considered an unusual time.)
    f. Legal. A department store collecting its own debts is not covered by the Act.
    g. Legal. A credit union collecting its own debts is not covered by the Act.
    h. Illegal. A debt collector cannot call a consumer at work if such contact is prohibited by the employer.
    i. Illegal. Because a debt collector legally cannot "throw a consumer in jail," he/she cannot threaten to do so.
    j. Legal. The creditor may repossess the furniture so it can be stated as possible consequence of nonpayment.

6. Cost of credit   APR
   a. $232   10.77%
   b. $114   22.62%
   c. $500   10.91%

7. The nominal rate of interest on the loan is 0 percent.

8. The real rate of interest is minus seven percent.

Chapter 8 Answers

Pretest *True-False*
1. F (p. 249)
2. F (p. 249)
3. T (p. 243)
4. F (p. 243)
5. T (p. 246)
6. T (p. 247)
7. F (p. 258)
8. T (p. 260)
9. T (p. 261)
10. F (p. 261)

Post Test *Completion*
1. unit pricing (p. 244)
2. Small claims court (p. 261)
3. mediation (p. 259)
4. Impulse buying (p. 243)
5. legal aid societies (p. 262)
6. Arbitration (p. 260)
7. service contract (p. 247)
8. class action suit (p. 261)
9. cooperative (p. 243)
10. warranty (p. 246)

Multiple Choice
1. C (p. 242)
2. B (p. 249)
3. C (p. 243)
4. D (p. 244)
5. C (p. 246)
6. B (p. 246)
7. A (p. 258)
8. B (p. 260)
9. C (p. 261)
10. B (p. 261)

Problems, Applications, and Cases

1. Answers will vary.

2. Scoring results: Brand A 5.3; Brand B 6.2; Brand C 5.9.

   Based on this analysis, John would buy Brand B, but he should also consider other factors in his purchasing decision, such as comments from friends, ratings by consumer organizations, and brand reputation.

3. Answers will vary.

4. a. Highway Traffic Safety Administration
   b. U.S. Postal Service or Federal Trade Commission
   c. Food and Drug Administration
   d. State Consumer Protection Office and Securities and Exchange Commission

Chapter 9 Answers

Pretest *True-False*
1. T (p. 273)
2. T (p. 277)
3. F (p. 278)
4. T (p. 281)
5. T (p. 283)
6. T (p. 286)
7. T (p. 287)
8. F (p. 288)
9. T (p. 292)
10. T (p. 294)

Post Test *Completion*
1. Amortization (p. 289)
2. condominium (p. 281)
3. balloon (p. 290)
4. deed (p. 294)
5. lease (p. 277)
6. Points (p. 288)
7. buy-down (p. 293)
8. escrow account (p. 294)
9. Earnest money (p. 285)
10. closing costs (p. 294)

Multiple Choice
1. C (p. 276)
2. B (p. 277)
3. A (p. 281)
4. D (p. 281)
5. C (p. 283)
6. D (p. 283)
7. B (p. 288)
8. B (p. 289)
9. C (p. 293)
10. B (p. 294)

Problems, Applications, and Cases

1. (1) Total annual home purchase expenses ($790 x 12 x $420) — $9,900
   (2) Deductible portion of expenses ($8,900 + $1,575) — $10,475
   (3) Multiply deductible items by tax rate ($10,475 x 0.28) — $2,933
   (4) Subtract (3) from (1) to obtain after-tax cost of buying — $6,967
   (5) Multiply rent by 12 to obtain annual renting costs — $7,800

   In addition to these financial aspects, George and Alicia should also consider the money needed for a down payment, chances of having to move in the near future, freedom from being responsible for repairs, as well as other personal and financial factors.

2. Answers will vary.

3. Answers will vary.

4. Answers will vary.

5. a. an FHA mortgage or buy down
   b. a balloon mortgage or variable rate mortgage
   c. a second mortgage or variable rate mortgage
   d. a conventional mortgage
   e. a graduated payment mortgage

Chapter 10 Answers

Pretest *True-False*
1. F (p. 312)
2. T (p. 313)
3. T (p. 315)
4. F (p. 315)
5. F (p. 318)
6. T (p. 318)
7. F (p. 320)
8. T (p. 323)
9. T (p. 324)
10. F (p. 326)

Post Test *Completion*
1. Comprehensive physical damage (p. 324)
2. actual cash value (p. 318)
3. Property damage liability (p. 323)
4. Vicarious (p. 312)
5. Driver classification (p. 326)
6. Financial responsibility law (p. 320)
7. negligence (p. 312)
8. Collision (p. 323)
9. umbrella (p. 315)
10. Medical payments (p. 323)

Multiple Choice
1. C (p. 312)
2. C (p. 313)
3. B (p. 315)
4. A (p. 316)
5. C (p. 319)
6. B (p. 322)
7. D (p. 323)
8. C (p. 324)
9. C (p. 326)
10. A (p. 326)

Problems, Applications, and Cases

1. Student activity.
2. Student activity.
3. a. medical payments
   b. property damage liability
   c. bodily injury liability
   d. comprehensive physical damage
   e. uninsured motorists protection
   f. collision

Chapter 11 Answers

Pretest *True-False*
1. T (p. 336)
2. T (p. 339)
3. F (p. 339)
4. T (p. 341)
5. T (p. 342)
6. F (p. 343)
7. T (p. 351)
8. F (p. 358)
9. F (p. 361)
10. T (p. 362)

Post Test *Completion*
1. stay well (p. 339)
2. health insurance (p. 339)
3. Hospital expense insurance (p. 342)
4. Surgical expense insurance (p. 342)
5. Physical expense insurance (p. 342)
6. Blue Cross (p. 351)
7. Blue Shield (p. 351)
8. Medicare (p. 355)
9. Medicaid (p. 358)
10. Disability income insurance (p. 361)

Multiple Choice
1. D (p. 336)
2. D (p. 340)
3. C (p. 342)
4. A (p. 342)
5. B (p. 342)
6. A (p. 351)
7. B (p. 351)
8. C (p. 355)
9. A (p. 361)
10. C (p. 362)

Problems, Applications, and Cases

1. Answers will vary.

2. Answers will vary.

3. Answers will vary.

4.
   a. major medical
   b. basic protection
   c. basic protection; major medical; disability income
   d. basic protection
   e. supplemental policy (dental insurance)
   f. basic protection

5. Larry probably does not need health insurance because he is covered through Liz's employer-sponsored health insurance plan. However, Larry should obtain disability income insurance and possibly a decreasing term insurance.

6. Since Pam's ex-husband is responsible for the children's health care bills, she does not need additional health insurance coverage, but she should purchase disability insurance.

Chapter 12 Answers

Pretest *True-False*
1. F (p. 372)
2. T (p. 373)
3. F (p. 376)
4. F (p. 376)
5. T (p. 379)
6. F (p. 382)
7. T (p. 387)
8. T (p. 389)
9. F (p. 393)
10. T (p. 398)

Post Test *Completion*
1. life insurance (p. 372)
2. easy method (p. 376)
3. participating policy (p. 379)
4. Term insurance (p. 379)
5. whole life (p. 382)
6. group insurance (p. 386)
7. beneficiary (p. 387)
8. Interest-adjusted (p. 394)
9. annuity (p. 397)
10. annuity (p. 397)

Multiple Choice
1. B (p. 372)
2. B (p. 376)
3. A (p. 379)
4. D (p. 382)
5. C (p. 387)
6. A (p. 386)
7. B (p. 388)
8. C (p. 389)
9. D (p. 394)
10. A (p. 398)

Problems, Applications, and Cases

1. Student responses will vary depending on where they live.

2. Student responses will vary from state to state.

3. The answers given here are recommended. With more information, it would be possible to give logical reasons for other answers:
   a. straight life or term
   b. term
   c. straight life
   d. term

4. Answers will vary.

5. Single persons living alone or with their parents usually have little or no need for life insurance.

6. Households with small children most often have the greatest need for life insurance.

   Based on the insurance agent's rule of thumb that a "typical family" will need approximately 70 percent of the breadwinner's salary for seven years, Barry will need about $147,000 worth of life insurance on his life.

   Since Mary does not work, we can use a "non-working spouse" method of determining life insurance needs. The youngest child reaches age 18 in 16 years. Simply multiply 16 by $9,000; therefore, Barry needs $144,000 of life insurance.

Chapter 13 Answers

Pretest *True-False*
1. T (p. 408)
2. F (p. 409)
3. T (p. 409)
4. F (p. 412)
5. F (p. 419)
6. T (p. 419)
7. F (p. 422)
8. T (p. 423)
9. T (p. 423)
10. F (p. 431)

Post Test *Completion*
1. three (p. 409)
2. Safety, risk (p. 412)
3. rate return (p. 414)
4. interest rate (p. 416)
5. common stock (p. 422)
6. preferred stock (p. 422)
7. one, thirty (p. 423)
8. mutual fund (p. 423)
9. recordkeeping (p. 427)
10. search engine (p. 428)

Multiple Choice
1. B (p. 410)
2. B (p. 418)
3. B (p. 418)
4. D (p. 419)
5. B (p. 419)
6. D (p. 421)
7. C (p. 423)
8. B (p. 424)
9. C (p. 426)
10. A (p. 431)

Problems, Applications, and Cases

1. Answers will vary.
2. Answers will vary
3. Answers will vary.

Chapter 14 Answers

Pretest *True-False*
1. T (p. 443)
2. T (p. 444)
3. F (p. 447)
4. F (p. 448)
5. T (p. 449)
6. T (p. 455)
7. F (p. 456)
8. F (p. 466)
9. F (p. 467)
10. T (p. 470)

Post Test *Completion*
1. proxy (p. 443)
2. stock split (p. 445)
3. convertible (p. 447)
4. defensive (p. 449)
5. price-earnings (p. 455)
6. fundamental (p. 459)
7. securities exchange (p. 461)
8. account executive (p. 463)
9. direct investment (p. 468)
10. option (p. 471)

Multiple Choice
1. D (p. 442)
2. B (p. 447)
3. C (p. 449)
4. B (p. 455)
5. C (p. 459)
6. B (p. 460)
7. B (p. 462)
8. A (p. 466)
9. D (p. 467)
10. C (p. 470)

Problems, Applications, and Cases

1. Answers will vary.

2. Dividend payout = 18%

3. a. Book value = $8.80 per share
   b. Earnings per share = $3.20
   c. Price-earnings ratio = 14

4. a. Current yield = 3.1 percent
   b. Total return = $1,400
   c. Annualized holding period yield = 8 percent

Chapter 15 Answers

Pretest *True-False*
1. F (p. 482)
2. T (p. 483)
3. F (p. 484)
4. T (p. 484)
5. F (p. 487)
6. F (p. 488)
7. F (p. 493)
8. T (p. 495)
9. F (p. 500)
10. F (p. 500)

Post Test *Completion*
1. corporate bond (p. 482)
2. maturity date (p. 482)
3. subordinated debenture (p. 484)
4. sinking (p. 485)
5. interest, value, repayment (p. 487)
6. registered (p. 488)
7. $1,000 (p. 493)
8. general obligation (p. 495)
9. bid (p. 499)
10. market (p. 500)

Multiple Choice
1. B (p. 483)
2. A (p. 484)
3. D (p. 485)
4. B (p. 487)
5. B (p. 488)
6. B (p. 494)
7. B (p. 495)
8. D (p. 499)
9. A (p. 500)
10. C (p. 500)

Problems, Applications, and Cases

1. Answers will vary, but you may want to compare your answers with the material in Exhibit 15-6.

2. a. 6.67 percent
   b. 8.00 percent
   c. 8.67 percent
   d. 10.42 percent
   e. 11.11 percent

3. Answers will vary.

4. Answers will vary.

5. a. 8.42 percent
   b. 4.76 percent
   c. 11.67 percent
   d. 10.79 percent
   e. 15.29 percent

Chapter 16 Answers

Pretest *True-False*
1. T (p. 515)
2. F (p. 516)
3. F (p. 518)
4. T (p. 518)
5. F (p. 521)
6. T (p. 523)
7. F (p. 526)
8. F (p. 529)
9. T (p. 533)
10. T (p. 536)

Post Test *Completion*
1. professional, diversification (p. 515)
2. exchange-traded (p. 516)
3. net asset value (p. 517)
4. contingent deferred sales load (p. 518)
5. small cap (p. 522)
6. balanced (p. 523)
7. professional-advisory (p. 526)
8. prospectus (p. 529)
9. Capital gain (p. 533)
10. capital (p. 533)

Multiple Choice
1. D (p. 514)
2. C (p. 517)
3. B (p. 518)
4. D (p. 518)
5. C (p. 521)
6. D (p. 521)
7. B (p. 529)
8. D (p. 533)
9. A (p. 536)
10. A (p. 536)

Problems, Applications, and Cases

1. Matching questions
    1. c (p. 517)
    2. i (p. 518)
    3. b (p. 517)
    4. g (p. 518)
    5. d (p. 516)
    6. a (p. 516)
    7. e (p. 519)
    8. h (p. 518)
    9. f (p. 518)

2. Answers will vary, but you may want to review the material on pages 520-523 while completing this exercise.

3. Answers will vary.

4. a. The net asset value per share is $14.67.
      $590,000,000 − $1,400,000 = $588,600,000
      $588,600,000 ÷ 40,124,200 = $14.67 per share.
   b. The commission on a $2,000 investment would be $80.
      $2,000 x 0.04 = $80.

5. a. The current yield for this investment is 5.6 percent.
      $0.60 ÷ $10.75 = 5.6 percent.
   b. The total return for this investment would be $180 loss at the end of 12 months.
      200 shares x $0.60 = $120 current return.
      200 shares x $1.50 = $300 dollar loss ($12.25 purchase price - $10.75 selling price = $1.50 per share loss.)
      $120 current return - $300 future loss = $180 total loss on the transaction.

Chapter 17 Answers

Pretest *True-False*
1. T (p. 546)
2. T (p. 546)
3. T (p. 549)
4. F (p. 551)
5. F (p. 553)
6. T (p. 554)
7. F (p. 554)
8. T (p. 554)
9. T (p. 555)
10. F (p. 562)

Post Test *Completion*
1. direct investments (p. 546)
2. commercial property (p. 549)
3. syndicate (p. 550)
4. hybrid (p. 551)
5. limited partner (p. 554)
6. Financial leverage (p. 554)
7. Diversification (p. 555)
8. kilogram (p. 556)
9. Diamonds (p. 558)
10. Gemological Institute of America (p. 558)

Multiple Choice
1. C (p. 546)
2. A (p. 546)
3. D (p. 550)
4. C (p. 551)
5. B (p. 551)
6. A (p. 551)
7. C (p. 553)
8. D (p. 554)
9. B (p. 554)
10. C (p. 558)

Problems, Applications, and Cases

1. Responses will vary.
2. Responses will vary.
3. Responses will vary.
4. Responses will vary.
5. a. 13.6%
   b. 17.5%
   c. −11.4%

Chapter 18 Answers

Pretest *True-False*
1. F (p. 570)
2. F (p. 570)
3. T (p. 573)
4. F (p. 575)
5. F (p. 576)
6. T (p. 576)
7. T (p. 580)
8. F (p. 581)
9. F (p. 586)
10. F (p. 602)

Post Test *Completion*
1. 16 to 25 (p. 571)
2. financial (p. 571)
3. impossible (p. 576)
4. less (p. 576)
5. Social Security (p. 581)
6. defined-contribution plan (p. 588)
7. defined-benefit plan (p. 590)
8. Keogh plan (p. 597)
9. Immediate (p. 599)
10. deferred (p. 599)

Multiple Choice
1. B (p. 571)
2. C (p. 571)
3. C (p. 571)
4. A (p. 571)
5. D (p. 576)
6. C (p. 576)
7. A (p. 581)
8. D (p. 588)
9. B (p. 588)
10. C (p. 600)

Problems, Applications, and Cases

1. Student activity.

2. Student activity.

3. Answers will vary.

4. Answers will vary.

5. a. $647
   b. $368

6. Male: $2,249.95
   Female: $2,746.98

Chapter 19 Answers

Pretest *True-False*
1. T (p. 614)
2. F (p. 615)
3. T (p. 617)
4. T (p. 618)
5. F (p. 620)
6. F (p. 621)
7. T (p. 622)
8. T (p. 628)
9. T (p. 636)
10. F (p. 636)

Post Test *Completion*
1. five or ten (p. 616)
2. will (p. 618)
3. intestate (p. 618)
4. simple will (p. 620)
5. holographic will (p. 621)
6. codicil (p. 624)
7. prenuptial agreement (p. 624)
8. power of attorney (p. 626)
9. revocable (p. 628)
10. 5 to 8 (p. 638)

Multiple Choice
1. D (p. 614)
2. D (p. 618)
3. A (p. 620)
4. C (p. 621)
5. B (p. 621)
6. D (p. 624)
7. C (p. 622)
8. A (p. 626)
9. B (p. 630)
10. B (p. 638)

Problems, Applications, and Cases

1. Student activity.

2. Answers will vary.

3. Answers will vary.

4. Student activity.

5. Tax on $1,000,000 is $345,800
   Tax on additional $250,000 at 41 percent is $102,500
   Total tax is $448,300 ($345,800 plus $102,500)

6. Student activity.